SMITH AND THE PHARAOHS, AND OTHER TALES
BY H. RIDER HAGGARD

ORIGINALLY PUBLISHED IN 1921

This book edition was created and published by Mamba Press
©MambaPress. Print in 2024

Contents

Smith And The Pharaohs
    Magepa The Buck
    The Blue Curtains
    Little Flower
    Only A Dream
    Barbara Who Came Back

Smith And The Pharaohs

CHAPTER I

Scientists, or some scientists—for occasionally one learned person differs from other learned persons—tell us they know all that is worth knowing about man, which statement, of course, includes woman. They trace him from his remotest origin; they show us how his bones changed and his shape modified, also how, under the influence of his needs and passions, his intelligence developed from something very humble. They demonstrate conclusively that there is nothing in man which the dissecting-table will not explain; that his aspirations towards another life have their root in the fear of death, or, say others of them, in that of earthquake or thunder; that his affinities with the past are merely inherited from remote ancestors who lived in that past, perhaps a million years ago; and that everything noble about him is but the fruit of expediency or of a veneer of civilisation, while everything base must be attributed to the instincts of his dominant and primeval nature. Man, in short, is an animal who, like every other animal, is finally subdued by his environment and takes his colour from his surroundings, as cattle do from the red soil of Devon. Such are the facts, they (or some of them) declare; all the rest is rubbish.

At times we are inclined to agree with these sages, especially after it has been our privilege to attend a course of lectures by one of them. Then perhaps something comes within the range of our experience which gives us pause and causes doubts, the old divine doubts, to arise again deep in our hearts, and with them a yet diviner hope.

Perchance when all is said, so we think to ourselves, man *is* something more than an animal. Perchance he has known the past, the far past, and will know the future, the far, far future. Perchance the dream is true, and he does indeed possess what for convenience is called an immortal soul, that may manifest itself in one shape or another; that may sleep for ages, but, waking or sleeping, still remains itself, indestructible as the matter of the Universe.

An incident in the career of Mr. James Ebenezer Smith might well occasion such reflections, were any acquainted with its details, which until this, its setting forth, was not the case. Mr. Smith is a person who knows when to be silent. Still, undoubtedly it gave cause for thought to one individual—namely, to him to whom it happened. Indeed, James Ebenezer Smith is still thinking over it, thinking very hard indeed.

J. E. Smith was well born and well educated. When he was a good-looking and able young man at college, but before he had taken his degree, trouble came to him, the particulars of which do not matter, and he was thrown penniless, also friendless, upon the rocky bosom of the world. No, not quite friendless, for he had a godfather, a gentleman connected with business whose Christian name was Ebenezer. To him, as a last resource, Smith went, feeling that Ebenezer owed him something in return for the awful appellation wherewith he had been endowed in baptism.

To a certain extent Ebenezer recognised the obligation. He did nothing heroic, but he found his godson a clerkship in a bank of which he was one of the directors—a modest clerkship, no more. Also, when he died a year later, he left him a hundred pounds to be spent upon some souvenir.

Smith, being of a practical turn of mind, instead of adorning himself with memorial jewellery for which he had no use, invested the hundred pounds in an exceedingly promising speculation. As it happened, he was not misinformed, and his talent returned to him multiplied by ten. He repeated the experiment, and, being in a position to know what he was doing, with considerable success. By the time that he was thirty he found himself possessed of a fortune of something over twenty-five thousand pounds. Then (and this shows the wise and practical nature of the man) he stopped speculating and put out his money in such a fashion that it brought him a safe and clear four per cent.

By this time Smith, being an excellent man of business, was well up in the service of his bank—as yet only a clerk, it is true, but one who drew his four hundred pounds a year, with prospects. In short, he was in a position to marry had he wished to do so. As it happened, he did not wish—perhaps because, being very friendless, no lady who attracted him crossed his path; perhaps for other reasons.

Shy and reserved in temperament, he confided only in himself. None, not even his superiors at the bank or the Board of Management, knew how well off he had become. No one visited him at the flat which he was understood to occupy somewhere in the neighbourhood of Putney; he belonged to no club, and possessed not a single intimate. The blow which the world had dealt him in his early days, the harsh repulses and the rough treatment he had then experienced, sank so deep into his sensitive soul that never again did he seek close converse with his kind. In fact, while still young, he fell into a condition of old-bachelorhood of a refined type.

Soon, however, Smith discovered—it was after he had given up speculating—that a man must have something to occupy his mind. He tried philanthropy, but found himself too sensitive for a business which so often resolves itself into rude inquiry as to the affairs of other people. After a struggle, therefore, he compromised with his conscience by setting aside a liberal portion of his income for anonymous distribution among deserving persons and objects.

While still in this vacant frame of mind Smith chanced one day, when the bank was closed, to drift into the British Museum, more to escape the vile weather that prevailed without than for any other reason. Wandering hither and thither at hazard, he found himself in the great gallery devoted to Egyptian stone objects and sculpture. The place bewildered him somewhat, for he knew nothing of Egyptology; indeed, there remained upon his mind only a sense of wonderment not unmixed with awe. It must have been a great people, he thought to himself, that executed these works, and with the thought came a desire to know more about them. Yet he was going away when suddenly his eye fell on the sculptured head of a woman which hung upon the wall.

Smith looked at it once, twice, thrice, and at the third look he fell in love. Needless to say, he was not aware that such was his condition. He knew only that a change had come over him, and never, never could he forget the face which that carven mask portrayed. Perhaps it was not really beautiful save for its wondrous and mystic smile; perhaps the lips were too thick and the nostrils too broad. Yet to him that face was Beauty itself, beauty which drew him as with a cart-rope, and awoke within him all kinds of wonderful imaginings, some of them so strange and tender that almost they partook of the nature of memories. He stared at the image, and the image smiled back sweetly at him, as doubtless it, or rather its original—for this was but a plaster cast—had smiled at nothingness in some tomb or hiding-hole for over thirty centuries, and as the woman whose likeness it was had once smiled upon the world.

A short, stout gentleman bustled up and, in tones of authority, addressed some workmen who were arranging a base for a neighbouring statue. It occurred to Smith that he must be someone who knew about these objects. Overcoming his natural diffidence with an effort, he raised his hat and asked the gentleman if he could tell him who was the original of the mask.

The official—who, in fact, was a very great man in the Museum—glanced at Smith shrewdly, and, seeing that his interest was genuine, answered—

"I don't know. Nobody knows. She has been given several names, but none of them have authority. Perhaps one day the rest of the statue may be found, and then we shall learn—that is, if it is inscribed. Most likely, however, it has been burnt for lime long ago."

"Then you can't tell me anything about her?" said Smith.

"Well, only a little. To begin with, that's a cast. The original is in the Cairo Museum. Mariette found it, I believe at Karnac, and gave it a name after his fashion. Probably she was a queen—of the eighteenth dynasty, by the work. But you can see her rank for yourself from the broken *uraeus*." (Smith did not stop him to explain that he had not the faintest idea what a *uraeus* might be, seeing that he was utterly unfamiliar with the snake-headed crest of Egyptian royalty.) "You should go to Egypt and study the head for yourself. It is one of the most beautiful things that ever was found. Well, I must be off. Good day."

And he bustled down the long gallery.

Smith found his way upstairs and looked at mummies and other things. Somehow it hurt him to reflect that the owner of yonder sweet, alluring face must have become a mummy long, long before the Christian era. Mummies did not strike him as attractive.

He returned to the statuary and stared at his plaster cast till one of the workmen remarked to his fellow that if he were the gent he'd go and look at "a live'un" for a change.

Then Smith retired abashed.

On his way home he called at his bookseller's and ordered "all the best works on Egyptology". When, a day or two later, they arrived in a packing-case, together with a bill for thirty-eight pounds, he was somewhat dismayed. Still, he tackled those books like a man, and, being clever and industrious, within three months had a fair working knowledge of the subject, and had even picked up a smattering of hieroglyphics.

In January—that was, at the end of those three months—Smith astonished his Board of Directors by applying for ten weeks' leave, he who had hitherto been content with a fortnight in the year. When questioned he explained that he had been suffering from bronchitis, and was advised to take a change in Egypt.

"A very good idea," said the manager; "but I'm afraid you'll find it expensive. They fleece one in Egypt."

"I know," answered Smith; "but I've saved a little and have only myself to spend it upon."

So Smith went to Egypt and saw the original of the beauteous head and a thousand other fascinating things. Indeed, he did more. Attaching himself to some excavators who were glad of his intelligent assistance, he actually dug for a month in the neighbourhood of ancient Thebes, but without finding anything in particular.

It was not till two years later that he made his great discovery, that which is known as Smith's Tomb. Here it may be explained that the state of his health had become such as to necessitate an annual visit to Egypt, or so his superiors understood.

However, as he asked for no summer holiday, and was always ready to do another man's work or to stop overtime, he found it easy to arrange for these winter excursions.

On this, his third visit to Egypt, Smith obtained from the Director-General of Antiquities at Cairo a licence to dig upon his own account. Being already well known in the country as a skilled Egyptologist, this was granted upon the usual terms—namely, that the Department of Antiquities should have a right to take any of the objects which might be found, or all of them, if it so desired.

Such preliminary matters having been arranged by correspondence, Smith, after a few days spent in the Museum at Cairo, took the night train to Luxor, where he found his head-man, an ex-dragoman named Mahomet, waiting for him and his fellaheen labourers already hired. There were but forty of them, for his was a comparatively small venture. Three hundred pounds was the amount that he had made up his mind to expend, and such a sum does not go far in excavations.

During his visit of the previous year Smith had marked the place where he meant to dig. It was in the cemetery of old Thebes, at the wild spot not far from the temple of Medinet Habu, that is known as the Valley of the Queens. Here, separated from the resting-places of their royal lords by the bold mass of the intervening hill, some of the greatest ladies of Egypt have been laid to rest, and it was their tombs that Smith desired to investigate. As he knew well, some of these must yet remain to be discovered. Who could say? Fortune favours the bold. It might be that he would find the holy grave of that beauteous, unknown Royalty whose face had haunted him for three long years!

For a whole month he dug without the slightest success. The spot that he selected had proved, indeed, to be the mouth of a tomb. After twenty-five days of laborious exploration it was at length cleared out, and he stood in a rude, unfinished cave. The queen for whom it had been designed must have died quite young and been buried elsewhere; or she had chosen herself another sepulchre, or mayhap the rock had proved unsuitable for sculpture.

Smith shrugged his shoulders and moved on, sinking trial pits and trenches here and there, but still finding nothing. Two-thirds of his time and money had been spent when at last the luck turned. One day, towards evening, with some half-dozen of his best men he was returning after a fruitless morning of labour, when something seemed to attract him towards a little *wadi*, or bay, in the hillside that was filled with tumbled rocks and sand. There were scores of such places, and this one looked no more promising than any of the others had proved to be. Yet it attracted him. Thoroughly dispirited, he walked past it twenty paces or more, then turned.

"Where go you, sah?" asked his head-man, Mahomet.

He pointed to the recess in the cliff.

"No good, sah," said Mahomet. "No tomb there. Bed-rock too near top. Too much water run in there; dead queen like keep dry!"

But Smith went on, and the others followed obediently.

He walked down the little slope of sand and boulders and examined the cliff. It was virgin rock; never a tool mark was to be seen. Already the men were going, when the same strange instinct which had drawn him to the spot caused him to take a spade from one of them and begin to shovel away the sand from the face of the cliff—for here, for some unexplained reason, were no boulders or *debris*. Seeing their master, to whom they were attached, at work, they began to work too, and for twenty minutes or more dug on cheerfully enough, just to humour him, since all were sure that here there was no tomb. At length Smith ordered them to desist, for, although now they were six feet down, the rock remained of the same virgin character.

With an exclamation of disgust he threw out a last shovelful of sand. The edge of his spade struck on something that projected. He cleared away a little more sand, and there appeared a rounded ledge which seemed to be a cornice. Calling back the men, he pointed to it, and without a word all of them began to dig again. Five minutes more of work made it clear that it was a cornice, and half an hour later there appeared the top of the doorway of a tomb.

"Old people wall him up," said Mahomet, pointing to the flat stones set in mud for mortar with which the doorway had been closed, and to the undecipherable impress upon the mud of the scarab seals of the officials whose duty it had been to close the last resting-place of the royal dead for ever.

"Perhaps queen all right inside," he went on, receiving no answer to his remark.

"Perhaps," replied Smith, briefly. "Dig, man, dig! Don't waste time in talking."

So they dug on furiously till at length Smith saw something which caused him to groan aloud. There was a hole in the masonry—the tomb had been broken into. Mahomet saw it too, and examined the top of the aperture with his skilled eye.

"Very old thief," he said. "Look, he try build up wall again, but run away before he have time finish." And he pointed to certain flat stones which had been roughly and hurriedly replaced.

"Dig—dig!" said Smith.

Ten minutes more and the aperture was cleared. It was only just big enough to admit the body of a man.

By now the sun was setting. Swiftly, swiftly it seemed to tumble down the sky. One minute it was above the rough crests of the western hills behind them; the next, a great ball of glowing fire, it rested on their topmost ridge. Then it was gone. For an instant a kind of green spark shone where it had been. This too went out, and the sudden Egyptian night was upon them.

The fellaheen muttered among themselves, and one or two of them wandered off on some pretext. The rest threw down their tools and looked at Smith. "Men say they no like stop here. They afraid of ghost! Too many *afreet* live in these tomb. That what they say. Come back finish to-morrow morning when it light. Very foolish people, these common fellaheen," remarked Mahomet, in a superior tone.

"Quite so," replied Smith, who knew well that nothing that he could offer would tempt his men to go on with the opening of a tomb after sunset. "Let them go away. You and I will stop and watch the place till morning."

"Sorry, sah," said Mahomet, "but I not feel quite well inside; think I got fever. I go to camp and lie down and pray under plenty blanket."

"All right, go," said Smith; "but if there is anyone who is not a coward, let him bring me my big coat, something to eat and drink, and the lantern that hangs in my tent. I will meet him there in the valley."

Mahomet, though rather doubtfully, promised that this should be done, and, after begging Smith to accompany them, lest the spirit of whoever slept in the tomb should work him a mischief during the night, they departed quickly enough.

Smith lit his pipe, sat down on the sand, and waited. Half an hour later he heard a sound of singing, and through the darkness, which was dense, saw lights coming up the valley.

"My brave men," he thought to himself, and scrambled up the slope to meet them.

He was right. These were his men, no less than twenty of them, for with a fewer number they did not dare to face the ghosts which they believed haunted the valley after nightfall. Presently the light from the lantern which one of them carried (not Mahomet, whose sickness had increased too suddenly to enable him to come) fell upon the tall form of Smith, who, dressed in his white working clothes, was leaning against a rock. Down went the lantern, and with a howl of terror the brave company turned and fled.

"Sons of cowards!" roared Smith after them, in his most vigorous Arabic. "It is I, your master, not an *afreet*."

They heard, and by degrees crept back again. Then he perceived that in order to account for their number each of them carried some article. Thus one had the bread, another the lantern, another a tin of sardines, another the sardine-opener, another a box of matches, another a bottle of beer, and so on. As even thus there were not enough things to go round, two of them bore his big coat between them, the first holding it by the sleeves and the second by the tail as though it were a stretcher.

"Put them down," said Smith, and they obeyed. "Now," he added, "run for your lives; I thought I heard two *afreets* talking up there just now of what they would do to any followers of the Prophet who mocked their gods, if perchance they should meet them in their holy place at night."

This kindly counsel was accepted with much eagerness. In another minute Smith was alone with the stars and the dying desert wind.

Collecting his goods, or as many of them as he wanted, he thrust them into the pockets of the great-coat and returned to the mouth of the tomb. Here he made his simple meal by the light of the lantern, and afterwards tried to go to sleep. But sleep he could not. Something always woke him. First it was a jackal howling amongst the rocks; next a sand-fly bit him in the ankle so sharply that he thought he must have been stung by a scorpion. Then, notwithstanding his warm coat, the cold got hold of him, for the clothes beneath were wet through with perspiration, and it occurred to him that unless he did something he would probably contract an internal chill or perhaps fever. He rose and walked about.

By now the moon was up, revealing all the sad, wild scene in its every detail. The mystery of Egypt entered his soul and oppressed him. How much dead majesty lay in the hill upon which he stood? Were they all really dead, he wondered, or were those fellaheen right? Did their spirits still come forth at night and wander through the land where once they ruled? Of course that was the Egyptian faith according to which the *Ka*, or Double, eternally haunted the place where its earthly counterpart had been laid to rest. When one came to think of it, beneath a mass of unintelligible symbolism there was much in the Egyptian faith which it was hard for a Christian to disbelieve. Salvation through a Redeemer, for instance, and the resurrection of the body. Had he, Smith, not already written a treatise upon these points of similarity which he proposed to publish one day, not under his own name? Well, he would not think of them now; the occasion seemed scarcely fitting—they came home too pointedly to one who was engaged in violating a tomb.

His mind, or rather his imagination—of which he had plenty—went off at a tangent. What sights had this place seen thousands of years ago! Once, thousands of years ago, a procession had wound up along the roadway which was doubtless buried beneath the sand whereon he stood towards the dark door of this sepulchre. He could see it as it passed in and out between the rocks. The priests, shaven-headed and robed in leopards' skins, or some of them in pure white, bearing the mystic symbols of their office. The funeral sledge drawn by oxen, and on it the great rectangular case that contained the outer and the inner coffins, and within them the mummy of some departed Majesty; in the Egyptian formula, "the hawk that had spread its wings and flown into the bosom of Osiris," God of Death. Behind, the mourners, rending the air with their lamentations. Then those who bore the funeral furniture and offerings. Then the high officers of State and the first priests of Amen and of the other gods. Then the sister queens, leading by the hand a wondering child or two. Then the sons of Pharaoh, young men carrying the emblems of their rank.

Lastly, walking alone, Pharaoh himself in his ceremonial robes, his apron, his double crown of linen surmounted by the golden snake, his inlaid bracelets and his heavy, tinkling earrings. Pharaoh, his head bowed, his feet travelling wearily, and in his heart—what thoughts? Sorrow, perhaps, for her who had departed. Yet he had other queens and fair women without count. Doubtless she was sweet and beautiful, but sweetness and beauty were not given to her alone. Moreover, was she not wont to cross his will and to question his divinity? No, surely it is not only of her that he thinks, her for whom he had prepared this splendid tomb with all things needful to unite her with the gods. Surely he thinks also of himself and that other tomb on the farther side of the hill whereat the artists labour day by day—yes, and have laboured these many years; that tomb to which before so very long he too must travel in just this fashion, to seek his place beyond the doors of Death, who lays his equal hand on king and queen and slave.

The vision passed. It was so real that Smith thought he must have been dreaming. Well, he was awake now, and colder than ever. Moreover, the jackals had multiplied. There were a whole pack of them, and not far away. Look! One crossed in the ring of the lamplight, a slinking, yellow beast that smelt the remains of dinner. Or perhaps it smelt himself. Moreover, there were bad characters who haunted these mountains, and he was alone and quite unarmed. Perhaps he ought to put out the light which advertised his whereabouts. It would be wise, and yet in this particular he rejected wisdom. After all, the light was some company.

Since sleep seemed to be out of the question, he fell back upon poor humanity's other anodyne, work, which has the incidental advantage of generating warmth. Seizing a shovel, he began to dig at the doorway of the tomb, whilst the jackals howled louder than ever in astonishment. They were not used to such a sight. For thousands of years, as the old moon above could have told, no man, or at least no solitary man, had dared to rob tombs at such an unnatural hour.

When Smith had been digging for about twenty minutes something tinkled on his shovel with a noise which sounded loud in that silence.

"A stone which may come in handy for the jackals," he thought to himself, shaking the sand slowly off the spade until it appeared. There it was, and not large enough to be of much service. Still, he picked it up, and rubbed it in his hands to clear off the encrusting dirt. When he opened them he saw that it was no stone, but a bronze.

"Osiris," reflected Smith, "buried in front of the tomb to hallow the ground. No, an Isis. No, the head of a statuette, and a jolly good one, too—at any rate, in moonlight. Seems to have been gilded." And, reaching out for the lamp, he held it over the object.

Another minute, and he found himself sitting at the bottom of the hole, lamp in one hand and statuette, or rather head, in the other.

"The Queen of the Mask!" he gasped. "The same—the same! By heavens, the very same!"

Oh, he could not be mistaken. There were the identical lips, a little thick and pouted; the identical nostrils, curved and quivering, but a little wide; the identical arched eyebrows and dreamy eyes set somewhat far apart. Above all, there was the identical alluring and mysterious smile. Only on this masterpiece of ancient art was set a whole crown of *uraei* surrounding the entire head. Beneath the crown and pressed back behind the ears was a full-bottomed wig or royal head-dress, of which the ends descended to the breasts. The statuette, that, having been gilt, remained quite perfect and uncorroded, was broken just above the middle, apparently by a single violent blow, for the fracture was very clean.

At once it occurred to Smith that it had been stolen from the tomb by a thief who thought it to be gold; that outside of the tomb doubt had overtaken him and caused him to break it upon a stone or otherwise. The rest was clear. Finding that it was but gold-washed bronze he had thrown away the fragments, rather than be at the pains of carrying them. This was his theory, probably not a correct one, as the sequel seems to show.

Smith's first idea was to recover the other portion. He searched quite a long while, but without success. Neither then nor afterwards could it be found. He reflected that perhaps this lower half had remained in the thief's hand, who, in his vexation, had thrown it far away, leaving the head to lie where it fell. Again Smith examined this head, and more closely. Now he saw that just beneath the breasts was a delicately cut cartouche.

Being by this time a master of hieroglyphics, he read it without trouble. It ran: "Ma-Mee, Great Royal Lady. Beloved of ——" Here the cartouche was broken away.

"Ma-Mé, or it might be Ma-Mi," he reflected. "I never heard of a queen called Ma-Mé, or Ma-Mi, or Ma-Mu. She must be quite new to history. I wonder of whom she was beloved? Amen, or Horus, or Isis, probably. Of some god, I have no doubt, at least I hope so!"

He stared at the beautiful portrait in his hand, as once he had stared at the cast on the Museum wall, and the beautiful portrait, emerging from the dust of ages, smiled back at him there in the solemn moonlight as once the cast had smiled from the museum wall. Only that had been but a cast, whereas this was real. This had slept with the dead from whose features it had been fashioned, the dead who lay, or who had lain, within.

A sudden resolution took hold of Smith. He would explore that tomb, at once and alone. No one should accompany him on this his first visit; it would be a sacrilege that anyone save himself should set foot there until he had looked on what it might contain.

Why should he not enter? His lamp, of what is called the "hurricane" brand, was very good and bright, and would burn for many hours. Moreover, there had been time for the foul air to escape through the hole that they had cleared. Lastly, something seemed to call on him to come and see. He placed the bronze head in his breast-pocket over his heart, and, thrusting the lamp through the hole, looked down. Here there was no difficulty, since sand had drifted in to the level of the bottom of the aperture. Through it he struggled, to find himself upon a bed of sand that only just left him room to push himself along between it and the roof. A little farther on the passage was almost filled with mud.

Mahomet had been right when, from his knowledge of the bedrock, he said that any tomb made in this place must be flooded. It *had* been flooded by some ancient rain-storm, and Smith began to fear that he would find it quite filled with soil caked as hard as iron. So, indeed, it was to a certain depth, a result that apparently had been anticipated by those who hollowed it, for this entrance shaft was left quite undecorated. Indeed, as Smith found afterwards, a hole had been dug beneath the doorway to allow the mud to enter after the burial was completed. Only a miscalculation had been made. The natural level of the mud did not quite reach the roof of the tomb, and therefore still left it open.

After crawling for forty feet or so over this caked mud, Smith suddenly found himself on a rising stair. Then he understood the plan; the tomb itself was on a higher level.

Here began the paintings. Here the Queen Ma-Mee, wearing her crowns and dressed in diaphanous garments, was presented to god after god. Between her figure and those of the divinities the wall was covered with hieroglyphs as fresh to-day as on that when the artist had limned them. A glance told him that they were extracts from the Book of the Dead. When the thief of bygone ages had broken into the tomb, probably not very long after the interment, the mud over which Smith had just crawled was still wet. This he could tell, since the clay from the rascal's feet remained upon the stairs, and that upon his fingers had stained the paintings on the wall against which he had supported himself; indeed, in one place was an exact impression of his hand, showing its shape and even the lines of the skin.

At the top of the flight of steps ran another passage at a higher level, which the water had never reached, and to right and left were the beginnings of unfinished chambers. It was clear to him that this queen had died young. Her tomb, as she or the king had designed it, was never finished. A few more paces, and the passage enlarged itself into a hall about thirty feet square. The ceiling was decorated with vultures, their wings outspread, the looped Cross of Life hanging from their talons. On one wall her Majesty Ma-Mee stood expectant while Anubis weighed her heart against the feather of truth, and Thoth, the Recorder, wrote down the verdict upon his tablets. All her titles were given to her here, such as—"Great Royal Heiress, Royal Sister, Royal Wife, Royal Mother, Lady of the Two Lands, Palm-branch of Love, Beautiful-exceedingly."

Smith read them hurriedly and noted that nowhere could he see the name of the king who had been her husband. It would almost seem as though this had been purposely omitted. On the other walls Ma-Mee, accompanied by her *Ka*, or Double, made offerings to the various gods, or uttered propitiatory speeches to the hideous demons of the underworld, declaring their names to them and forcing them to say: "Pass on. Thou art pure!"

Lastly, on the end wall, triumphant, all her trials done, she, the justified Osiris, or Spirit, was received by the god Osiris, Saviour of Spirits.

All these things Smith noted hurriedly as he swung the lamp to and fro in that hallowed place. Then he saw something else which filled him with dismay. On the floor of the chamber where the coffins had been—for this was the burial chamber—lay a heap of black fragments charred with fire. Instantly he understood. After the thief had done his work he had burned the mummy-cases, and with them the body of the queen. There could be no doubt that this was so, for look! among the ashes lay some calcined human bones, while the roof above was blackened with the smoke and cracked by the heat of the conflagration. There was nothing left for him to find!

Oppressed with the closeness of the atmosphere, he sat down upon a little bench or table cut in the rock that evidently had been meant to receive offerings to the dead. Indeed, on it still lay the scorched remains of some votive flowers. Here, his lamp between his feet, he rested a while, staring at those calcined bones. See, yonder was the lower jaw, and in it some teeth, small, white, regular and but little worn. Yes, she had died young. Then he turned to go, for disappointment and the holiness of the place overcame him; he could endure no more of it that night.

Leaving the burial hall, he walked along the painted passage, the lamp swinging and his eyes fixed upon the floor. He was disheartened, and the paintings could wait till the morrow. He descended the steps and came to the foot of the mud slope. Here suddenly he perceived, projecting from some sand that had drifted down over the mud, what seemed to be the corner of a reed box or basket. To clear away the sand was easy, and—yes, it was a basket, a foot or so in length, such a basket as the old Egyptians used to contain the funeral figures which are called *ushaptis*, or other objects connected with the dead. It looked as though it had been dropped, for it lay upon its side. Smith opened it—not very hopefully, for surely nothing of value would have been abandoned thus.

The first thing that met his eyes was a mummied hand, broken off at the wrist, a woman's little hand, most delicately shaped. It was withered and paper-white, but the contours still remained; the long fingers were perfect, and the almond-shaped nails had been stained with henna, as was the embalmers' fashion. On the hand were two gold rings, and for those rings it had been stolen. Smith looked at it for a long while, and his heart swelled within him, for here was the hand of that royal lady of his dreams.

Indeed, he did more than look; he kissed it, and as his lips touched the holy relic it seemed to him as though a wind, cold but scented, blew upon his brow. Then, growing fearful of the thoughts that arose within him, he hurried his mind back to the world, or rather to the examination of the basket.

Here he found other objects roughly wrapped in fragments of mummy-cloth that had been torn from the body of the queen. These it is needless to describe, for are they not to be seen in the gold room of the Museum, labelled "Bijouterie de la Reine Ma-Mé, XVIIIème Dynastie. Thebes (Smith's Tomb)"? It may be mentioned, however, that the set was incomplete. For instance, there was but one of the great gold ceremonial ear-rings fashioned like a group of pomegranate blooms, and the most beautiful of the necklaces had been torn in two—half of it was missing.

It was clear to Smith that only a portion of the precious objects which were buried with the mummy had been placed in this basket. Why had these been left where he found them? A little reflection made that clear also. Something had prompted the thief to destroy the desecrated body and its coffin with fire, probably in the hope of hiding his evil handiwork. Then he fled with his spoil. But he had forgotten how fiercely mummies and their trappings can burn. Or perhaps the thing was an accident. He must have had a lamp, and if its flame chanced to touch this bituminous tinder!

At any rate, the smoke overtook the man in that narrow place as he began to climb the slippery slope of clay. In his haste he dropped the basket, and dared not return to search for it. It could wait till the morrow, when the fire would be out and the air pure. Only for this desecrator of the royal dead that morrow never came, as was discovered afterwards.

When at length Smith struggled into the open air the stars were paling before the dawn. An hour later, after the sky was well up, Mahomet (recovered from his sickness) and his myrmidons arrived.

"I have been busy while you slept," said Smith, showing them the mummied hand (but not the rings which he had removed from the shrunk fingers), and the broken bronze, but not the priceless jewellery which was hidden in his pockets.

For the next ten days they dug till the tomb and its approach were quite clear. In the sand, at the head of a flight of steps which led down to the doorway, they found the skeleton of a man, who evidently had been buried there in a hurried fashion. His skull was shattered by the blow of an axe, and the shaven scalp that still clung to it suggested that he might have been a priest.

Mahomet thought, and Smith agreed with him, that this was the person who had violated the tomb. As he was escaping from it the guards of the holy place surprised him after he had covered up the hole by which he had entered and purposed to return. There they executed him without trial and divided up the plunder, thinking that no more was to be found. Or perhaps his confederates killed him.

Such at least were the theories advanced by Mahomet. Whether they were right or wrong none will ever know. For instance, the skeleton may not have been that of the thief, though probability appears to point the other way.

Nothing more was found in the tomb, not even a scarab or a mummy-bead. Smith spent the remainder of his time in photographing the pictures and copying the inscriptions, which for various reasons proved to be of extraordinary interest. Then, having reverently buried the charred bones of the queen in a secret place of the sepulchre, he handed it over to the care of the local Guardian of Antiquities, paid off Mahomet and the fellaheen, and departed for Cairo. With him went the wonderful jewels of which he had breathed no word, and another relic to him yet more precious—the hand of her Majesty Ma-Mee, Palm-branch of Love.

And now follows the strange sequel of this story of Smith and the queen Ma-Mee.

CHAPTER II

Smith was seated in the sanctum of the distinguished Director-General of Antiquities at the new Cairo Museum. It was a very interesting room. Books piled upon the floor; objects from tombs awaiting examination, lying here and there; a hoard of Ptolemaic silver coins, just dug up at Alexandria, standing on a table in the pot that had hidden them for two thousand years; in the corner the mummy of a royal child, aged six or seven, not long ago discovered, with some inscription scrawled upon the wrappings (brought here to be deciphered by the Master), and the withered lotus-bloom, love's last offering, thrust beneath one of the pink retaining bands.

"A touching object," thought Smith to himself. "Really, they might have left the dear little girl in peace."

Smith had a tender heart, but even as he reflected he became aware that some of the jewellery hidden in an inner pocket of his waistcoat (designed for bank-notes) was fretting his skin. He had a tender conscience also.

Just then the Director, a French savant, bustled in, alert, vigorous, full of interest.

"Ah, my dear Mr. Smith!" he said, in his excellent English. "I am indeed glad to see you back again, especially as I understand that you are come rejoicing and bringing your sheaves with you. They tell me you have been extraordinarily successful. What do you say is the name of this queen whose tomb you have found—Ma-Mee? A very unusual name. How do you get the extra vowel? Is it for euphony, eh? Did I not know how good a scholar you are, I should be tempted to believe that you had misread it. Me-Mee, Ma-Mee! That would be pretty in French, would it not? *Ma mie*—my darling! Well, I dare say she was somebody's *mie* in her time. But tell me the story."

Smith told him shortly and clearly; also he produced his photographs and copies of inscriptions.

"This is interesting—interesting truly," said the Director, when he had glanced through them. "You must leave them with me to study. Also you will publish them, is it not so? Perhaps one of the Societies would help you with the cost, for it should be done in facsimile. Look at this vignette! Most unusual. Oh, what a pity that scoundrelly priest got off with the jewellery and burnt her Majesty's body!"

"He didn't get off with all of it."

"What, Mr. Smith? Our inspector reported to me that you found nothing."

"I dare say, sir; but your inspector did not know what I found."

"Ah, you are a discreet man! Well, let us see."

Slowly Smith unbuttoned his waistcoat. From its inner pocket and elsewhere about his person he extracted the jewels wrapped in mummy-cloth as he had found them. First he produced a sceptre-head of gold, in the shape of a pomegranate fruit and engraved with the throne name and titles of Ma-Mee.

"What a beautiful object!" said the Director. "Look! the handle was of ivory, and that *sacré* thief of a priest smashed it out at the socket. It was fresh ivory then; the robbery must have taken place not long after the burial. See, this magnifying-glass shows it. Is that all?"

Smith handed him the surviving half of the marvellous necklace that had been torn in two.

"I have re-threaded it," he muttered, "but every bead is in its place."

"Oh, heavens! How lovely! Note the cutting of those cornelian heads of Hathor and the gold lotus-blooms between—yes, and the enamelled flies beneath. We have nothing like it in the Museum."

So it went on.

"Is that all?" gasped the Director at last, when every object from the basket glittered before them on the table.

"Yes," said Smith. "That is—no. I found a broken statuette hidden in the sand outside the tomb. It is of the queen, but I thought perhaps you would allow me to keep this."

"But certainly, Mr. Smith; it is yours indeed. We are not niggards here. Still, if I might see it——"

From yet another pocket Smith produced the head. The Director gazed at it, then he spoke with feeling.

"I said just now that you were discreet, Mr. Smith, and I have been reflecting that you are honest. But now I must add that you are very clever. If you had not made me promise that this bronze should be yours before you showed it me—well, it would never have gone into that pocket again. And, in the public interest, won't you release me from the promise?"

"*No*," said Smith.

"You are perhaps not aware," went on the Director, with a groan, "that this is a portrait of Mariette's unknown queen whom we are thus able to identify. It seems a pity that the two should be separated; a replica we could let you have."

"I am quite aware," said Smith, "and I will be sure to send *you* a replica, with photographs. Also I promise to leave the original to some museum by will."

The Director clasped the image tenderly, and, holding it to the light, read the broken cartouche beneath the breasts.

"'Ma-Mé, Great Royal Lady. Beloved of ——' Beloved of whom? Well, of Smith, for one. Take it, monsieur, and hide it away at once, lest soon there should be another mummy in this collection, a modern mummy called Smith; and, in the name of Justice, let the museum which inherits it be not the British, but that of Cairo, for this queen belongs to Egypt. By the way, I have been told that you are delicate in the lungs. How is your health now? Our cold winds are very trying. Quite good? Ah, that is excellent! I suppose that you have no more articles that you can show me?"

"I have nothing more except a mummied hand, which I found in the basket with the jewels. The two rings off it lie there. Doubtless it was removed to get at that bracelet. I suppose you will not mind my keeping the hand——"

"Of the beloved of Smith," interrupted the Director drolly. "No, I suppose not, though for my part I should prefer one that was not quite so old. Still, perhaps *you* will not mind my seeing it. That pocket of yours still looks a little bulky; I thought that it contained books!"

Smith produced a cigar-box; in it was the hand wrapped in cotton wool.

"Ah," said the Director, "a pretty, well-bred hand. No doubt this Ma-Mee was the real heiress to the throne, as she describes herself. The Pharaoh was somebody of inferior birth, half-brother—she is called 'Royal Sister,' you remember—son of one of the Pharaoh's slave-women, perhaps. Odd that she never mentioned him in the tomb. It looks as though they didn't get on in life, and that she was determined to have done with him in death. Those were the rings upon that hand, were they not?"

He replaced them on the fingers, then took off one, a royal signet in a cartouche, and read the inscription on the other: "'Bes Ank, Ank Bes.' 'Bes the Living, the Living Bes.'

"Your Ma-Mee had some human vanity about her," he added. "Bes, among other things, as you know, was the god of beauty and of the adornments of women. She wore that ring that she might remain beautiful, and that her dresses might always fit, and her rouge never cake when she was dancing before the gods. Also it fixes her period pretty closely, but then so do other things. It seems a pity to rob Ma-Mee of her pet ring, does it not? The royal signet will be enough for us."

With a little bow he gave the hand back to Smith, leaving the Bes ring on the finger that had worn it for more than three thousand years. At least, Smith was so sure it was the Bes ring that at the time he did not look at it again.

Then they parted, Smith promising to return upon the morrow, which, owing to events to be described, he did not do.

"Ah!" said the Master to himself, as the door closed behind his visitor. "He's in a hurry to be gone. He has fear lest I should change my mind about that ring. Also there is the bronze. Monsieur Smith was *ruse* there. It is worth a thousand pounds, that bronze. Yet I do not believe he was thinking of the money. I believe he is in love with that Ma-Mee and wants to keep her picture. *Mon Dieu!* A well-established affection. At least he is what the English call an odd fish, one whom I could never make out, and of whom no one seems to know anything. Still, honest, I am sure—quite honest. Why, he might have kept every one of those jewels and no one have been the wiser. And what things! What a find! *Ciel!* what a find! There has been nothing like it for years. Benedictions on the head of Odd-fish Smith!"

Then he collected the precious objects, thrust them into an inner compartment of his safe, which he locked and double-locked, and, as it was nearly five o'clock, departed from the Museum to his private residence in the grounds, there to study Smith's copies and photographs, and to tell some friends of the great things that had happened.

When Smith found himself outside the sacred door, and had presented its venerable guardian with a baksheesh of five piastres, he walked a few paces to the right and paused a while to watch some native labourers who were dragging a huge sarcophagus upon an improvised tramway. As they dragged they sang an echoing rhythmic song, whereof each line ended with an invocation to Allah.

Just so, reflected Smith, had their forefathers sung when, millenniums ago, they dragged that very sarcophagus from the quarries to the Nile, and from the Nile to the tomb whence it reappeared to-day, or when they slid the casing blocks of the pyramids up the great causeway and smooth slope of sand, and laid them in their dizzy resting-places. Only then each line of the immemorial chant of toil ended with an invocation to Amen, now transformed to Allah. The East may change its masters and its gods, but its customs never change, and if to-day Allah wore the feathers of Amen one wonders whether the worshippers would find the difference so very great.

Thus thought Smith as he hurried away from the sarcophagus and those blue-robed, dark-skinned fellaheen, down the long gallery that is filled with a thousand sculptures. For a moment he paused before the wonderful white statue of Queen Amenartas, then, remembering that his time was short, hastened on to a certain room, one of those which opened out of the gallery.

In a corner of this room, upon the wall, amongst many other beautiful objects, stood that head which Mariette had found, whereof in past years the cast had fascinated him in London. Now he knew whose head it was; to him it had been given to find the tomb of her who had sat for that statue. Her very hand was in his pocket—yes, the hand that had touched yonder marble, pointing out its defects to the sculptor, or perhaps swearing that he flattered her. Smith wondered who that sculptor was; surely he must have been a happy man. Also he wondered whether the statuette was also this master's work. He thought so, but he wished to make sure.

Near to the end of the room he stopped and looked about him like a thief. He was alone in the place; not a single student or tourist could be seen, and its guardian was somewhere else. He drew out the box that contained the hand. From the hand he slipped the ring which the Director-General had left there as a gift to himself. He would much have preferred the other with the signet, but how could he say so, especially after the episode of the statuette?

Replacing the hand in his pocket without looking at the ring—for his eyes were watching to see whether he was observed—he set it upon his little finger, which it exactly fitted. (Ma-Mee had worn both of them upon the third finger of her left hand, the Bes ring as a guard to the signet.) He had the fancy to approach the effigy of Ma-Mee wearing a ring which she had worn and that came straight from her finger to his own.

Smith found the head in its accustomed place. Weeks had gone by since he looked upon it, and now, to his eyes, it had grown more beautiful than ever, and its smile was more mystical and living. He drew out the statuette and began to compare them point by point. Oh, no doubt was possible! Both were likenesses of the same woman, though the statuette might have been executed two or three years later than the statue. To him the face of it looked a little older and more spiritual. Perhaps illness, or some premonition of her end had then thrown its shadow on the queen. He compared and compared. He made some rough measurements and sketches in his pocket-book, and set himself to work out a canon of proportions.

So hard and earnestly did he work, so lost was his mind that he never heard the accustomed warning sound which announces that the Museum is about to close. Hidden behind an altar as he was, in his distant, shadowed corner, the guardian of the room never saw him as he cast a last perfunctory glance about the place before departing till the Saturday morning; for the morrow was Friday, the Mohammedan Sabbath, on which the Museum remains shut, and he would not be called upon to attend. So he went. Everybody went. The great doors clanged, were locked and bolted, and, save for a watchman outside, no one was left in all that vast place except Smith in his corner, engaged in sketching and in measurements.

The difficulty of seeing, owing to the increase of shadow, first called his attention to the fact that time was slipping away. He glanced at his watch and saw that it was ten minutes to the hour.

"Soon be time to go," he thought to himself, and resumed his work.

How strangely silent the place seemed! Not a footstep to be heard or the sound of a human voice. He looked at his watch again, and saw that it was six o'clock, not five, or so the thing said. But that was impossible, for the Museum shut at five; evidently the desert sand had got into the works. The room in which he stood was that known as Room I, and he had noticed that its Arab custodian often frequented Room K or the gallery outside. He would find him and ask what was the real time.

Passing round the effigy of the wonderful Hathor cow, perhaps the finest example of an ancient sculpture of a beast in the whole world, Smith came to the doorway and looked up and down the gallery. Not a soul to be seen. He ran to Room K, to Room H, and others. Still not a soul to be seen. Then he made his way as fast as he could go to the great entrance. The doors were locked and bolted.

"Watch must be right after all. I'm shut in," he said to himself. "However, there's sure to be someone about somewhere. Probably the *salle des ventes* is still open. Shops don't shut till they are obliged."

Thither he went, to find its door as firmly closed as a door can be. He knocked on it, but a sepulchral echo was the only answer.

"I know," he reflected. "The Director must still be in his room. It will take him a long while to examine all that jewellery and put it away."

So for the room he headed, and, after losing his path twice, found it by help of the sarcophagus that the Arabs had been dragging, which now stood as deserted as it had done in the tomb, a lonesome and impressive object in the gathering shadows. The Director's door was shut, and again his knockings produced nothing but an echo. He started on a tour round the Museum, and, having searched the ground floors, ascended to the upper galleries by the great stairway.

Presently he found himself in that devoted to the royal mummies, and, being tired, rested there a while. Opposite to him, in a glass case in the middle of the gallery, reposed Rameses II. Near to, on shelves in a side case, were Rameses' son, Meneptah, and above, his son, Seti II, while in other cases were the mortal remains of many more of the royalties of Egypt. He looked at the proud face of Rameses and at the little fringe of white locks turned yellow by the embalmer's spices, also at the raised left arm. He remembered how the Director had told him that when they were unrolling this mighty monarch they went away to lunch, and that presently the man who had been left in charge of the body rushed into the room with his hair on end, and said that the dead king had lifted his arm and pointed at him.

Back they went, and there, true enough, was the arm lifted; nor were they ever able to get it quite into its place again. The explanation given was that the warmth of the sun had contracted the withered muscles, a very natural and correct explanation.

Still, Smith wished that he had not recollected the story just at this moment, especially as the arm seemed to move while he contemplated it —a very little, but still to move.

He turned round and gazed at Meneptah, whose hollow eyes stared at him from between the wrappings carelessly thrown across the parchment-like and ashen face. There, probably, lay the countenance that had frowned on Moses. There was the heart which God had hardened. Well, it was hard enough now, for the doctors said he died of ossification of the arteries, and that the vessels of the heart were full of lime!

Smith stood upon a chair and peeped at Seti II. above. His weaker countenance was very peaceful, but it seemed to wear an air of reproach. In getting down Smith managed to upset the heavy chair. The noise it made was terrific. He would not have thought it possible that the fall of such an article could produce so much sound. Satisfied with his inspection of these particular kings, who somehow looked quite different now from what they had ever done before—more real and imminent, so to speak—he renewed his search for a living man.

On he went, mummies to his right, mummies to his left, of every style and period, till he began to feel as though he never wished to see another dried remnant of mortality. He peeped into the room where lay the relics of Iouiya and Touiyou, the father and mother of the great Queen Taia. Cloths had been drawn over these, and really they looked worse and more suggestive thus draped than in their frigid and unadorned blackness. He came to the coffins of the priest-kings of the twentieth dynasty, formidable painted coffins with human faces. There seemed to be a vast number of these priest-kings, but perhaps they were better than the gold masks of the great Ptolemaic ladies which glinted at him through the gathering gloom.

Really, he had seen enough of the upper floors. The statues downstairs were better than all these dead, although it was true that, according to the Egyptian faith, every one of those statues was haunted eternally by the *Ka*, or Double, of the person whom it represented. He descended the great stairway. Was it fancy, or did something run across the bottom step in front of him—an animal of some kind, followed by a swift-moving and indefinite shadow? If so, it must have been the Museum cat hunting a Museum mouse. Only then what on earth was that very peculiar and unpleasant shadow?

He called, "Puss! puss! puss!" for he would have been quite glad of its company; but there came no friendly "miau" in response. Perhaps it was only the *Ka* of a cat and the shadow was—oh! never mind what. The Egyptians worshipped cats, and there were plenty of their mummies about on the shelves. But the shadow!

Once he shouted in the hope of attracting attention, for there were no windows to which he could climb. He did not repeat the experiment, for it seemed as though a thousand voices were answering him from every corner and roof of the gigantic edifice.

Well, he must face the thing out. He was shut in a museum, and the question was in what part of it he should camp for the night. Moreover, as it was growing rapidly dark, the problem must be solved at once. He thought with affection of the lavatory, where, before going to see the Director, only that afternoon he had washed his hands with the assistance of a kindly Arab who watched the door and gracefully accepted a piastre. But there was no Arab there now, and the door, like every other in this confounded place, was locked. He marched on to the entrance.

Here, opposite to each other, stood the red sarcophagi of the great Queen Hatshepu and her brother and husband, Thotmes III. He looked at them. Why should not one of these afford him a night's lodging? They were deep and quiet, and would fit the human frame very nicely. For a while Smith wondered which of these monarchs would be the more likely to take offence at such a use of a private sarcophagus, and, acting on general principles, concluded that he would rather throw himself on the mercy of the lady.

Already one of his legs was over the edge of that solemn coffer, and he was squeezing his body beneath the massive lid that was propped above it on blocks of wood, when he remembered a little, naked, withered thing with long hair that he had seen in a side chamber of the tomb of Amenhotep II. in the Valley of Kings at Thebes. This caricature of humanity many thought, and he agreed with them, to be the actual body of the mighty Hatshepu as it appeared after the robbers had done with it.

Supposing now, that when he was lying at the bottom of that sarcophagus, sleeping the sleep of the just, this little personage should peep over its edge and ask him what he was doing there! Of course the idea was absurd; he was tired, and his nerves were a little shaken. Still, the fact remained that for centuries the hallowed dust of Queen Hatshepu had slept where he, a modern man, was proposing to sleep.

He scrambled down from the sarcophagus and looked round him in despair. Opposite to the main entrance was the huge central hall of the Museum. Now the cement roof of this hall had, he knew, gone wrong, with the result that very extensive repairs had become necessary. So extensive were they, indeed, that the Director-General had informed him that they would take several years to complete. Therefore this hall was boarded up, only a little doorway being left by which the workmen could enter. Certain statues, of Seti II. and others, too large to be moved, were also roughly boarded over, as were some great funeral boats on either side of the entrance. The rest of the place, which might be two hundred feet long with a proportionate breadth, was empty save for the colossi of Amenhotep III. and his queen Taia that stood beneath the gallery at its farther end.

It was an appalling place in which to sleep, but better, reflected Smith, than a sarcophagus or those mummy chambers. If, for instance, he could creep behind the deal boards that enclosed one of the funeral boats he would be quite comfortable there. Lifting the curtain, he slipped into the hall, where the gloom of evening had already settled. Only the skylights and the outline of the towering colossi at the far end remained visible. Close to him were the two funeral boats which he had noted when he looked into the hall earlier on that day, standing at the head of a flight of steps which led to the sunk floor of the centre. He groped his way to that on the right. As he expected, the projecting planks were not quite joined at the bow. He crept in between them and the boat and laid himself down.

Presumably, being altogether tired out, Smith did ultimately fall asleep, for how long he never knew. At any rate, it is certain that, if so, he woke up again. He could not tell the time, because his watch was not a repeater, and the place was as black as the pit. He had some matches in his pocket, and might have struck one and even have lit his pipe. To his credit be it said, however, he remembered that he was the sole tenant of one of the most valuable museums in the world, and his responsibilities with reference to fire. So he refrained from striking that match under the keel of a boat which had become very dry in the course of five thousand years.

Smith found himself very wide awake indeed. Never in all his life did he remember being more so, not even in the hour of its great catastrophe, or when his godfather, Ebenezer, after much hesitation, had promised him a clerkship in the bank of which he was a director. His nerves seemed strung tight as harp-strings, and his every sense was painfully acute. Thus he could even smell the odour of mummies that floated down from the upper galleries and the earthy scent of the boat which had been buried for thousands of years in sand at the foot of the pyramid of one of the fifth dynasty kings.

Moreover, he could hear all sorts of strange sounds, faint and far-away sounds which at first he thought must emanate from Cairo without. Soon, however, he grew sure that their origin was more local. Doubtless the cement work and the cases in the galleries were cracking audibly, as is the unpleasant habit of such things at night.

Yet why should these common manifestations be so universal and affect him so strangely? Really, it seemed as though people were stirring all about him. More, he could have sworn that the great funeral boat beneath which he lay had become re-peopled with the crew that once it bore.

He heard them at their business above him. There were trampings and a sound as though something heavy were being laid on the deck, such, for instance, as must have been made when the mummy of Pharaoh was set there for its last journey to the western bank of the Nile. Yes, and now he could have sworn again that the priestly crew were getting out the oars.

Smith began to meditate flight from the neighbourhood of that place when something occurred which determined him to stop where he was.

The huge hall was growing light, but not, as at first he hoped, with the rays of dawn. This light was pale and ghostly, though very penetrating. Also it had a blue tinge, unlike any other he had ever seen. At first it arose in a kind of fan or fountain at the far end of the hall, illumining the steps there and the two noble colossi which sat above.

But what was this that stood at the head of the steps, radiating glory? By heavens! it was Osiris himself or the image of Osiris, god of the Dead, the Egyptian saviour of the world!

There he stood, in his mummy-cloths, wearing the feathered crown, and holding in his hands, which projected from an opening in the wrappings, the crook and the scourge of power. Was he alive, or was he dead? Smith could not tell, since he never moved, only stood there, splendid and fearful, his calm, benignant face staring into nothingness.

Smith became aware that the darkness between him and the vision of this god was peopled; that a great congregation was gathering, or had gathered there. The blue light began to grow; long tongues of it shot forward, which joined themselves together, illumining all that huge hall.

Now, too, he saw the congregation. Before him, rank upon rank of them, stood the kings and queens of Egypt. As though at a given signal, they bowed themselves to the Osiris, and ere the tinkling of their ornaments had died away, lo! Osiris was gone. But in his place stood another, Isis, the Mother of Mystery, her deep eyes looking forth from beneath the jewelled vulture-cap. Again the congregation bowed, and, lo! she was gone. But in her place stood yet another, a radiant, lovely being, who held in her hand the Sign of Life, and wore upon her head the symbol of the shining disc—Hathor, Goddess of Love. A third time the congregation bowed, and she, too, was gone; nor did any other appear in her place.

The Pharaohs and their queens began to move about and speak to each other; their voices came to his ears in one low, sweet murmur.

In his amaze Smith had forgotten fear. From his hiding-place he watched them intently. Some of them he knew by their faces. There, for instance, was the long-necked Khu-en-aten, talking somewhat angrily to the imperial Rameses II. Smith could understand what he said, for this power seemed to have been given to him. He was complaining in a high, weak voice that on this, the one night of the year when they might meet, the gods, or the magic images of the gods who were put up for them to worship, should not include *his* god, symbolized by the "Aten," or the sun's disc.

"I have heard of your Majesty's god," replied Rameses; "the priests used to tell me of him, also that he did not last long after your Majesty flew to heaven. The Fathers of Amen gave you a bad name; they called you 'the heretic' and hammered out your cartouches. They were quite rare in my time. Oh, do not let your Majesty be angry! So many of us have been heretics. My grandson, Seti, there"—and he pointed to a mild, thoughtful-faced man—"for example. I am told that he really worshipped the god of those Hebrew slaves whom I used to press to build my cities. Look at that lady with him. Beautiful, isn't she? Observe her large, violet eyes! Well, she was the one who did the mischief, a Hebrew herself. At least, they tell me so."

"I will talk with him," answered Khu-en-aten. "It is more than possible that we may agree on certain points. Meanwhile, let me explain to your Majesty——"

"Oh, I pray you, not now. There is my wife."

"Your wife?" said Khu-en-aten, drawing himself up. "Which wife? I am told that your Majesty had many and left a large family; indeed, I see some hundreds of them here to-night. Now, I—but let me introduce Nefertiti to your Majesty. I may explain that she was my *only* wife."

"So I have understood. Your Majesty was rather an invalid, were you not? Of course, in those circumstances, one prefers the nurse whom one can trust. Oh, pray, no offence! Nefertari, my love—oh, I beg pardon! —Astnefert—Nefertari has gone to speak to some of her children—let me introduce you to your predecessor, the Queen Nefertiti, wife of Amenhotep IV.—I mean Khu-en-aten (he changed his name, you know, because half of it was that of the father of the gods). She is interested in the question of plural marriage. Good-bye! I wish to have a word with my grandfather, Rameses I. He was fond of me as a little boy."

At this moment Smith's interest in that queer conversation died away, for of a sudden he beheld none other than the queen of his dreams, Ma-Mee. Oh! there she stood, without a doubt, only ten times more beautiful than he had ever pictured her. She was tall and somewhat fair-complexioned, with slumbrous, dark eyes, and on her face gleamed the mystic smile he loved. She wore a robe of simple white and a purple-broidered apron, a crown of golden *uraei* with turquoise eyes was set upon her dark hair as in her statue, and on her breast and arms were the very necklace and bracelets that he had taken from her tomb. She appeared to be somewhat moody, or rather thoughtful, for she leaned by herself against a balustrade, watching the throng without much interest.

Presently a Pharaoh, a black-browed, vigorous man with thick lips, drew near.

"I greet your Majesty," he said.

She started, and answered: "Oh, it is you! I make my obeisance to your Majesty," and she curtsied to him, humbly enough, but with a suggestion of mockery in her movements.

"Well, you do not seem to have been very anxious to find me, Ma-Mee, which, considering that we meet so seldom——"

"I saw that your Majesty was engaged with my sister queens," she interrupted, in a rich, low voice, "and with some other ladies in the gallery there, whose faces I seem to remember, but who I think were *not* queens. Unless, indeed, you married them after I was drawn away."

"One must talk to one's relations," replied the Pharaoh.

"Quite so. But, you see, I have no relations—at least, none whom I know well. My parents, you will remember, died when I was young, leaving me Egypt's heiress, and they are still vexed at the marriage which I made on the advice of my counsellors. But, is it not annoying? I have lost one of my rings, that which had the god Bes on it. Some dweller on the earth must be wearing it to-day, and that is why I cannot get it back from him."

"Him! Why 'him'? Hush; the business is about to begin."

"What business, my lord?"

"Oh, the question of the violation of our tombs, I believe."

"Indeed! That is a large subject, and not a very profitable one, I should say. Tell me, who is that?" And she pointed to a lady who had stepped forward, a very splendid person, magnificently arrayed.

"Cleopatra the Greek," he answered, "the last of Egypt's Sovereigns, one of the Ptolemys. You can always know her by that Roman who walks about after her."

"Which?" asked Ma-Mee. "I see several—also other men. She was the wretch who rolled Egypt in the dirt and betrayed her. Oh, if it were not for the law of peace by which we must abide when we meet thus!"

"You mean that she would be torn to shreds, Ma-Mee, and her very soul scattered like the limbs of Osiris? Well, if it were not for that law of peace, so perhaps would many of us, for never have I heard a single king among these hundreds speak altogether well of those who went before or followed after him."

"Especially of those who went before if they happen to have hammered out their cartouches and usurped their monuments," said the queen, dryly, and looking him in the eyes.

At this home-thrust the Pharaoh seemed to wince. Making no answer, he pointed to the royal woman who had mounted the steps at the end of the hall.

Queen Cleopatra lifted her hand and stood thus for a while. Very splendid she was, and Smith, on his hands and knees behind the boarding of the boat, thanked his stars that alone among modern men it had been his lot to look upon her rich and living loveliness. There she shone, she who had changed the fortunes of the world, she who, whatever she did amiss, at least had known how to die.

Silence fell upon that glittering galaxy of kings and queens and upon all the hundreds of their offspring, their women, and their great officers who crowded the double tier of galleries around the hall.

"Royalties of Egypt," she began, in a sweet, clear voice which penetrated to the farthest recesses of the place, "I, Cleopatra, the sixth of that name and the last monarch who ruled over the Upper and the Lower Lands before Egypt became a home of slaves, have a word to say to your Majesties, who, in your mortal days, all of you more worthily filled the throne on which once I sat. I do not speak of Egypt and its fate, or of our sins—whereof mine were not the least—that brought her to the dust. Those sins I and others expiate elsewhere, and of them, from age to age, we hear enough. But on this one night of the year, that of the feast of him whom we call Osiris, but whom other nations have known and know by different names, it is given to us once more to be mortal for an hour, and, though we be but shadows, to renew the loves and hates of our long-perished flesh. Here for an hour we strut in our forgotten pomp; the crowns that were ours still adorn our brows, and once more we seem to listen to our people's praise. Our hopes are the hopes of mortal life, our foes are the foes we feared, our gods grow real again, and our lovers whisper in our ears. Moreover, this joy is given to us—to see each other as we are, to know as the gods know, and therefore to forgive, even where we despise and hate. Now I have done, and I, the youngest of the rulers of ancient Egypt, call upon him who was the first of her kings to take my place."

She bowed, and the audience bowed back to her. Then she descended the steps and was lost in the throng. Where she had been appeared an old man, simply-clad, long-bearded, wise-faced, and wearing on his grey hair no crown save a plain band of gold, from the centre of which rose the snake-headed *uraeus* crest.

"Your Majesties who came after me," said the old man, "I am Menes, the first of the accepted Pharaohs of Egypt, although many of those who went before me were more truly kings than I. Yet as the first who joined the Upper and the Lower Lands, and took the royal style and titles, and ruled as well as I could rule, it is given to me to talk with you for a while this night whereon our spirits are permitted to gather from the uttermost parts of the uttermost worlds and see each other face to face. First, in darkness and in secret, let us speak of the mystery of the gods and of its meanings. Next, in darkness and in secret, let us speak of the mystery of our lives, of whence they come, of where they tarry by the road, and whither they go at last. And afterwards, let us speak of other matters face to face in light and openness, as we were wont to do when we were men. Then hence to Thebes, there to celebrate our yearly festival. Is such your will?"

"Such is our will," they answered.

It seemed to Smith that dense darkness fell upon the place, and with it a silence that was awful. For a time that he could not reckon, that might have been years or might have been moments, he sat there in the utter darkness and the utter silence.

At length the light came again, first as a blue spark, then in upward pouring rays, and lastly pervading all. There stood Menes on the steps, and there in front of him was gathered the same royal throng.

"The mysteries are finished," said the old king. "Now, if any have aught to say, let it be said openly."

A young man dressed in the robes and ornaments of an early dynasty came forward and stood upon the steps between the Pharaoh Menes and all those who had reigned after him. His face seemed familiar to Smith, as was the side lock that hung down behind his right ear in token of his youth. Where had he seen him? Ah, he remembered. Only a few hours ago lying in one of the cases of the Museum, together with the bones of the Pharaoh Unas.

"Your Majesties," he began, "I am the King Metesuphis. The matter that I wish to lay before you is that of the violation of our sepulchres by those men who now live upon the earth. The mortal bodies of many who are gathered here to-night lie in this place to be stared at and mocked by the curious. I myself am one of them, jawless, broken, hideous to behold. Yonder, day by day, must my *Ka* sit watching my desecrated flesh, torn from the pyramid that, with cost and labour, I raised up to be an eternal house wherein I might hide till the hour of resurrection. Others of us lie in far lands. Thus, as he can tell you, my predecessor, Man-kau-ra, he who built the third of the great pyramids, the Pyramid of Her, sleeps, or rather wakes in a dark city, called London, across the seas, a place of murk where no sun shines. Others have been burnt with fire, others are scattered in small dust. The ornaments that were ours are stole away and sold to the greedy; our sacred writings and our symbols are their jest. Soon there will not be one holy grave in Egypt that remains undefiled."

"That is so," said a voice from the company. "But four months gone the deep, deep pit was opened that I had dug in the shadow of the Pyramid of Cephren, who begat me in the world. There in my chamber I slept alone, two handfuls of white bones, since when I died they did not preserve the body with wrappings and with spices. Now I see those bones of mine, beside which my Double has watched for these five thousand years, hid in the blackness of a great ship and tossing on a sea that is strewn with ice."

"It is so," echoed a hundred other voices.

"Then," went on the young king, turning to Menes, "I ask of your Majesty whether there is no means whereby we may be avenged on those who do us this foul wrong."

"Let him who has wisdom speak," said the old Pharaoh.

A man of middle age, short in stature and of a thoughtful brow, who held in his hand a wand and wore the feathers and insignia of the heir to the throne of Egypt and of a high priest of Amen, moved to the steps. Smith knew him at once from his statues. He was Khaemuas, son of Rameses the Great, the mightiest magician that ever was in Egypt, who of his own will withdrew himself from earth before the time came that he should sit upon the throne.

"I have wisdom, your Majesties, and I will answer," he said. "The time draws on when, in the land of Death which is Life, the land that we call Amenti, it will be given to us to lay our wrongs as to this matter before Those who judge, knowing that they will be avenged. On this night of the year also, when we resume the shapes we were, we have certain powers of vengeance, or rather of executing justice. But our time is short, and there is much to say and do before the sun-god Ra arises and we depart each to his place. Therefore it seems best that we should leave these wicked ones in their wickedness till we meet them face to face beyond the world."

Smith, who had been following the words of Khaemuas with the closest attention and considerable anxiety, breathed again, thanking Heaven that the engagements of these departed monarchs were so numerous and pressing. Still, as a matter of precaution, he drew the cigar-box which contained Ma-Mee's hand from his pocket, and pushed it as far away from him as he could. It was a most unlucky act. Perhaps the cigar-box grated on the floor, or perhaps the fact of his touching the relic put him into psychic communication with all these spirits. At any rate, he became aware that the eyes of that dreadful magician were fixed upon him, and that a bone had a better chance of escaping the search of a Röntgen ray than he of hiding himself from their baleful glare.

"As it happens, however," went on Khaemuas, in a cold voice, "I now perceive that there is hidden in this place, and spying on us, one of the worst of these vile thieves. I say to your Majesties that I see him crouched beneath yonder funeral barge, and that he has with him at this moment the hand of one of your Majesties, stolen by him from her tomb at Thebes."

Now every queen in the company became visibly agitated (Smith, who was watching Ma-Mee, saw her hold up her hands and look at them), while all the Pharaohs pointed with their fingers and exclaimed together, in a voice that rolled round the hall like thunder:

"Let him be brought forth to judgment!"

Khaemuas raised his wand and, holding it towards the boat where Smith was hidden, said:

"Draw near, Vile One, bringing with thee that thou hast stolen."

Smith tried hard to remain where he was. He sat himself down and set his heels against the floor. As the reader knows, he was always shy and retiring by disposition, and never had these weaknesses oppressed him more than they did just then. When a child his favourite nightmare had been that the foreman of a jury was in the act of proclaiming him guilty of some dreadful but unstated crime. Now he understood what that nightmare foreshadowed. He was about to be convicted in a court of which all the kings and queens of Egypt were the jury, Menes was Chief Justice, and the magician Khaemuas played the *role* of Attorney-General.

In vain did he sit down and hold fast. Some power took possession of him which forced him first to stretch out his arm and pick up the cigar-box containing the hand of Ma-Mee, and next drew him from the friendly shelter of the deal boards that were about the boat.

Now he was on his feet and walking down the flight of steps opposite to those on which Menes stood far away. Now he was among all that throng of ghosts, which parted to let him pass, looking at him as he went with cold and wondering eyes. They were very majestic ghosts; the ages that had gone by since they laid down their sceptres had taken nothing from their royal dignity. Moreover, save one, none of them seemed to have any pity for his plight. She was a little princess who stood by her mother, that same little princess whose mummy he had seen and pitied in the Director's room with a lotus flower thrust beneath her bandages. As he passed Smith heard her say:

"This Vile One is frightened. Be brave, Vile One!"

Smith understood, and pride came to his aid. He, a gentleman of the modern world, would not show the white feather before a crowd of ancient Egyptian ghosts. Turning to the child, he smiled at her, then drew himself to his full height and walked on quietly. Here it may be stated that Smith was a tall man, still comparatively young, and very good-looking, straight and spare in frame, with dark, pleasant eyes and a little black beard.

"At least he is a well-favoured thief," said one of the queens to another.

"Yes," answered she who had been addressed. "I wonder that a man with such a noble air should find pleasure in disturbing graves and stealing the offerings of the dead," words that gave Smith much cause for thought. He had never considered the matter in this light.

Now he came to the place where Ma-Mee stood, the black-browed Pharaoh who had been her husband at her side. On his left hand which held the cigar-box was the gold Bes ring, and that box he felt constrained to carry pressed against him just over his heart.

As he went by he turned his head, and his eyes met those of Ma-Mee. She started violently. Then she saw the ring upon his hand and again started still more violently.

"What ails your Majesty?" asked the Pharaoh.

"Oh, naught," she answered. "Yet does this earth-dweller remind you of anyone?"

"Yes, he does," answered the Pharaoh. "He reminds me very much of that accursed sculptor about whom we had words."

"Do you mean a certain Horu, the Court artist; he who worked the image that was buried with me, and whom you sent to carve your statues in the deserts of Kush, until he died of fevers—or was it poison?"

"Aye; Horu and no other, may Set take and keep him!" growled the Pharaoh.

Then Smith passed on and heard no more. Now he stood before the venerable Menes. Some instinct caused him to bow to this Pharaoh, who bowed back to him. Then he turned and bowed to the royal company, and they also bowed back to him, coldly, but very gravely and courteously.

"Dweller on the world where once we had our place, and therefore brother of us, the dead," began Menes, "this divine priest and magician"—and he pointed to Khaemuas—"declares that you are one of those who foully violate our sepulchres and desecrate our ashes. He declares, moreover, that at this very moment you have with you a portion of the mortal flesh of a certain Majesty whose spirit is present here. Say, now, are these things true?"

To his astonishment Smith found that he had not the slightest difficulty in answering in the same sweet tongue.

"O King, they are true, and not true. Hear me, rulers of Egypt. It is true that I have searched in your graves, because my heart has been drawn towards you, and I would learn all that I could concerning you, for it comes to me *now* that once I was one of you—no king, indeed, yet perchance of the blood of kings. Also—for I would hide nothing even if I could—I searched for one tomb above all others."

"Why, O man?" asked the Judge.

"Because a face drew me, a lovely face that was cut in stone."

Now all that great audience turned their eyes towards him and listened as though his words moved them.

"Did you find that holy tomb?" asked Menes. "If so, what did you find therein?"

"Aye, Pharaoh, and in it I found these," and he took from the box the withered hand, from his pocket the broken bronze, and from his finger the ring.

"Also I found other things which I delivered to the keeper of this place, articles of jewellery that I seem to see to-night upon one who is present here among you."

"Is the face of this figure the face you sought?" asked the Judge.

"It is the lovely face," he answered.

Menes took the effigy in his hand and read the cartouche that was engraved beneath its breast.

"If there be here among us," he said, presently, "one who long after my day ruled as queen in Egypt, one who was named Ma-Mé, let her draw near."

Now from where she stood glided Ma-Mee and took her place opposite to Smith.

"Say, O Queen," asked Menes, "do you know aught of this matter?"

"I know that hand; it was my own hand," she answered. "I know that ring; it was my ring. I know that image in bronze; it was my image. Look on me and judge for yourselves whether this be so. A certain sculptor fashioned it, the son of a king's son, who was named Horu, the first of sculptors and the head artist of my Court. There, clad in strange garments, he stands before you. Horu, or the Double of Horu, he who cut the image when I ruled in Egypt, is he who found the image and the man who stands before you; or, mayhap, his Double cast in the same mould."

The Pharaoh Menes turned to the magician Khaemuas and said:—

"Are these things so, O Seer?"

"They are so," answered Khaemuas. "This dweller on the earth is he who, long ago, was the sculptor Horu. But what shall that avail? He, once more a living man, is a violator of the hallowed dead. I say, therefore, that judgment should be executed on his flesh, so that when the light comes here to-morrow he himself will again be gathered to the dead."

Menes bent his head upon his breast and pondered. Smith said nothing. To him the whole play was so curious that he had no wish to interfere with its development. If these ghosts wished to make him of their number, let them do so. He had no ties on earth, and now when he knew full surely that there was a life beyond this of earth he was quite prepared to explore its mysteries. So he folded his arms upon his breast and awaited the sentence.

But Ma-Mee did not wait. She raised her hand so swiftly that the bracelets jingled on her wrists, and spoke out with boldness.

"Royal Khaemuas, prince and magician," she said, "hearken to one who, like you, was Egypt's heir centuries before you were born, one also who ruled over the Two Lands, and not so ill—which, Prince, never was your lot. Answer me! Is all wisdom centred in your breast? Answer me! Do you alone know the mysteries of Life and Death? Answer me! Did your god Amen teach you that vengeance went before mercy? Answer me! Did he teach you that men should be judged unheard? That they should be hurried by violence to Osiris ere their time, and thereby separated from the dead ones whom they loved and forced to return to live again upon this evil Earth?

"Listen: when the last moon was near her full my spirit sat in my tomb in the burying-place of queens. My spirit saw this man enter into my tomb, and what he did there. With bowed head he looked upon my bones that a thief of the priesthood had robbed and burnt within twenty years of their burial, in which he himself had taken part. And what did this man with those bones, he who was once Horu? I tell you that he hid them away there in the tomb where he thought they could not be found again. Who, then, was the thief and the violator? He who robbed and burnt my bones, or he who buried them with reverence? Again, he found the jewels that the priest of your brotherhood had dropped in his flight, when the smoke of the burning flesh and spices overpowered him, and with them the hand which that wicked one had broken off from the body of my Majesty. What did this man then? He took the jewels. Would you have had him leave them to be stolen by some peasant? And the hand? I tell you that he kissed that poor dead hand which once had been part of the body of my Majesty, and that now he treasures it as a holy relic. My spirit saw him do these things and made report thereof to me. I ask you, therefore, Prince, I ask you all, Royalties of Egypt—whether for such deeds this man should die?"

Now Khaemuas, the advocate of vengeance, shrugged his shoulders and smiled meaningly, but the congregation of kings and queens thundered an answer, and it was:—

"*No!*"

Ma-Mee looked to Menes to give judgment. Before he could speak the dark-browed Pharaoh who had named her wife strode forward and addressed them.

"Her Majesty, Heiress of Egypt, Royal Wife, Lady of the Two Lands, has spoken," he cried. "Now let me speak who was the husband of her Majesty. Whether this man was once Horu the sculptor I know not. If so he was also an evil-doer who, by my decree, died in banishment in the land of Kush. Whatever be the truth as to that matter, he admits that he violated the tomb of her Majesty and stole what the old thieves had left. Her Majesty says also—and he does not deny it—that he dared to kiss her hand, and for a man to kiss the hand of a wedded Queen of Egypt the punishment is death. I claim that this man should die to the World before his time, that in a day to come again he may live and suffer in the World. Judge, O Menes."

Menes lifted his head and spoke, saying:—

"Repeat to me the law, O Pharaoh, under which a living man must die for the kissing of a dead hand. In my day and in that of those who went before me there was no such law in Egypt. If a living man, who was not her husband, or of her kin, kissed the living hand of a wedded Queen of Egypt, save in ceremony, then perchance he might be called upon to die. Perchance for such a reason a certain Horu once was called upon to die. But in the grave there is no marriage, and therefore even if he had found her alive within the tomb and kissed her hand, or even her lips, why should he die for the crime of love?

"Hear me, all; this is my judgment in the matter. Let the soul of that priest who first violated the tomb of the royal Ma-Mee be hunted down and given to the jaws of the Destroyer, that he may know the last depths of Death, if so the gods declare. But let this man go from among us unharmed, since what he did he did in reverent ignorance and because Hathor, Goddess of Love, guided him from of old. Love rules this world wherein we meet to-night, with all the worlds whence we have gathered or whither we still must go. Who can defy its power? Who can refuse its rites? Now hence to Thebes!"

There was a rushing sound as of a thousand wings, and all were gone.

No, not all, since Smith yet stood before the draped colossi and the empty steps, and beside him, glorious, unearthly, gleamed the vision of Ma-Mee.

"I, too, must away," she whispered; "yet ere I go a word with you who once were a sculptor in Egypt. You loved me then, and that love cost you your life, you who once dared to kiss this hand of mine that again you kissed in yonder tomb. For I was Pharaoh's wife in name only; understand me well, in name only; since that title of Royal Mother which they gave me is but a graven lie. Horu, I never was a wife, and when you died, swiftly I followed you to the grave. Oh, you forget, but I remember! I remember many things. You think that the priestly thief broke this figure of me which you found in the sand outside my tomb. Not so. *I* broke it, because, daring greatly, you had written thereon, 'Beloved,' not 'of *Horus* the God,' as you should have done, but 'of *Horu* the Man.' So when I came to be buried, Pharaoh, knowing all, took the image from my wrappings and hurled it away. I remember, too, the casting of that image, and how you threw a gold chain I had given you into the crucible with the bronze, saying that gold alone was fit to fashion me. And this signet that I bear—it was you who cut it. Take it, take it, Horu, and in its place give me back that which is on your hand, the Bes ring that I also wore. Take it and wear it ever till you die again, and let it go to the grave with you as once it went to the grave with me.

"Now hearken. When Ra the great sun arises again and you awake you will think that you have dreamed a dream. You will think that in this dream you saw and spoke with a lady of Egypt who died more than three thousand years ago, but whose beauty, carved in stone and bronze, has charmed your heart to-day. So let it be, yet know, O man, who once was named Horu, that such dreams are ofttimes a shadow of the truth. Know that this Glory which shines before you is mine indeed in the land that is both far and near, the land wherein I dwell eternally, and that what is mine has been, is, and shall be yours for ever. Gods may change their kingdoms and their names; men may live and die, and live again once more to die; empires may fall and those who ruled them be turned to forgotten dust. Yet true love endures immortal as the souls in which it was conceived, and from it for you and me, the night of woe and separation done, at the daybreak which draws on, there shall be born the splendour and the peace of union. Till that hour foredoomed seek me no more, though I be ever near you, as I have ever been. Till that most blessed hour, Horu, farewell."

She bent towards him; her sweet lips touched his brow; the perfume from her breath and hair beat upon him; the light of her wondrous eyes searched out his very soul, reading the answer that was written there.

He stretched out his arms to clasp her, and lo! she was gone.

It was a very cold and a very stiff Smith who awoke on the following morning, to find himself exactly where he had lain down—namely, on a cement floor beneath the keel of a funeral boat in the central hall of the Cairo Museum. He crept from his shelter shivering, and looked at this hall, to find it quite as empty as it had been on the previous evening. Not a sign or a token was there of Pharaoh Menes and all those kings and queens of whom he had dreamed so vividly.

Reflecting on the strange phantasies that weariness and excited nerves can summon to the mind in sleep, Smith made his way to the great doors and waited in the shadow, praying earnestly that, although it was the Mohammedan Sabbath, someone might visit the Museum to see that all was well.

As a matter of fact, someone did, and before he had been there a minute—a watchman going about his business. He unlocked the place carelessly, looking over his shoulder at a kite fighting with two nesting crows. In an instant Smith, who was not minded to stop and answer questions, had slipped past him and was gliding down the portico, from monument to monument, like a snake between boulders, still keeping in the shadow as he headed for the gates.

The attendant caught sight of him and uttered a yell of fear; then, since it is not good to look upon an *afreet*, appearing from whence no mortal man could be, he turned his head away. When he looked again Smith was through those gates and had mingled with the crowd in the street beyond.

The sunshine was very pleasant to one who was conscious of having contracted a chill of the worst Egyptian order from long contact with a damp stone floor. Smith walked on through it towards his hotel—it was Shepheard's, and more than a mile away—making up a story as he went to tell the hall-porter of how he had gone to dine at Mena House by the Pyramids, missed the last tram, and stopped the night there.

Whilst he was thus engaged his left hand struck somewhat sharply against the corner of the cigar-box in his pocket, that which contained the relic of the queen Ma-Mee. The pain caused him to glance at his fingers to see if they were injured, and to perceive on one of them the ring he wore. Surely, surely it was not the same that the Director-General had given him! *That* ring was engraved with the image of the god Bes. On *this* was cut the cartouche of her Majesty Ma-mee! And he had dreamed—oh, he had dreamed——!

To this day Smith is wondering whether, in the hurry of the moment, he made a mistake as to which of those rings the Director-General had given him as part of his share of the spoil of the royal tomb he discovered in the Valley of Queens. Afterwards Smith wrote to ask, but the Director-General could only remember that he gave him one of the two rings, and assured him that that inscribed "*Bes Ank, Ank Bes*," was with Ma-Mee's other jewels in the Gold Room of the Museum.

Also Smith is wondering whether any other bronze figure of an old Egyptian royalty shows so high a percentage of gold as, on analysis, the broken image of Ma-Mee was proved to do. For had she not seemed to tell him a tale of the melting of a golden chain when that effigy was cast?

Was it all only a dream, or was it—something more—by day and by night he asks of Nothingness?

But, be she near or far, no answer comes from the Queen Ma-Mee, whose proud titles were "Her Majesty the Good God, the justified Dweller in Osiris; Daughter of Amen, Royal Heiress, Royal Sister, Royal Wife, Royal Mother; Lady of the Two Lands; Wearer of the Double Crown; of the White Crown, of the Red Crown; Sweet Flower of Love, Beautiful Eternally."

So, like the rest of us, Smith must wait to learn the truth concerning many things, and more particularly as to which of those two circles of ancient gold the Director-General gave him yonder at Cairo.

It seems but a little matter, yet it is more than all the worlds to him!

To the astonishment of his colleagues in antiquarian research, Smith has never returned to Egypt. He explains to them that his health is quite restored, and that he no longer needs this annual change to a more temperate clime.

Now, *which* of the two royal rings did the Director-General return to Smith on the mummied hand of her late Majesty Ma-Mee?

Magepa The Buck

In a preface to a story of the early life of the late Allan Quatermain, known in Africa as Macumazahn, which has been published under the name of "Marie," Mr. Curtis, the brother of Sir Henry Curtis, tells of how he found a number of manuscripts that were left by Mr. Quatermain in his house in Yorkshire. Of these "Marie" was one, but in addition to it and sundry other completed records I, the Editor to whom it was directed that these manuscripts should be handed for publication, have found a quantity of unclassified notes and papers. Some of these deal with matters that have to do with sport and game, or with historical events, and some are memoranda of incidents connected with the career of the writer, or with remarkable occurrences that he had witnessed of which he does not speak elsewhere.

One of these notes—it is contained in a book much soiled and worn that evidently its owner had carried about with him for years—reminds me of a conversation that I had with Mr. Quatermain long ago when I was his guest in Yorkshire. The note itself is short; I think that he must have jotted it down within an hour or two of the event to which it refers. It runs thus:—

"I wonder whether in the 'Land Beyond' any recognition is granted for acts of great courage and unselfish devotion—a kind of spiritual Victoria Cross. If so I think it ought to be accorded to that poor old savage, Magepa, as it would be if I had any voice in the matter. Upon my word he has made me feel proud of humanity. And yet he was nothing but a 'nigger,' as so many call the Kaffirs."

For a while I, the Editor, wondered to what this entry could allude. Then of a sudden it all came back to me. I saw myself, as a young man, seated in the hall of Quatermain's house one evening after dinner. With me were Sir Henry Curtis and Captain Good. We were smoking, and the conversation had turned upon deeds of heroism. Each of us detailed such acts as he could remember which had made the most impression on him. When we had finished, old Allan said:—

"With your leave I'll tell you a story of what I think was one of the bravest things I ever saw. It happened at the beginning of the Zulu War, when the troops were marching into Zululand. Now at that time, as you know, I was turning an honest penny transport-riding for the Government, or rather for the military authorities. I hired them three wagons with the necessary voorloopers and drivers, sixteen good salted oxen to each wagon, and myself in charge of the lot. They paid me, well, never mind how much—I am rather ashamed to mention the amount. The truth is that the Imperial officers bought in a dear market during that Zulu War; moreover, things were not always straight. I could tell you stories of folk, not all of them Colonials, who got rich quicker than they ought, commissions and that kind of thing. But perhaps these are better forgotten. As for me, I asked a good price for my wagons, or rather for the hire of them, of a very well-satisfied young gentleman in uniform who had been exactly three weeks in the country, and to my surprise, got it. But when I went to those in command and warned them what would happen if they persisted in their way of advance, then in their pride they would not listen to the old hunter and transport-rider, but politely bowed me out. If they had, there would have been no Isandhlwana disaster."

He brooded awhile, for, as I knew, this was a sore subject with him, one on which he would rarely talk. Although he escaped himself, Quatermain had lost friends on that fatal field. He went on:—

"To return to old Magepa. I had known him for many years. The first time we met was in the battle of the Tugela. I was fighting for the king's son, Umbelazi the Handsome, in the ranks of the Tulwana regiment—I mean to write all that story, for it should not be lost. Well, as I have told you before, the Tulwana were wiped out; of the three thousand or so of them I think only about fifty remained alive after they had annihilated the three of Cetewayo's regiments that set upon them. But as it chanced Magepa was one who survived.

"I met him afterwards at old King Panda's kraal and recognised him as having fought by my side. Whilst I was talking to him the Prince Cetewayo came by; to me he was civil enough, for he knew how I chanced to be in the battle, but he glared at Magepa, and said:

"'Why, Macumazahn, is not this man one of the dogs with which you tried to bite me by the Tugela not long ago? He must be a cunning dog also, one who can run fast, for how comes it that he lives to snarl when so many will never bark again? *Ow!* if I had my way I would find a strip of hide to fit his neck.'

"'Not so,' I answered, 'he has the King's peace and he is a brave man —braver than I am, anyway, Prince, seeing that I ran from the ranks of the Tulwana, while he stood where he was.'

"'You mean that your horse ran, Macumazahn. Well, since you like this dog, I will not hurt him,' and with a shrug he went his way.

"'Yet soon or late he *will* hurt me,' said Magepa, when the Prince had gone. 'U'Cetewayo has a memory long as the shadow thrown by a tree at sunset. Moreover, as he knows well, it is true that I ran, Macumazahn, though not till all was finished and I could do no more by standing still. You remember how, after we had eaten up the first of Cetewayo's regiments, the second charged us and we ate that up also. Well, in that fight I got a tap on the head from a kerry. It struck me on my man's ring which I had just put on, for I think I was the youngest soldier in that regiment of veterans. The ring saved me; still, for a while I lost my mind and lay like one dead. When I found it again the fight was over and Cetewayo's people were searching for our wounded that they might kill them. Presently they found me and saw that there was no hurt on me.

""Here is one who shams dead like a stink-cat," said a big fellow, lifting his spear.

"'Then it was that I sprang up and ran, who was but just married and desired to live. He struck at me, but I jumped over the spear, and the others that they threw missed me. Then they began to hunt me, but, Macumazahn, I who am named "The Buck," because I am swifter of foot than any man in Zululand, outpaced them all and got away safe.'

"'Well done, Magepa,' I said. 'Still, remember the saying of your people, "At last the strong swimmer goes with the stream and the swift runner is run down."'

"'I know it, Macumazahn,' he answered, with a nod, 'and perhaps in a day to come I shall know it better.'

"I took little heed of his words at the time, but more than thirty years afterwards I remembered them.

"Such was my first acquaintance with Magepa. Now, friends, I will tell you how it was renewed at the time of the Zulu War.

"As you know, I was attached to the centre column that advanced into Zululand by Rorke's Drift on the Buffalo River. Before war was declared, or at any rate before the advance began, while it might have been and many thought it would be averted, I was employed transport-riding goods to the little Rorke's Drift Station, that which became so famous afterwards, and incidentally in collecting what information I could of Cetewayo's intentions. Hearing that there was a kraal a mile or so the other side of the river, of which the people were said to be very friendly to the English, I determined to visit it. You may think this was rash, but I was so well known in Zululand, where for many years, by special leave of the king, I was allowed to go whither I would quite unmolested and, indeed, under the royal protection, that I felt no fear for myself so long as I went alone.

"Accordingly one evening I crossed the drift and headed for a kloof in which I was told the kraal stood. Ten minutes' ride brought me in sight of it. It was not a large kraal; there may have been six or eight huts and a cattle enclosure surrounded by the usual fence. The situation, however, was very pretty, a knoll of rising ground backed by the wooded slopes of the kloof. As I approached, I saw women and children running to the kraal to hide, and when I reached the gateway for some time no one would come out to meet me. At length a small boy appeared who informed me that the kraal was 'empty as a gourd.'

"'Quite so,' I answered; 'still, go and tell the headman that Macumazahn wishes to speak with him.'

"The boy departed, and presently I saw a face that seemed familiar to me peeping round the edge of the gateway. After a careful inspection its owner emerged.

"He was a tall, thin man of indefinite age, perhaps between sixty and seventy, with a finely-cut face, a little grey beard, kind eyes and very well-shaped hands and feet, the fingers, which twitched incessantly, being remarkably long.

"'Greeting, Macumazahn,' he said, 'I see you do not remember me. Well, think of the battle of the Tugela, and of the last stand of the Tulwana, and of a certain talk at the kraal of our Father-who-is-dead' (that is King Panda), 'and of how he who sits in his place' (he meant Cetewayo), 'told you that if he had his way he would find a hide rope to fit the neck of a certain one.'

"'Ah!' I said, 'I know you now, you are Magepa the Buck. So the Runner has not yet been run down.'

"'No, Macumazahn, not yet, but there is still time. I think that many swift feet will be at work ere long.'

"'How have you prospered?' I asked him.

"'Well enough, Macumazahn, in all ways except one. I have three wives, but my children have been few and are dead, except one daughter, who is married and lives with me, for her husband, too, is dead. He was killed by a buffalo, and she has not yet married again. But enter and see.'

"So I went in and saw Magepa's wives, old women all of them. Also, at his bidding, his daughter, whose name was Gita, brought me some *maas*, or curdled milk, to drink. She was a well-formed woman, very like her father, but sad-faced, perhaps with a prescience of evil to come. Clinging to her finger was a beautiful boy of something under two years of age, who, when he saw Magepa, ran to him and threw his little arms about his legs. The old man lifted the child and kissed him tenderly, saying:

"'It is well that this toddler and I should love one another, Macumazahn, seeing that he is the last of my race. All the other children here are those of the people who have come to live in my shadow.'

"'Where are their fathers?' I asked, patting the little boy who, his mother told me, was named Sinala, upon the cheek, an attention that he resented.

"'They have been called away on duty,' answered Magepa shortly; and I changed the subject.

"Then we began to talk about old times, and I asked him if he had any oxen to sell, saying that this was my reason for visiting the kraal.

"'Nay, Macumazahn,' he answered in a meaning voice. 'This year all the cattle are the king's.'

"I nodded and replied that, as it was so, I had better be going, whereon, as I half expected, Magepa announced that he would see me safe to the drift. So I bade farewell to the wives and the widowed daughter, and we started.

"As soon as we were clear of the kraal Magepa began to open his heart to me.

"'Macumazahn,' he said, looking up at me earnestly, for I was mounted, and he walked beside my horse, 'there is to be war. Cetewayo will not consent to the demands of the great White Chief from the Cape,'—he meant Sir Bartle Frere—'he will fight with the English; only he will let them begin the fighting. He will draw them on into Zululand and then overwhelm them with his impis and stamp them flat, and eat them up; and I, who love the English, am very sorry. Yes, it makes my heart bleed. If it were the Boers now, I should be glad, for we Zulus hate the Boers; but the English we do not hate; even Cetewayo likes them; still, he will eat them up if they attack him.'

"'Indeed,' I answered; and then as in duty bound I proceeded to get what I could out of him, and that was not a little. Of course, however, I did not swallow it all, since that I suspected that Magepa was feeding me with news that he had been ordered to disseminate.

"Presently we came to the mouth of the kloof in which the kraal stood, and here, for greater convenience of conversation, we halted, for I thought it as well that we should not be seen in close talk on the open plain beyond. The path here, I should add, ran past a clump of green bushes; I remember they bore a white flower that smelt sweet, and were backed by some tall grass, elephant-grass I think it was, among which grew mimosa trees.

"'Magepa,' I said, 'if in truth there is to be fighting, why don't you move over the river one night with your people and cattle, and get into Natal?'

"'I would if I could, Macumazahn, who have no stomach for this war against the English. But there I should not be safe, since presently the king will come into Natal too, or send thirty thousand assegais as his messengers. Then what will happen to those who have left him?'

"'Oh! if you think that,' I answered, laughing, 'you had better stay where you are.'

"'Also, Macumazahn, the husbands of those women at my kraal have been called up to their regiments and if their wives fled to the English they would be killed. Again, the king has sent for nearly all our cattle "to keep them safe." He fears lest we Border Zulus might join our people in Natal, and that is why he is keeping our cattle "safe."'

"'Life is more than cattle, Magepa. At least you might come.'

"'What! And leave my people to be killed? Macumazahn, you did not use to talk so. Still, hearken. Macumazahn, will you do me a service? I will pay you well for it. I would get my daughter Gita and my little grandson Sinala into safety. If I and my wives are wiped out it does not matter, for we are old. But her I would save, and the boy I would save, so that one may live who will remember my name. Now if I were to send them across the drift, say at the dawn, not to-morrow and not the next day, but the day after, would you receive them into your wagon and deliver them safe to some place in Natal? I have money hidden, fifty pieces of gold, and you may take half of these and also half of the cattle if ever I live to get them back out of the keeping of the king.'

"'Never mind about the money, and we will speak of the cattle afterwards,' I said. 'I understand that you wish to send your daughter and your little grandson out of danger; and I think you wise, very wise. When once the advance begins, if there is an advance, who knows what may happen? War is a rough game, Magepa. It is not the custom of you black people to spare women and children; and there will be Zulus fighting on our side as well as on yours; do you understand?'

"'*Ow!* I understand, Macumazahn. I have known the face of war and seen many a little one like my grandson Sinala assegaied upon his mother's back.'

"'Very good. But if I do this for you, you must do something for me. Say, Magepa, does Cetewayo *really* mean to fight, and if so, how? Oh yes, I know all you have been telling me, but I want not words but truth from the heart?'

"'You ask secrets,' said the old fellow, peering about him into the gathering gloom. 'Still, "a spear for a spear and a shield for a shield," as our saying runs. I have spoken no lie. The king *does* mean to fight, not because he wants to, but because the regiments swear that they will wash their assegais; they who have never seen blood since that battle of the Tugela in which we two played a part, and if he will not suffer it, well, there are more of his race! Also he means to fight thus,' and he gave me some very useful information, that is, information which would have been useful if those in authority had deigned to pay any attention to it when I passed it on.

"Just as he had finished speaking I thought that I heard a sound in the dense green bush behind us. It reminded me of the noise a man makes when he tries to stifle a cough, and frightened me. For if we had been overheard by a spy, Magepa was as good as dead, and the sooner I was across the river the better.

"'What's that?' I asked.

"'A bush buck, Macumazahn. There are lots of them about here.'

"Not being satisfied, though it is true that buck do cough like this, I turned my horse to the bush, seeking an opening. Thereon something crashed away and vanished into the long grass. In those shadows, of course, I could not see what it was, but such light as remained glinted on what might have been the polished tip of the horn of an antelope or—an assegai.

"'I told you it was a buck, Macumazahn,' said Magepa. 'Still, if you smell danger, let us come away from the bush, though the orders are that no white man is to be touched as yet.'

"Then, while we walked on towards the ford, he set out with great detail, as Kaffirs do, the exact arrangements that he proposed to make for the handing over of his daughter and her child into my care. I remember that I asked him why he would not send her on the following morning, instead of two mornings later. He answered because he expected an outpost of scouts from one of the regiments at his kraal that night, who would probably remain there over the morrow and perhaps longer. While they were in the place it would be difficult, if not impossible, for him to send away Gita and her son without exciting suspicion.

"Near the drift we parted, and I returned to our provisional camp and wrote a beautiful report of all that I had learned, of which report, I may add, no one took the slightest notice.

"I think it was the morning before that whereon I had arranged to meet Gita and the little boy at the drift that just about dawn I went down to the river for a wash. Having taken my dip, I climbed on to a flat rock to dress myself, and looked at the billows of beautiful, pearly mist which hid the face of the water, and considered—I almost said listened to—the great silence, for as yet no live thing was stirring.

"Ah! if I had known of the hideous sights and sounds that were destined to be heard ere long in this same haunt of perfect peace! Indeed, at that moment there came a kind of hint or premonition of them, since suddenly through the utter quiet broke the blood-curdling wail of a woman. It was followed by other wails and shouts, distant and yet distinct. Then the silence fell again.

"Now, I thought to myself, that noise might very well have come from old Magepa's kraal; luckily, however, sounds are deceptive in mist.

"Well, the end of it was that I waited there till the sun rose. The first thing on which its bright beams struck was a mighty column of smoke rising to heaven from where Magepa's kraal had stood!

"I went back to my wagons very sad—so sad that I could scarcely eat my breakfast. While I walked I wondered hard whether the light had glinted upon the tip of a buck's horn in that patch of green bush with the sweet-smelling white flowers a night or two ago. Or had it perchance fallen upon the point of the assegai of some spy who was watching my movements! In that event yonder column of smoke and the horrible cries that preceded it were easy to explain. For had not Magepa and I talked secrets together, and in Zulu?

"On the following morning at dawn I attended at the drift in the faint hope that Gita and her boy might arrive there as arranged. But nobody came, which was not wonderful, seeing that Gita lay dead, stabbed through and through, as I saw afterwards, (she made a good fight for the child), and that her spirit had gone to wherever go the souls of the brave-hearted, be they white or black. Only on the farther bank of the river I saw some Zulu scouts who seemed to know my errand, for they called to me, asking mockingly where was the pretty woman I had come to meet?

"After that I tried to put the matter out of my head, which indeed was full enough of other things, since now definite orders had arrived as to the advance, and with these many troops and officers.

"It was just then that the Zulus began to fire across the river at such of our people as they saw upon the bank. At these they took aim, and, as a result, hit nobody. A raw Kaffir with a rifle, in my experience, is only dangerous when he aims at nothing, for then the bullet looks after itself and may catch you. To put a stop to this nuisance a regiment of the friendly natives—there may have been several hundred of them—was directed to cross the river and clear the kloofs and rocks of the Zulu skirmishers who were hidden among them. I watched them go off in fine style, and in the course of the afternoon heard a good deal of shouting and banging of guns on the farther side of the river.

"Towards evening someone told me that our *impi*, as he called it grandiloquently, was returning victorious. Having at the moment nothing else to do, I walked down to the river at a point where the water was deep and the banks were high. Here I climbed to the top of a pile of boulders, whence with my field-glasses I could sweep a great extent of plain which stretched away on the Zululand side till at length it merged into hills and bush.

"Presently I saw some of our natives marching homewards in a scattered and disorganised fashion, but evidently very proud of themselves, for they were waving their assegais and singing scraps of war-songs. A few minutes later, a mile or more away, I caught sight of a man running.

"Watching him through the glasses I noted three things: First, that he was tall; secondly, that he ran with extraordinary swiftness; and, thirdly, that he had something tied upon his back. It was evident, further, that he had good reason to run, since he was being hunted by a number of our Kaffirs, of whom more and more continually joined the chase. From every side they poured down upon him, trying to cut him off and kill him, for as they got nearer I could see the assegais which they threw at him flash in the sunlight.

"Very soon I understood that the man was running with a definite object and to a definite point; he was trying to reach the river. I thought the sight very pitiful, this one poor creature being hunted to death by so many. Also I wondered why he did not free himself from the bundle on his back, and came to the conclusion that he must be a witch-doctor, and that the bundle contained his precious charms or medicines.

"This was while he was yet a long way off, but when he came nearer, within three or four hundred yards, of a sudden I caught the outline of his face against a good background, and knew it for that of Magepa.

"'My God!' I said to myself, 'it is old Magepa the Buck, and the bundle in the mat will be his grandson, Sinala!'

"Yes, even then I felt certain that he was carrying the child upon his back.

"What was I to do? It was impossible for me to cross the river at that place, and long before I could get round by the ford all would be finished. I stood up on my rock and shouted to those brutes of Kaffirs to let the man alone. They were so excited that they did not hear my words; at least, they swore afterwards that they thought I was encouraging them to hunt him down.

"But Magepa heard me. At the moment he seemed to be failing, but the sight of me appeared to give him fresh strength. He gathered himself together and leapt forward at a really surprising speed. Now the river was not more than three hundred yards away from him, and for the first two hundred of these he quite outdistanced his pursuers, although they were most of them young men and comparatively fresh. Then once more his strength began to fail.

"Watching through the glasses, I could see that his mouth was wide open, and that there was red foam upon his lips. The burden on his back was dragging him down. Once he lifted his hands as though to loose it; then with a wild gesture let them fall again.

"Two of the pursuers who had outpaced the others crept up to him—lank, lean men of not more than thirty years of age. They had stabbing spears in their hands, such as are used at close quarters, and these of course they did not throw. One of them gained a little on the other.

"Now Magepa was not more than fifty yards from the bank, with the first hunter about ten paces behind him and coming up rapidly. Magepa glanced over his shoulder and saw, then put out his last strength. For forty yards he went like an arrow, running straight away from his pursuers, until he was within a few feet of the bank, when he stumbled and fell.

"'He's done,' I said, and, upon my word, if I had had a rifle in my hand I think I would have stopped one or both of those bloodhounds and taken the consequences.

"But no! Just as the first man lifted his broad spear to stab him through the back on which the bundle lay, Magepa leapt up and wheeled round to take the thrust in the chest. Evidently he did not wish to be speared in the back—for a certain reason. He took it sure enough, for the assegai was wrenched out of the hand of the striker. Still, as he was reeling backwards, it did not go through Magepa, or perhaps it hit a bone. He drew out the spear and threw it at the man, wounding him. Then he staggered on, back and back, to the edge of the little cliff.

"It was reached at last. With a cry of 'Help me, Macumazahn!' Magepa turned, and before the other man could spear him, leapt straight into the deep water. He rose. Yes, the brave old fellow rose and struck out for the other bank, leaving a little line of red behind him.

"I rushed, or rather sprang and rolled down to the edge of the stream to where a point of shingle ran out into the water. Along this I clambered, and beyond it up to my middle. Now Magepa was being swept past me. I caught his outstretched hand and pulled him ashore.

"'The boy!' he gasped; 'the boy! Is he dead?'

"I severed the lashings of the mat that had cut right into the old fellow's shoulders. Inside of it was little Sinala, spluttering out water, but very evidently alive and unhurt, for presently he set up a yell.

"'No,' I said, 'he lives, and will live.'

"'Then all is well, Macumazahn.' (*A pause.*) 'It *was* a spy in the bush, not a buck. He overheard our talk. The King's slayers came. Gita held the door of the hut while I took the child, cut a hole through the straw with my assegai, and crept out at the back. She was full of spears before she died, but I got away with the boy. Till your Kaffirs found me I lay hid in the bush, hoping to escape to Natal. Then I ran for the river, and saw you on the farther bank. *I* might have got away, but that child is heavy.' (*A pause.*) 'Give him food, Macumazahn, he must be hungry.' (*A pause.*) 'Farewell. That was a good saying of yours—the swift runner is outrun at last. Ah! yet I did not run in vain.' (*Another pause, the last.*) Then he lifted himself upon one arm and with the other saluted, first the boy Sinala and next me, muttering, 'Remember your promise, Macumazahn.'

"That is how Magepa the Buck died. I never saw anyone carrying weight who could run quite so well as he," and Quatermain turned his head away as though the memory of this incident affected him somewhat.

"What became of the child Sinala?" I asked presently.

"Oh! I sent him to an institution in Natal, and afterwards was able to get some of his property back for him. I believe that he is being trained as an interpreter."

The Blue Curtains

CHAPTER I

In his regiment familiarly they called him "Bottles," nobody quite knew why. It was, however, rumoured that he had been called "Bottles" at Harrow on account of the shape of his nose. Not that his nose was particularly like a bottle, but at the end of it was round and large and thick. In reality, however, the sobriquet was more ancient than that, for it had belonged to the hero of this story from babyhood. Now, when a man has a nickname, it generally implies two things: first, that he is good-tempered, and, secondly, that he is a good fellow. Bottles, *alias* John George Peritt, of a regiment it is unnecessary to name, amply justified both these definitions, for a kindlier-tempered or better fellow never breathed. But unless a thick round nose, a pair of small light-coloured eyes, set under bushy brows, and a large but not badly shaped mouth can be said to constitute beauty, he was not beautiful. On the other hand, however, he was big and well-formed, and a pleasant-mannered if a rather silent companion.

Many years ago Bottles was in love; all the regiment knew it, he was so very palpably and completely in love. Over his bed in his tidy quarters hung the photograph of a young lady who was known to be *the* young lady; which, when the regiment, individually and collectively, happened to see it, left no doubt in its mind as to their comrade's taste. It was evident even from that badly-coloured photograph that Miss Madeline Spenser had the makings of a lovely figure and a pair of wonderful eyes. It was said, however, that she had not a sixpence; and as our hero had but very few, the married ladies of the battalion used frequently to speculate how Mr. Peritt would "manage" when it came to matrimony.

At this date the regiment was quartered in Maritzburg, Natal, but its term of foreign service had expired, and it expected to be ordered home immediately.

One morning Bottles had been out buck hunting with the scratch pack kept in those days by the garrison at Maritzburg. The run had been a good one, and after a seven or eight-mile gallop over the open country they had actually killed their buck—a beautiful Oribe. This was a thing that did not often happen, and Bottles returned filled with joy and pride with the buck fastened behind his saddle, for he was whip to the pack. The hounds had met at dawn, and it was nine o'clock or so, when, as he was riding hot and tired up the shadier side of broad and dusty Church Street, a gun fired at the Fort beyond Government House announced the arrival of the English mail.

With a beaming smile—for to him the English mail meant one if not two letters from Madeline, and possibly the glad news of sailing orders—he pushed on to his quarters, tubbed and dressed, and then went down to the mess-house for breakfast, expecting to find the letters delivered. But the mail was a heavy one, and he had ample time to eat his breakfast, also to sit and smoke a pipe upon the pleasant verandah under the shade of the bamboos and camellia bushes before the orderly arrived with the bag. Bottles went at once into the room that opened on to the veranda and stood by calmly, not being given to betraying his emotions, while slowly and clumsily the mess sergeant sorted the letters. At last he got his packet—it only consisted of some newspapers and a single letter—and went away back to his seat on the veranda, feeling rather disappointed, for he had expected to hear from his only brother as well as from his lady-love. Having relit his pipe—for he was of a slow and deliberate mind, and it rather enhances a pleasure to defer it a little—and settled himself in the big chair opposite the camellia bush just now covered with sealing-wax-like blooms, he opened his letter and read:—

"My dear George——"

"Good heavens!" he thought to himself, "what can be the matter? She always calls me 'Darling Bottles!'"

"My dear George," he began again, "I hardly know how to begin this letter—I can scarcely see the paper for crying, and when I think of you reading it out in that horrid country it makes me cry more than ever. There! I may as well get it out at once, for it does not improve by keeping—it is all over between you and me, my dear, dear old Bottles."

"All over!" he gasped to himself.

"I hardly know how to tell the miserable story," went on the letter, "but as it must be told I suppose I had better begin from the beginning. A month ago I went with my father and my aunt to the Hunt Ball at Atherton, and there I met Sir Alfred Croston, a middle-aged gentleman, who danced with me several times. I did not care about him much, but he made himself very agreeable, and when I got home aunt—you know her nasty way—congratulated me on my conquest. Well, next day he came to call, and papa asked him to stop to dinner, and he took me in, and before he went away he told me that he was coming to stop at the George Inn to fish for trout in the lake. After that he came here every day, and whenever I went out walking he always met me, and really was kind and nice. At last one day he asked me to marry him, and I was very angry and told him that I was engaged to a gentleman in the army, who was in South Africa. He laughed, and said South Africa was a long way off, and I hated him for it. That evening papa and aunt set on me—you know they neither of them liked our engagement—and told me that our affair was perfectly silly, and that I must be mad to refuse such an offer. And so it went on, for he would not take 'no' for an answer; and at last, dear, I had to give in, for they gave me no peace, and papa implored me to consent for his sake. He said the marriage would be the making of him, and now I suppose I am engaged. Dear, dear

George, don't be angry with me, for it is not my fault, and I suppose after all we could not have got married, for we have so little money. I do love you, but I can't help myself. I hope you won't forget me, or marry anybody else—at least, not just at present—for I cannot bear to think about it. Write to me and tell me you won't forget me, and that you are not angry with me. Do you want your letters back? If you burn mine that will do. Good-bye, dear! If you only knew what I suffer! It is all very well to talk like aunt does about settlements and diamonds, but they can't make up to me for you. Good-bye, dear, I cannot write any more because my head aches so.—Ever yours,

"Madeline Spenser."

When George Peritt, *alias* Bottles, had finished reading and re-reading this letter, he folded it up neatly and put it, after his methodical fashion, into his pocket. Then he sat and stared at the red camellia blooms before him, that somehow looked as indistinct and misty as though they were fifty yards off instead of so many inches.

"It is a great blow," he said to himself. "Poor Madeline! How she must suffer!"

Presently he rose and walked—rather unsteadily, for he felt much upset—to his quarters, and, taking a sheet of notepaper, wrote the following letter to catch the outgoing mail:—

"My dear Madeline,—I have got your letter putting an end to our engagement. I don't want to dwell on myself when you must have so much to suffer, but I must say that it has been, and is, a great blow to me. I have loved you for so many years, ever since we were babies, I think; it does seem hard to lose you now after all. I thought that when we got home I might get the adjutancy of a militia regiment, and that we might have been married. I think we might have managed on five hundred a year, though perhaps I have no right to expect you to give up comforts and luxuries to which you are accustomed; but I am afraid that when one is in love one is apt to be selfish. However, all that is done with now, as, of course, putting everything else aside, I could not think of standing in your way in life. I love you much too well for that, dear Madeline, and you are too beautiful and delicate to be the wife of a poor subaltern with little beside his pay. I can honestly say that I hope you will be happy. I don't ask you to think of me too often, as that might make you less so, but perhaps sometimes when you are quiet you will spare your old lover a thought or two, because I am sure nobody could care for you more than I do. You need not be afraid that I shall forget you or marry anybody else. I shall do neither the one nor the other. I must close this now to catch the mail; I don't know that there is anything more to say. It is a hard trial—very; but it is no good being weak and giving way, and it consoles me to think that you are 'bettering yourself' as the servants say. Good-bye, dear Madeline. May God bless you, is now and ever my earnest prayer.

"J. G. Peritt."

Scarcely was this letter finished and hastily dispatched when a loud voice was heard calling, "Bottles, Bottles, my boy, come rejoice with me; the orders have come—we sail in a fortnight;" followed by the owner of the voice, another subaltern, and our hero's bosom friend. "Why, you don't seem very elated," said he of the voice, noting his friend's dejected and somewhat dazed appearance.

"No—that is, not particularly. So you sail in a fortnight, do you?"

"'You sail?' What do you mean? Why, we *all* sail, of course, from the colonel down to the drummer-boy."

"I don't think that I—I am going to sail, Jack," was the hesitating answer.

"Look here, old fellow, are you off your head, or have you been liquoring up, or what?"

"No—that is, I don't think so; certainly not the first—the second, I mean."

"Then what do you mean?"

"I mean that, in short, I am sending in my papers. I like this climate —I, in short, am going to take to farming."

"Sending in your papers! Going to take to farming! And in this God-forsaken hole, too. You *must* be screwed."

"No, indeed. It is only ten o'clock."

"And how about getting married, and the girl you are engaged to, and whom you are looking forward so much to seeing. Is she going to take to farming?"

Bottles winced visibly.

"No, you see—in short, we have put an end to that. I am not engaged now."

"Oh, indeed," said the friend, and awkwardly departed.

CHAPTER II

Twelve years have passed since Bottles sent in his papers, and in twelve years many things happen. Amongst them recently it had happened that our hero's only and elder brother had, owing to an unexpected development of consumption among the expectant heirs, tumbled into a baronetcy and eight thousand a year, and Bottles himself into a modest but to him most ample fortune of as many hundred. When the news reached him he was the captain of a volunteer corps engaged in one of the numerous Basuto wars in the Cape Colony. He served the campaign out, and then, in obedience to his brother's entreaties and a natural craving to see his native land, after an absence of nearly fourteen years, resigned his commission and returned to England.

Thus it came to pass that the next scene of this little history opens, not upon the South African veld, or in a whitewashed house in some half-grown, hobbledehoy colonial town, but in a set of the most comfortable chambers in the Albany, the local and appropriate habitation of the bachelor brother aforesaid, Sir Eustace Peritt.

In a very comfortable arm-chair in front of a warm fire (for the month is November) sits the Bottles of old days—bigger, uglier, shyer than ever, and in addition, disfigured by an assegai wound through the cheek. Opposite to him, and peering at him occasionally with fond curiosity through an eyeglass, is his brother, a very different stamp of man. Sir Eustace Peritt is a well-preserved, London-looking gentleman, of apparently any age between thirty and fifty. His eye is so bright, his figure so well preserved, that to judge from appearances alone you would put him down to the former age. But when you come to know him so as to be able to measure his consummate knowledge of the world, and to have the opportunity of reflecting upon the good-natured but profound cynicism which pleasantly pervades his talk as absolutely as the flavour of lemon pervades rum punch, you would be inclined to assign his natal day to a much earlier date. In reality he was forty, neither more nor less, and had both preserved his youthful appearance and gained the mellowness of his experience by a judicious use of the opportunities of life.

"Well, my dear George," said Sir Eustace, addressing his brother—determined to take this occasion of meeting after so long a time to be rid of the nickname "Bottles," which he hated—"I haven't had such a pleasure for years."

"As—as what?"

"As meeting you again, of course. When I saw you on the vessel I knew you at once. You have not changed at all, unless expansion can be called a change."

"Nor have you, Eustace, unless contraction can be called a change. Your waist used to be bigger, you know."

"Ah, George, I drank beer in those days; it is one of those things of which I have lived to see the folly. In fact, there are not many things of which I have not lived to see the folly."

"Except living itself, I suppose?"

"Exactly—except living. I have no wish to follow the example of our poor cousins," he answered with a sigh, "to whose considerate behaviour, however," he added, brightening, "we owe our present improved position." Then came a pause.

"Fourteen years is a long time, George; you must have had a rough time of it."

"Yes, pretty rough. I have seen a good deal of irregular service, you know."

"And never got anything out of it, I suppose?"

"Oh, yes; I have got my bread and butter, which is all I am worth."

Sir Eustace looked at his brother doubtfully through his eyeglass. "You are modest," he said; "that does not do. You must have a better opinion of yourself if you want to get on in the world."

"I don't want to get on. I am quite content to earn a living, and I am modest because I have seen so many better men fare worse."

"But now you need not earn a living any more. What do you propose to do? Live in town? I can set you going in a very good lot. You will be quite a lion with that hole in your cheek—by the way, you must tell me the story. And then, you see, if anything happens to me you stand in for the title and estates. That will be quite enough to float you."

Bottles writhed uneasily in his chair. "Thank you, Eustace; but really I must ask you—in short, I don't want to be floated or anything of the sort. I would rather go back to South Africa and my volunteer corps. I would indeed. I hate strangers, and society, and all that sort of thing. I'm not fit for it like you."

"Then what do you mean to do—get married and live in the country?"

Bottles coloured a little through his sun-tanned skin—a fact that did not escape the eyeglass of his observant brother. "No, I am not going to get married, certainly not."

"By the way," said Sir Eustace carelessly, "I saw your old flame, Lady Croston, yesterday, and told her you were coming home. She makes a charming widow."

"*What!*" ejaculated his brother, slowly raising himself out of his chair in astonishment. "Is her husband dead?"

"Dead? Yes, died a year ago, and a good riddance too. He appointed me one of his executors; I am sure I don't know why, for we never liked each other. I think he was the most disagreeable fellow I ever knew. They say he gave his wife a roughish time of it occasionally. Serve her right, too."

"Why did it serve her right?"

Sir Eustace shrugged his shoulders.

"When a heartless girl jilts the fellow she is engaged to in order to sell herself to an elderly beast, I think she deserves all she gets. This one did not get half enough; indeed, she has made a good thing of it—better than she expected."

His brother sat down again before he answered in a constrained voice, "Don't you think you are rather hard on her, Eustace?"

"Hard on her? No, not a bit of it. Of all the worthless women that I know, I think Madeline Croston is the most worthless. Look how she treated you."

"Eustace," broke in his brother almost sharply, "if you don't mind, I wish you would not talk of her like that to me. I can't—in short, I don't like it."

Sir Eustace's eyeglass dropped out of Sir Eustace's eye—he had opened it so wide to stare at his brother. "Why, my dear fellow," he ejaculated, "you don't mean to tell me you still care for that woman?"

His brother twisted his great form about uncomfortably in the low chair as he answered, "I don't know, I'm sure, about caring for her, but I don't like to hear you say such things about her."

Sir Eustace whistled softly. "I am sorry if I offended you, old fellow," he said. "I had no idea that it was still a sore point with you. You must be a faithful people in South Africa. Here the 'holy feelings of the heart' are shorter lived. We wear out several generations of them in twelve years."

CHAPTER III

Bottles did not go to bed till late that night. Long after Sir Eustace —who, always careful of his health, never stopped up late if he could avoid it—had vanished, yawning, his brother sat smoking pipe after pipe and thinking. He had sat many times in the same way on a wagon-box in the African veld, or up where the moonlight turned the falls of the Zambesi into a rushing cataract of silver, or alone in his tent when all the camp was sleeping round him. It was a habit of this queer, silent man to sit and think for hours at night, and arose to a great extent from an incapacity to sleep, that was the weak point in his constitution.

As for his meditations, they were various, but mostly the outcome of a curious speculative side to his nature, which he never revealed to the outside world. Dreams of a happiness of which heretofore his hard life had given him no glimpse; semi-mystical, religious meditations upon the great unknown around us; and grand schemes for the regeneration of mankind—all formed part of them.

But there was one central thought, the fixed star of his mind, round which all the others continually revolved, taking their light and colour from it, and that was the thought of Madeline Croston, the woman to whom he had been engaged. Years and years had passed since he had seen her face, and yet it was always present to him. Beyond the occasional mention of her name in some society paper—several of which, by the way, he took in for years and conscientiously searched on the chance of finding it—till this evening he had never even seen it or heard it spoken; and yet with all the tenacity of his strong, deep nature he clung to her dear memory. That she had left him to marry another man weighed as nothing in the balance of his love. Once she had loved him, and thereby he was repaid for the devotion of his life. He had no ambitions. Madeline had been his great ambition; and when that had fallen, all the others had fallen with it, even to the dust. He simply did his duty, whatever it might be, as well as in him lay, without fear of blame or hope of praise—shunning men, and never, if he could avoid it, speaking to a woman, content to earn his livelihood, and for the rest rendered colourless by his secret and pathetic passion.

And now it appeared that Madeline was a widow, which meant—and his heart beat fast at the thought—that she was a free woman. Madeline was a free woman, and he was within a few minutes' walk of her. No thousands of miles of ocean rolled between them now. He rose, went to the table, and consulted a Red book that lay on it. There was the address—a house in Grosvenor Street. Overcome by an uncontrollable impulse, he went out of the room. Going to his own he found his mackintosh and a round hat, and softly left the house. It was then past two in the morning, pouring with rain, and blowing hard.

He had been a little in London as a lad and remembered the main thoroughfares, so had no great difficulty in finding his way up Piccadilly till he came to Park Lane, into which the Red book told him Grosvenor Square opened. But to find Grosvenor Street itself was a more difficult matter, and at such a time on such a night there was naturally nobody to ask—least of all a policeman. At last he found it, and hurried on down the street with a quickening pulse. What he was hurrying to he could not tell, but that over-mastering impulse forced him on quicker and quicker yet.

Suddenly he halted, and examined the number of one of the houses by the faint and struggling light from the nearest lamp. It was *her* house; now there was nothing between them but a few feet of space and fourteen inches of brickwork. He crossed over to the other side of the street, and looked up at the house, but could scarcely make it out through the driving rain. There was no light in the house, and no sign of life about the street. But there were both light and life in the heart of this watcher. All the pulses of his blood were astir, keeping time with the commotion of his mind. He stood there in the shadow, gazing at the murky house, heedless of the bitter wind and pelting rain, and felt his life and spirit pass out of his control into an unknown dominion. The storm that raged around him was nothing to the convulsion of his inner self in that hour of madness, which was yet happiness. Yet as it had arisen thus suddenly, so with equal swiftness it died away, and left him standing there with a chill sense of folly in his mind and of the bitter weather in his body; for on such a night a mackintosh and a dress coat were not adapted to keep the most ardent lover warm. He shivered, and turning, made his way back to Albany, feeling heartily ashamed of himself and his midnight expedition, and heartily glad that no one knew of it except himself.

On the following day Bottles—for convenience' sake we still call him by his old nickname—was obliged to see a lawyer with reference to the money which he had inherited, and to search for a box which had gone astray aboard the steamer; also to buy a tall hat, such as he had not worn for fourteen years; so that between one thing and another it was half-past four before he got back to the Albany. Here he donned the new hat, which did not fit very well, and a new black coat which fitted so well that it seemed to cut into his large frame in every possible direction, and departed, furiously struggling with a pair of gloves, also new, for Grosvenor Street.

A quarter of an hour's walk, for he knew the road this time, brought him to the house. Glancing for a while at the spot where he had stood on the previous night, he walked up the steps and pulled the bell. Though he looked bold enough outwardly—indeed, rather imposing than otherwise—with his broad shoulders and the great scar on his bronzed face, his breast was full of terrors. In these, however, he had not much time to indulge, for a footman, still decked in the trappings of vicarious grief, opened the door with the most startling promptitude, and he was ushered upstairs into a small but richly furnished room.

Madeline was not in the room, though to judge from the lace handkerchief lying on the floor by a low chair, and the open novel on a little wicker table alongside, she had not left it long. The footman departed, saying, in a magnificent undertone, that "her ladyship" should be informed, and left our hero to enjoy his sensations. Being one of those people whom suspense of any sort makes fidgety, he employed himself in looking at the pictures and china, even going so far as to walk to a pair of very heavy blue velvet curtains that apparently communicated with another room, and peep through them at a much larger apartment of which the furniture was done up in ghostly-looking bags.

Retreating from this melancholy sight, finally he took up a position on the hearthrug and waited. Would she be angry with him for coming? he wondered. Would it recall things she had rather forget? But perhaps she had already forgotten them—it was so long ago. Would she be very much changed? Perhaps he should not know her. Perhaps—but here he happened to lift his eyes, and there, standing between the two blue velvet curtains, was Madeline, now a woman in the full splendour of a remarkable beauty, and showing as yet, at any rate in that dull November twilight, no traces of her years. There she stood, her large dark eyes fixed upon him with a look of wistful curiosity, her shapely lips just parted to speak, and her bosom gently heaving, as though with trouble.

Poor Bottles! One look was enough. There was no chance of his attaining the blessed haven of disillusionment. In five seconds he was farther out to sea than ever. When she knew that he had seen her she dropped her eyes a little—he saw the long curved lashes appear against her cheek, and moved forward.

"How do you do?" she said softly, extending her slim, cool hand.

He took the hand and shook it, but for the life of him could think of nothing to say. Not one of the little speeches he had prepared would come into his mind. Yet the desperate necessity of saying something forced itself upon him.

"How do you do?" he ejaculated with a jerk. "It—it's very cold, isn't it?"

This remark was such an utter and ludicrous *fiasco* that Lady Croston could not choose but laugh a little.

"I see," she said, "that you have not got over your shyness."

"It is a long while since we met," he blurted out.

"I am very glad to see you," was her simple answer. "Now sit down and talk to me; tell me all about yourself. Stop; before you begin—how very curious it is! Do you know I dreamed about you last night—such a curious, painful dream. I dreamed that I was asleep in my room—which indeed I was—and that it was blowing a gale and raining in torrents—which I believe it was also—so there is nothing very wonderful about that. But now comes the odd part. I dreamed that you were standing out in the rain and wind and yet looking at me as though you saw me. I could not see your face because you were in the dark, but I knew it was you. Then I woke up with a start. It was a most vivid dream. And now to-day you have come to see me after all these years."

He shifted his legs uneasily. Considering the facts of the case, her dream frightened him, which was not strange. Fortunately, at that moment the impressive footman arrived with the tea-things and asked whether he should light the lamps.

"No," said Lady Croston; "put some wood on the fire." She knew that she looked her very best in those half-lights.

Then, when she had given him his tea, delighting him by remembering that he did not like sugar, she fell to drawing him out about the wild life he had been leading.

"By the way," she said presently, "perhaps you can tell me—a few days ago I bought a book for my boy"—she had two children—"all about brave deeds and that sort of thing, and in it there was a story of a volunteer officer in South Africa (the name was not mentioned) which interested me very much. Did you ever hear of it? It was this: The officer was in command of a fort containing a force that was operating against a native chief. While he was away the chief sent a flag of truce down to the fort, which was fired on by some of the volunteers in the fort, because there was a man among the truce party against whom they had a spite. Just afterwards the officer returned, and was very angry that such a thing had been done by Englishmen, whose duty it was, he said, to teach all the world what honour meant.

"Now comes the brave part of the story. Without saying any more, and notwithstanding the entreaties of his men, who knew that in all probability he was going to a death by torture, for he was so brave that the natives had set a great price upon him, wishing to kill him and use his body for medicine, which they thought would make them as brave as he was, that officer rode out far away into the mountains with only an interpreter and a white handkerchief, till he came to the chief's stronghold. But when the natives saw him coming, holding up his white handkerchief, they did not fire at him as his men had fired at them, because they were so astonished at his bravery that they thought he must be mad or inspired. So he came straight on to the walls of the stronghold, called to the chief and begged his pardon for what had happened, and then rode away again unharmed. Shortly afterwards, the chief, having captured some of the officer's volunteers, whom in the ordinary course of affairs he would have tortured to death, sent them back again untouched, with a message to the effect that he would show the English officer that he was not the only man who could behave 'like a gentleman.' I should like to know that man. Do you know who he was?"

Bottles looked uncomfortable, as well he might, for it was an incident in his own career; but her praise and enthusiasm sent a flush of pride into his face.

"I believe it was some fellow in the Basuto War," he said, prevaricating with peculiar awkwardness.

"Oh, then it *is* a true story?"

"Yes—that is, it is partially true. There was nothing heroic about it. It was a necessary act if our honour as fair opponents was to continue to be worth anything."

"But who was the man?" she asked, fixing her dark eyes on him suspiciously.

"The man!" he stammered. "Oh, the man—well, in short——" and he stopped.

"In short, *George*," she put in, for the first time calling him by his Christian name, "that man was *you*, and I am so proud of you, George."

It was very hateful to him in a way, for he loathed that kind of personal adulation, even from her. He was so intensely modest he had never even reported the incident in question; it had come out in some roundabout way. Yet he could not but feel happy that she had found him out. It was a great deal to him to have moved her, and her sparkling eyes and heaving bosom showed that she was somewhat moved.

He looked up and his eyes caught hers; the room was nearly dark now, but the bright flame from the wood the servant had put on the fire played upon her face. His eyes caught hers, and there was a look in them from which he could not escape, even if he had wished to do so. She had thrown her head back so that the coronet of her glossy hair rested upon the back of her low seat, and thus, without strain, could look straight up into his face. He had risen, and was standing by the mantelpiece. A slow, sweet smile grew upon the perfect face, and the dark eyes became soft and luminous as though they shone through tears.

In another second it had ended, as she thought that it would end and had intended that it should end. The great strong man was down—yes, down on his knees before her, one trembling hand catching at the arm of her chair, and the other clasping her tapering fingers. There was no hesitation or awkwardness about him now, the greatness of his long-pent passion inspired him, and he told her all without let or stop—all that he had suffered for her sake throughout those lonely years, all his wretched hopelessness, keeping nothing back.

Much she did not understand; such a passion as this was too deep to be fathomed by her shallow lines, too soaring for her to net in her world-straitened imagination. Once or twice even his exalted notions made her smile: it seemed ridiculous, knowing the world as she did, that any man should think thus of *any* woman. Nor, when at length he had finished, did she attempt an answer, feeling that her strength lay in silence, for she had a poor case. At least, the only argument that she used was a purely feminine one, but perfectly effective. She bent her beautiful face towards him, and he kissed it again and again.

CHAPTER IV

The revulsion of feeling experienced by Bottles as he hurried back to the Albany to dress for dinner—for he was to dine with his brother at one of his clubs that night—was so extraordinary and overwhelming that it took him, figuratively speaking, off his legs. As yet his mind, so long accustomed to perpetual misfortune in this, the ruling passion of his life, could not quite grasp his luck. That he should, after all, have won back his lost Madeline seemed altogether too good to be true.

As it happened, Sir Eustace had asked one or two men to meet him, amongst them an Under-Secretary for the Colonies, who, having to prepare for a severe cross-examination in the House upon South African affairs, had jumped at the opportunity of sucking the brains of a man thoroughly acquainted with the subject. But the expectant Under-Secretary was destined to meet with a grievous disappointment, for out of Bottles came no good thing. For the most part of the dinner he sat silent, only speaking when directly addressed, and then answering so much at random that the Under-Secretary quickly came to the conclusion that Sir Eustace's brother was either a fool or that he had drunk too much.

Sir Eustace himself saw that his brother's taciturnity had spoilt his little dinner, and his temper was not improved thereby. He was not accustomed to have his dinners spoiled, and felt that, so far as the Under-Secretary was concerned, he had put himself into a false position.

"My dear George," he said in a tone of bland exasperation when they had got back to the Albany, "I wonder what can be the matter with you? I told Atherleigh that you would be able to post him up thoroughly about all this Bechuana mess, and he could not get a word out of you."

His brother absently filled his pipe before he answered:

"The Bechuanas? Oh, yes, I know all about them. I lived among them for a year."

"Then why on earth didn't you tell him what you knew? You put me in rather a false position."

"I am very sorry, Eustace," he answered humbly. "I will go and see him if you like, and explain the thing to him to-morrow. The fact of the matter is, I was thinking of something else."

Sir Eustace interrogated him with a look.

"I was thinking," he went on slowly, "about Mad—about Lady Croston."

"Oh!"

"I went to see her this afternoon, and I think, I hope, that I am going to marry her."

If Bottles expected that this great news would be received by his elder brother as such news ought to be received—with congratulatory rejoicing—he was destined to be disappointed.

"Good heavens!" ejaculated Sir Eustace shortly, letting his eyeglass drop.

"Why do you say that, Eustace?" Bottles asked uneasily.

"Because—because," answered his brother in the emphatic tone which was his equivalent for strong language, "you must be mad to think of such a thing."

"Why must I be mad?"

"Because you, still a young man, with all your life before you, deliberately propose to tie yourself up to a middle-aged and *passée* woman—she is extremely *passée* by daylight, let me tell you—who has already treated you like a dog, and is burdened with a couple of children, and who, if she marries again, will bring you very little except her luxurious tastes. But I expected this. I thought she would try to catch you with those languishing black eyes of hers. You are not the first; I know her of old."

"If," said his brother, rising in dudgeon, "you are going to abuse Madeline to me, I think I had better say good night, for we shall quarrel—which I would not do for anything."

Sir Eustace shrugged his shoulders. "Those whom the gods wish to destroy they first make mad," he muttered, as he lit his hand candle. "This is what comes of a course of South Africa."

But Sir Eustace was an amenable man. His favourite motto was "Live and let live"; and having given the matter his best consideration during the lengthy process of shaving himself on the following morning, he came to the conclusion, reluctantly enough it must be owned, that it was evident that his brother meant to have his own way, and therefore the best thing to be done was to fall in with his views and trust to the chapter of accidents to bring the thing to naught. Sir Eustace, for all his apparent worldliness and cynicism, was a good fellow at heart, and cherished a warm affection for his awkward, taciturn brother. He also cherished a great dislike for Lady Croston, whose character he thoroughly understood. He saw a good deal of her, it is true, because he happened to be one of the executors of her husband's will; and since he had come into the baronetcy it had struck him that she had developed a considerable partiality for his society.

The idea of a marriage between his brother and his brother's old flame was in every way distasteful to him. In the first place, under her husband's will, Madeline would bring, comparatively speaking, relatively little with her should she marry again. That was one objection. Another, and still more forcible one from Sir Eustace's point of view, was that at her time of life she was not likely to present the house of Peritt with an heir. Now, Sir Eustace had not the slightest intention of marrying. Matrimony was, he considered, an excellent institution, and necessary to the carrying on of the world in a respectable manner, but it was not one with which he was anxious to identify himself. Therefore, if his brother married at all, it was his earnest desire that the union should bring children to inherit the title and estates. Prominent above both these excellent reasons, stood his intense distrust and dislike of the lady.

Needs must, however, when the devil (by whom he understood Madeline) drives. He was not going to quarrel with his only brother and presumptive heir because he chose to marry a woman who was not to his taste. So he shrugged his shoulders—having finished his shaving and his reflections together—and determined to put the best possible face on his disappointment.

"Well, George," he said to his brother at breakfast, "so you are going to marry Lady Croston?"

Bottles looked up surprised. "Yes, Eustace," he answered, "if she will marry me."

Sir Eustace glanced at him. "I thought the affair was settled," he said.

Bottles rubbed his big nose reflectively as he answered, "Well, no. I don't think that marriage was mentioned. But I suppose she means to marry me. In short, I don't see how she could mean anything else."

Sir Eustace breathed more freely, guessing what had taken place. So there was as yet no actual engagement.

"When are you going to see her again?"

"To-morrow. She is engaged all to-day."

His brother took out a pocket-book and consulted it. "Then I am more fortunate than you are," he said; "I have an appointment with Lady Croston this evening after dinner. Don't look jealous, old fellow, it is only about some executor's business. I think I told you that I am one of her husband's executors, blessings on his memory. She is a peculiar woman, your *inamorata*, and swears that she won't trust her lawyers, so I have to do all the dirty work myself, worse luck. You had better come too."

"Shan't I be in the way?" asked Bottles doubtfully, struggling feebly against the bribe.

"It is evident, my dear fellow, that you cannot be *de trop*. I shall present my papers for signature and vanish. You ought to be infinitely obliged to me for giving you such a chance. We will consider that settled. We will dine together, and go round to Grosvenor Street afterwards."

Bottles agreed. Could he have seen the little scheme that was dawning in his brother's brain, perhaps he would not have assented so readily.

When her old lover went away reluctantly to dress for dinner on the previous day, Madeline Croston sat down to have a good think, and the result was not entirely satisfactory. It had been very pleasant to see him, and his passionate declaration of enduring love thrilled her through and through, and even woke an echo in her own breast. It made her proud to think that this man, who, notwithstanding his ugliness and awkwardness, was yet, her instinct told her, worth half a dozen smart London fashionables, still loved her and had never ceased to love her. Poor Bottles! she had been very fond of him once. They had grown up together, and it really gave her some cruel hours when a sense of what she owed to herself and her family had forced her to discard him.

She remembered, as she sat there this evening, how at the time she had wondered if it was worth it—if life would not be brighter and happier if she made up her mind to fight through it by her honest lover's side. Well, she could answer that question now. It had been well worth it. She had not liked her husband, it is true; but on the whole she had enjoyed a good time and plenty of money, and the power that money brings. The wisdom of her later days had confirmed the judgment of her youth. As regards Bottles himself, she had soon got over that fancy; for years she had scarcely thought of him, till Sir Eustace told her that he was coming home, and she had that curious dream about him. Now he had come and made love to her, not in a civilised, philandering sort of a way, such as she was accustomed to, but with a passion and a fire and an utter self-abandonment which, while it thrilled her nerves with a curious sensation of mingled pleasure and pain, not unlike that she once experienced at a Spanish bull-fight when she saw a man tossed, was yet extremely awkward to deal with and rather alarming.

Now, too, the old question had come up again, and what was to be done? She had sheered him off the question that afternoon, but he would want to marry her, she felt sure of that. If she consented, what were they to live on? Her own juncture, in the event of her re-marriage, would be cut down to a thousand a year—she had four now, and was pinched on that; and as for Bottles, she knew what he had—eight hundred, for Sir Eustace had told her. He was next heir to the baronetcy, it was true, but Sir Eustace looked as though he would live for ever, and besides, he might marry after all.

For a few minutes Lady Croston contemplated the possibility of existing on eighteen hundred a year, and what Chancery would give her as guardian of her children in a poky house somewhere down at Kensington. Soon she realised that the thing was not to be done.

"Unless Sir Eustace will do something for him, it is very clear that we cannot be married," she said to herself with a sigh. "However, I need not tell him that just yet, or he will be rushing back to South Africa or something."

CHAPTER V

Sir Eustace and his brother carried out their programme. They dined together, and about half-past nine drove round to Grosvenor Street. Here they were shown into the drawing-room by the solemn footman, who informed Sir Eustace that her ladyship was upstairs in the nursery and had left a message for him that she would be down presently.

"All right; there is no hurry," said Sir Eustace absently, and the man went downstairs.

Bottles, being nervous, was fidgeting round the room as usual, and his brother, being very much at ease, was standing with his back to the fire, and staring about him. Presently his glance lit upon the blue velvet curtains which shut off the room they were in from the larger saloon that had not been used since Lady Croston's widowhood, and an idea which had been floating about in his brain suddenly took definite shape and form. He was a prompt man, and in another second he had acted up to that idea.

"George," he said in a quick, low voice, "listen to me, and for Heaven's sake don't interrupt for a minute. You know that I do not like the idea of your marrying Lady Croston. You know that I think her worthless—no, wait a minute, don't interrupt—I am only saying what I think. You believe in her; you believe that she is in love with you and will marry you, and have good reason to believe it, have you not?"

Bottles nodded.

"Very well. Supposing that I can show you within half an hour that she is perfectly ready to marry somebody else—myself, for instance—would you still believe in her?"

Bottles turned pale. "The thing is impossible," he said.

"That is not the question. Would you still believe in her, and would you still marry her?"

"Great heavens! no."

"Good. Then I tell you what I will do for you, and it will perhaps give you some idea of how deeply I feel in the matter; I will sacrifice myself."

"Sacrifice yourself?"

"Yes. I mean that I will this very evening propose to Madeline Croston under your nose, and I bet you five pounds she accepts me."

"Impossible," said Bottles again. "Besides, if she did you don't want to marry her."

"Marry her! No, indeed. *I* am not mad. I shall have to get out of the scrape as best I can—always supposing my view of the lady is correct."

"Excuse me," said Bottles with a gasp, "but I must ask you—in short, have *you* ever been on affectionate terms with Madeline?"

"Never, on my honour."

"And yet you think she will marry you if you ask her, even after what took place with me yesterday?"

"Yes, I do."

"Why?"

"Because, my boy," replied Sir Eustace with a cynical smile, "I have eight thousand a year and you have eight hundred—because I have a title and you have none. That you may happen to be the better fellow of the two will, I fear, not make up for those deficiencies.

Bottles with a motion of his hand waved his brother's courtly compliment away, as it were, and turned on him with a set white face.

"I do not believe you, Eustace," he said. "Do you understand what you make out this lady to be when you say that she could kiss me and tell me that she loved me—for she did both yesterday—and promise to marry you to-day?"

Sir Eustace shrugged his shoulders. "I think that the lady in question has done something like that before, George."

"That was years ago and under pressure. Now, Eustace, you have made this charge; you have upset my faith in Madeline, whom I hope to marry, and I say, prove it—prove it if you can. I will stake my life you cannot."

"Don't agitate yourself, my dear fellow; and as to betting, I would not risk more than a fiver. Now oblige me by stepping behind those velvet curtains—*a la* 'School for Scandal'—and listening in perfect silence to my conversation with Lady Croston. She does not know that you are here, so she will not miss you. You can escape when you have had enough of it, for there is a door through on to the landing, and as we came up I noticed that it was ajar. Or if you like you can appear from between the curtains like an infuriated husband on the stage and play whatever *role* occasion may demand. Really the situation has a laughable side. I should enjoy it immensely if *I* were behind the curtain too. Come, in you go."

Bottles hesitated. "I can't hide," he said.

"Nonsense; remember how much depends on it. All is fair in love or war. Quick; here she comes."

Bottles grew flurried and yielded, scarcely knowing what he did. In another second he was in the darkened room behind the curtains, through the crack in which he could command the lighted scene before him, and Sir Eustace was back at his place before the fire, reflecting that in his ardour to extricate his brother from what he considered a suicidal engagement he had let himself in for a very pretty undertaking. Suppose she accepted him, his brother would be furious, and he would probably have to go abroad to get out of the lady's way; and suppose she refused him, he would look a fool.

Meanwhile the sweep, sweep of Madeline's dress as she passed down the stairs was drawing nearer, and in another instant she was in the room. She was beautifully dressed in silver-grey silk, plentifully trimmed with black lace, and cut square back and front so as to show her rounded shoulders. She wore no ornaments, being one of the few women who are able to dispense with them, unless indeed a red camellia pinned in the front of her dress can be called an ornament. Bottles, shivering with shame and doubt behind his curtain, marked that red camellia, and wondered of what it reminded him.

Then in a flash it all came back, the scene of years and years ago—the verandah in far-away Natal, with himself sitting on it, an open letter in his hand and staring with all his eyes at the camellia bush covered with bloom before him. It seemed a bad omen to him—that camellia in Madeline's bosom. Next second she was speaking.

"Oh, Sir Eustace, I owe you a thousand apologies. You must have been here for quite ten minutes, for I heard the front door bang when you came. But my poor little girl Effie is ill with a sore throat which has made her feverish, and she absolutely refused to go to sleep unless she had my hand to hold."

"Lucky Effie," said Sir Eustace, with his politest bow; "I am sure I can understand her fancy."

At the moment he was holding Madeline's hand himself, and gave emphasis to his words by communicating the gentlest possible pressure to it as he let it fall. But knowing his habits, she did not take much notice. Comparative strangers when Sir Eustace shook hands with them were sometimes in doubt whether he was about to propose to them or to make a remark upon the weather. Alas! it had always been the weather.

"I come as a man of business besides, and men of business are accustomed to being kept waiting," he went on.

"You are really very good, Sir Eustace, to take so much trouble about my affairs."

"It is a pleasure, Lady Croston."

"Ah, Sir Eustace, you do not expect me to believe that," laughed the radiant creature at his side. "But if you only knew how I detest lawyers, and what you spare me by the trouble you take, I am sure you would not grudge me your time."

"Do not talk of it, Lady Croston. I would do a great deal more than that for you; in fact," here he dropped his voice a little, "there are few things that I would not do for you, *Madeline*."

She raised her delicate eyebrows till they looked like notes of interrogation, and blushed a little. This was quite a new style for Sir Eustace. Was he in earnest? she wondered. Impossible!

"And now for business," he continued; "not that there is much business; as I understand it, you have only to sign this document, which I have already witnessed, and the stock can be transferred."

She signed the paper which he had brought in a big envelope almost without looking at it, for she was thinking of Sir Eustace's remark, and he put it back in the envelope.

"Is that all the business, Sir Eustace?" she asked.

"Yes; quite all. Now I suppose that as I have done my duty I had better go away."

"I wish to Heaven he would!" groaned Bottles to himself behind the curtains. He did not like his brother's affectionate little ways or Madeline's tolerance of them.

"Indeed, no; you had better sit down and talk to me—that is, if you have got nothing pleasanter to do."

We can guess Sir Eustace's prompt reply and Madeline's smiling reception of the compliment, as she seated herself in a low chair—that same low chair she had occupied the day before.

"Now for it," said Sir Eustace to himself. "I wonder how George is getting on?"

"My brother tells me that he came to see you yesterday," he began.

"Yes," she answered, smiling again, but wondering in her heart how much he had told him.

"Do you find him much changed?"

"Not much."

"You used to be very fond of each other once, if I remember right?" said he.

"Yes, once."

"I often think how curious it is," went on Sir Eustace in a reflective tone, "to watch the various changes time brings about, especially where the affections are concerned. One sees children at the seaside making little mounds of sand, and they think, if they are very young children, that they will find them there to-morrow. But they reckon without their tide. To-morrow the sands will have swept as level as ever, and the little boys will have to begin again. It is like that with our youthful love affairs, is it not? The tide of time comes up and sweeps them away, fortunately for ourselves. Now in your case, for instance, it is, I think, a happy thing for both of you that your sand-house did not last. Is it not?"

Madeline sighed softly. "Yes, I suppose so," she answered.

Bottles, behind the curtains, rapidly reviewed the past, and came to a different conclusion.

"Well, that is all done with," said Sir Eustace cheerfully.

Madeline did not contradict him; she did not see her way to doing so just at present.

Then came a pause.

"Madeline," said Sir Eustace presently, in a changed voice, "I have something to say to you."

"Indeed, Sir Eustace," she answered, lifting her eyebrows again in her note of interrogation manner, "what is it?"

"It is this, Madeline—I want to ask you to be my wife."

The blue velvet curtains suddenly gave a jump as though they were assisting at a spiritualistic *séance*.

Sir Eustace looked at the curtains with warning in his eye.

Madeline saw nothing.

"Really, Sir Eustace!"

"I dare say I surprise you," went on this ardent lover; "my suit may seem a sudden one, but in truth it is nothing of the sort."

"O Lord, what a lie!" groaned the distracted Bottles.

"I thought, Sir Eustace," murmured Madeline in her sweet low voice, "that you told me not very long ago that you never meant to marry."

"Nor did I, Madeline, because I thought there was no chance of my marrying you" ("which I am sure I hope there isn't," he added to himself). "But—but, Madeline, I love you." ("Heaven forgive me for that!") "Listen to me, Madeline, before you answer," and he drew his chair closer to her own. "I feel the loneliness of my position, and I want to get married. I think that we should suit each other very well. At our age, now that our youth is past" (he could not resist this dig, at which Madeline winced), "probably neither of us would wish to marry anybody much our junior. I have had many opportunities lately, Madeline, of seeing the beauty of your character, and to the beauties of your person no man could be blind. I can offer you a good position, a good fortune, and myself, such as I am. Will you take me?" and he laid his hand upon hers and gazed earnestly into her eyes.

"Really, Sir Eustace," she murmured, "this is so very unexpected and sudden."

"Yes, Madeline, I know it is. I have no right to take you by storm in this way, but I trust you will not allow my precipitancy to weight against me. Take a little time to think it over—a week say" ("by which time," he reflected, "I hope to be in Algiers.") "Only, if you can, Madeline, tell me that I may hope."

She made no immediate answer, but, letting her hands fall idly in her lap, looked straight before her, her beautiful eyes fixed upon vacancy, and her mind amply occupied in considering the pros and cons of the situation. Then Sir Eustace took heart of grace; bending down, he kissed the Madonna-like face. Still there was no response. Only very gently she pushed him from her, whispering:

"Yes, Eustace, I think I shall be able to tell you that you may hope."

Bottles waited to see no more. With set teeth and flaming eyes he crept, a broken man, through the door that led on to the landing, crept down the stairs and into the hall. On the pegs were his hat and coat; he took them and passed into the street.

"I have done a disgraceful thing," he thought, "and I have paid for it."

Softly as the door closed Sir Eustace heard it; and then he too left the room, murmuring, "I shall soon come for my answer, Madeline."

When he reached the street his brother was gone.

CHAPTER VI

Sir Eustace did not go straight back to the Albany, but, calling a hansom, drove down to his club.

"Well," he thought to himself, "I have played a good many curious parts in my time, but I never had to do with anything like this before. I only hope George is not much cut up. His eyes ought to be opened now. What a woman——" but we will not repeat Sir Eustace's comments upon the lady to whom he was nominally half engaged.

At the club Sir Eustace met his friend the Under-Secretary, who had just escaped from the House. Thanks to information furnished to him that morning by Bottles, who had been despatched by Sir Eustace, in a penitent mood, to the Colonial Office to see him, he had just succeeded in confusing, if not absolutely in defeating, the impertinent people who "wanted to know." Accordingly he was jubilant, and greeted Sir Eustace with enthusiasm, and they sat talking together for an hour or more.

Then Sir Eustace, being, as has been said, of early habits, made his way home.

In his sitting-room he found his brother smoking and contemplating the fire.

"Hullo, old fellow!" he said, "I wish you had come to the club with me. Atherleigh was there, and is delighted with you. What you told him this morning enabled him to smash up his enemies, and as the smashing lately has been rather the other way he is jubilant. He wants you to go to see him again to-morrow. Oh, by the way, you made your escape all right. I only hope I may be as lucky. Well, what do you think of your lady-love now?"

"I think," said Bottles slowly—"that I had rather not say what I do think."

"Well, you are not going to marry her now, I suppose?"

"No, I shall not marry her."

"That is all right; but I expect that it will take *me* all I know to get clear of her. However, there are some occasions in life when one is bound to sacrifice one's own convenience, and this is one of them. After all, she is really very pretty in the evening, so it might have been worse."

Bottles winced, and Sir Eustace took a cigarette.

"By the way, old fellow," he said, as he settled himself in his chair again, "I hope you are not put out with me over this. Believe me, you have no cause to be jealous; she does not care a hang about me, it is only the title and the money. If a fellow who was a lord and had a thousand a year more proposed to her to-morrow she would chuck me up and take him."

"No; I am not angry with you," said Bottles; "you meant kindly, but I am angry with myself. It was not honourable to—in short, play the spy upon a woman's weakness."

"You are very scrupulous," yawned Sir Eustace; "all means are fair to catch a snake. Dear me, I nearly exploded once or twice; it was better than [yawn] any [yawn] play," and Sir Eustace went to sleep.

Bottles sat still and stared at the fire.

Presently his brother woke up with a start. "Oh, you are there, are you, Bottles?" (it was the first time he had called him by that name since his return.) "Odd thing; but do you know that I was dreaming that we were boys again, and trout-fishing in the old Cantlebrook stream. I dreamt that I hooked a big fish, and you were so excited that you jumped right into the river after it—you did once, you remember—and the river swept you away and left me on the bank; most unpleasant dream. Well, good night, old boy. I vote we go down and have some trout-fishing together in the spring. God bless you!"

"Good night," said Bottles, gazing affectionately after his brother's departing form.

Then he too rose and went to his bedroom. On a table stood a battered old tin despatch-box—the companion of all his wanderings. He opened it and took from it first a little bottle of chloral.

"Ah," he said, "I shall want you if I am to sleep again." Setting the bottle down, he extracted from a dirty envelope one or two letters and a faded photograph. It was the same that used to hang over his bed in his quarters at Maritzburg. These he destroyed, tearing them into small bits with his strong brown fingers.

Then he shut the box and sat down at the table to think, opening the sluice-gates of his mind and letting the sea of misery flow in, as it were.

This, then, was the woman whom he had forgiven and loved and honoured for all these years. This was the end and this the reward of all his devotion and of all his hopes. And he smiled in bitterness of his pain and self-contempt.

What was he to do? Go back to South Africa? He had not the heart for it. Live here? He could not. His existence had been wasted. He had lost his delusion—the beautiful delusion of his life—and he felt as though it would drive him mad, as the man whose shadow left him went mad.

He rose from the chair, opened the window, and looked out. It was a clear frosty night, and the stars shone brightly. For some while he stood looking at them; then he undressed himself. Generally, for he was different to most men, he said his prayers. For years, indeed, he had not missed doing so, any more than he had missed praying Providence in them to watch over and bless his beloved Madeline. But to-night he said no prayers. He could not pray. The three angels, Faith, Hope, and Love, whose whisperings heretofore had been ever in his ears, had taken wing, and left him as he played the eavesdropper behind those blue velvet curtains.

So he swallowed his sleeping-draught and laid himself down to rest.

*****

When Madeline Croston heard the news at a dinner-party on the following evening she was much shocked, and made up her mind to go home early. To this day she tells the story as a frightful warning against the careless use of chloral.

Little Flower

CHAPTER I

The Rev. Thomas Bull was a man of rock-like character with no more imagination than a rock. Of good birth, good abilities, good principles and good repute, really he ought to have been named not Thomas but John Bull, being as he was a typical representative of the British middle class. By nature a really religious man and, owing to the balance of his mind, not subject to most of the weaknesses which often afflict others, very early in his career he determined that things spiritual were of far greater importance than things temporal, and that as Eternity is much longer than Time, it was wise to devote himself to the spiritual and leave the temporal to look after itself. There are quite a number of good people, earnest believers in the doctrine of rewards and punishments, who take that practical view. With such

"Repaid a thousand-fold shall be,"

is a favourite line of a favourite hymn.

It is true that his idea of the spiritual was limited. Perhaps it would be more accurate to say that it was unlimited, since he accepted without doubt or question everything that was to be found within the four corners of what he had been taught. As a boy he had been noted for his prowess in swallowing the largest pills.

"Don't think," he would say to his weaker brothers and sisters, especially one of the latter whose throat seemed to be so constituted that she was obliged to cut up these boluses with a pair of scissors, "Don't think, but gulp 'em down!"

So it was with everything else in life; Thomas did not think, he gulped it down. Thus in these matters of faith, if other young folk ventured to talk of "allegory" or even to cast unhallowed doubts upon such points as those of the exact method of the appearance on this earth of their Mother Eve, or whether the sun actually did stand still at the bidding of Joshua, or the ark, filled with countless pairs of living creatures, floated to the top of Ararat, or Jonah, defying digestive juices, in fact abode three days in the interior of a whale, Thomas looked on them with a pitying smile and remarked that what had been written by Moses and other accepted prophets was enough for him.

Indeed a story was told of him when he was a boy at school which well exemplified this attitude. By way of lightening their labours a very noted geologist who had the art of interesting youthful audiences and making the rocks of the earth tell their own secular story, was brought to lecture to his House. This eminent man lectured extremely well. He showed how beyond a doubt the globe we inhabit, one speck of matter, floating in the sea of space, had existed for millions upon millions of years, and how by the evolutionary changes of countless ages it had at length become fitted to be the habitation of men, who probably themselves had lived and moved and had their being there for at least a million of years, perhaps much longer.

At the conclusion of the entrancing story the boys were invited to ask questions. Thomas Bull, a large, beetle-browed youth, rose at once and inquired of their titled and aged visitor, a man of world-wide reputation, why he thought it funny to tell them fairy tales. The old gentleman, greatly interested, put on his spectacles, and while the rest of the school gasped and the head master and other pedagogues stared amazed, studied this strange lad, then said:

"I am outspoken myself, and I like those who speak out when they do so from conviction; but, my young friend, why do you consider that I—well, exaggerate?"

"Because the Bible says so," replied Thomas unabashed. "The Bible tells us that the world was made in six days, not in millions of years, and that the sun and the moon and the stars were put in the sky to light it; also that man was created four thousand years B.C.

Therefore, either you are wrong, sir, or the Bible is, and *I* prefer the Bible."

The eminent scientist took off his spectacles and carefully put them away, remarking:

"Most logical and conclusive. Pray, young gentleman, do not allow any humble deductions of my own or others to interfere with your convictions. Only I believe it was Archbishop Ussher, not the Bible, who said that the world began about 4,000 B.C. I think that one day you may become a great man—in your own way. Meanwhile I might suggest that a certain sugaring of manners sweetens controversy."

After this no more questions were asked, and the meeting broke up in confusion.

From all of which it will be gathered that since none of us is perfect, even in Thomas there were weak points. For instance, he had what is known as a "temper," also he was blessed with a good idea of himself and his own abilities, and had a share of that intolerance by which this is so often accompanied.

In due course Thomas Bull became a theological student. Rarely was there such a student. He turned neither to left nor right, worked eight hours a day when he did not work ten, and took the highest possible degrees on every subject. Then he was ordained. About this time he chanced to hear a series of sermons by a Colonial bishop that directed his mind towards the mission-field. This was after he had served as a deacon in an East End parish and become acquainted with savagery in its western form.

He consulted with his friends and his superiors as to whether his true call were not to the far parts of the earth. Unanimously they answered that they thought so; so unanimously that a mild fellow-labourer whom he bullied was stung to the uncharitable remark that almost it looked as though they wanted to be rid of him. Perhaps they did; perhaps they held that for energy so gigantic there was no fitting outlet in this narrow land.

But as it chanced there was another to be consulted, for by this time the Rev. Thomas Bull had become engaged to the only daughter of a deceased London trader—in fact, he had been a shop-keeper upon a large scale. This worthy citizen had re-married late in life, choosing, or being chosen by a handsome and rather fashionable lady of a somewhat higher class than his own, who was herself a widow. By her he had no issue, his daughter, Dorcas, being the child of his first marriage. Mr. Humphreys, for that was his name, made a somewhat peculiar will, leaving all his fortune, which was considerable, to his young widow, charged, however, with an annuity of 300 pounds settled on his daughter Dorcas.

On the day before his death, however, he added a codicil which angered Mrs. Humphreys very much when she saw it, to the effect that if she re-married, three-fourths of the fortune were to pass to Dorcas at once, and that she or her heirs were ultimately to receive it all upon the decease of his wife.

The result of these testamentary dispositions was that one house, although it chanced to be large, proved too small to hold Mrs. Humphreys and her stepdaughter, Dorcas. The latter was a mild and timid little creature with a turned-up nose, light-coloured fluffy hair and an indeterminate mouth. Still there was a degree of annoyance and fashionable scorn at which her spirit rose. The end of it was that she went to live on her three hundred a year and to practise good works in the East End, being laudably determined to make a career for herself, which she was not in the least fitted to do.

Thus it was that Dorcas came into contact with the Rev. Thomas Bull. From the first time she saw her future husband he dominated and fascinated her. He was in the pulpit and really looked very handsome there with his burly form, his large black eyes and his determined, clean-shaven face. Moreover, he preached well in his own vigorous fashion.

On this occasion he was engaged in denouncing the vices and pettiness of modern woman—upper-class modern woman—of whom he knew nothing at all, a topic that appealed to an East End congregation. He showed how worthless was this luxurious stamp of females, what a deal they thought of dress and of other more evil delights. He compared them to the Florentines whom Savonarola (in his heart Thomas saw resemblances between himself and that great if narrow man) scourged till they wept in repentance and piled up their jewels and fripperies to be burned.

What do they do with their lives, he asked. Is there one in ten thousand of them who would abandon her luxuries and go forth to spread the light in the dark places of earth, or would even pinch herself to support others who did? And so on for thirty minutes.

Dorcas, listening and, reflecting on her stepmother, thought how marvellously true it all was. Had he known her personally, which so far as she was aware was not the case, the preacher could not have described her better. Also it was certain that Mrs. Humphreys and her friends had not the slightest intention of spreading any kind of light, unless it were that of their own eyes and jewels, or of going anywhere to do so, except perhaps to Monte Carlo in the spring.

How noble too was the picture he painted of the life of self-sacrifice and high endeavour that lay open to her sex. She would like to lead that higher life, being in truth a good-hearted little thing full of righteous impulses; only unfortunately she did not know how, for her present mild and tentative efforts had been somewhat disappointing in their fruits.

Then an inspiration seized her; she would consult Mr. Bull.

She did so, with results that might have been anticipated. Within three months she and her mentor were engaged and within six married.

It was during those fervid weeks of engagement that the pair agreed, not without a little hesitation upon the part of Dorcas, that in due course he would become a missionary and set forth to convert the heathen in what he called "Blackest Africa." First, however, there was much to be done; he must go through a long course of training; he must acquaint himself with various savage languages, such as Swahili and Zulu, and so must she.

Oh! how poor Dorcas, who was not very clever and had no gift of tongues came to loathe those barbaric dialects. Still she worked away at them like a heroine, confining herself ultimately, with a wise and practical prescience, to learning words and sentences that dealt with domestic affairs, such as "Light the fire." "Put the kettle on to boil." "Sister, have you chopped the wood?" "Cease making so much noise in the kitchen-hut." "Wake me if you hear the lion eating our cow." And so forth.

For more than a year after their marriage these preliminaries continued while Thomas worked like a horse, though it is true that Dorcas slackened her attention to Swahili and Zulu grammar in the pressure of more immediate affairs. Especially was this so after the baby was born, a girl, flaxen-haired like her mother, whom Thomas christened by the name of Tabitha, and who in after years became the "Little Flower" of this history. Then as the time of departure drew near another thing happened. Her stepmother, Mrs. Humphreys, insisted upon going to a ball in Lent, where she caught a chill that developed into inflammation of the lungs and killed her.

The result of this visitation of Providence, as Thomas called it, was that Dorcas suddenly found herself a rich woman with an income of quite 2000 pounds a year, for her father had been wealthier than she knew. Now temptation took hold of her. Why, she asked herself, should Thomas depart to Africa to teach black people, when with his gifts and her means he could stop at home comfortably and before very long become a bishop, or at the least a dean?

Greatly daring, she propounded this matter to her husband, only to find that she might better have tried to knock down a stone wall with her head than induce him to change his plans. He listened to her patiently—unless over-irritated, a perfectly exasperating patience was one of his gifts—then said in a cold voice that he was astonished at her.

"When you were poor," he went on, "you vowed yourself to this service, and now because we are rich you wish to turn traitor and become a seeker after the fleshpots of Egypt. Never let me hear you mention the matter again."

"But there is the baby," she exclaimed. "Africa is hot and might not agree with her."

"Heaven will look after the baby," he answered.

"That's just what I am afraid of," wailed Dorcas.

Then they had their first quarrel, in the course of which, be it admitted, she said one or two spiteful things. For instance, she suggested that the real reason he wished to go abroad was because he was so unpopular with his brother clergymen at home, and especially with his superiors, to whom he was fond of administering lectures and reproofs.

It ended, of course, in her being crushed as flat as is a broken-winged butterfly that comes in the path of a garden roller. He stood up and towered over her.

"Dorcas," he said, "do what you will. Stay here if you wish, and enjoy your money and your luxuries. I sail on the first of next month for Africa. Because you are weak, do I cease to be strong?"

"I think not," she replied, sobbing, and gave in.

So they sailed, first class—this was a concession, for he had intended to go third—but without a nurse; on that point he stood firm.

"You must learn to look after your own children," he said, a remark at which she made a little face that meant more than he knew.

CHAPTER II

The career of Mr. and Mrs. Bull during the next eight years calls for but little comment. Partly because Tabitha was delicate at first and must be within reach of doctors, they lived for the most part at various coast cities in Africa, where Thomas worked with his usual fervour and earnestness, acquiring languages which he learned to speak with considerable perfection, though Dorcas never did, and acquainting himself thoroughly with the local conditions in so far as they affected missionary enterprise.

He took no interest in anything else, not even in the history of the natives, or their peculiar forms of culture, since for the most part they have a secret culture of their own. All that was done with, he said, a turned page of the black and barbarous past; it was his business to write new things upon a new sheet. Perhaps it was for this reason that Thomas Bull never really came to understand or enter into the heart of a Zulu, or a Basuto, or a Swahili, or indeed of any dark-skinned man, woman, or child. To him they were but brands to be snatched from the burning, desperate and disagreeable sinners who must be saved, and he set to work to save them with fearful vigour.

His wife, although her vocabulary was still extremely limited and much eked out with English or Dutch words, got on much better with them.

"You know, Thomas," she would say, "they have all sorts of fine ideas which we don't understand, and are not so bad in their way, only you must find out what their way is."

"I have found out," he said grimly; "it is a very evil way, the way of destruction. I wish you would not make such a friend of that sly black nurse-girl who tells me a lie once out of every three times she opens her mouth."

For the rest Dorcas was fairly comfortable, as with their means she was always able to have a nice house in whatever town they might be stationed, where she could give tennis parties and even little lunches and dinners, that is if her husband chanced to be away, as often he was visiting up-country districts, or taking the duty there for another missionary who was sick or on leave. Indeed, in these conditions she came to like Africa fairly well, for she was a chilly little thing who loved its ample, all-pervading sunshine, and made a good many friends, especially among young men, to whom her helplessness and rather forlorn little face appealed.

The women, too, liked her, for she was kindly and always ready to help in case of poverty or other distresses. Luckily, in a way, she was her own mistress, since her fortune came to her unfettered by any marriage settlements; moreover, it was in the hands of trustees, so that the principal could not be alienated. Therefore she had her own account and her own cheque-book and used her spare money as she liked. More than one poor missionary's wife knew this and called her blessed, as through her bounty they once again looked upon the shores of England or were able to send a sick child home for treatment. But of these good deeds Dorcas never talked, least of all to her husband. If he suspected them, after one encounter upon some such matter, in which she developed a hidden strength and purpose, he had the sense to remain silent.

So things went on for years, not unhappily on the whole, for as they rolled by the child Tabitha grew acclimatised and much stronger. By this time, although Dorcas loved her husband as all wives should, obeying him in all, or at any rate in most things, she had come to recognise that he and she were very differently constituted. Of course, she knew that he was infinitely her superior, and indeed that of most people. Like everybody else she admired his uprightness, his fixity of purpose and his devouring energy and believed him to be destined to great things. Still, to tell the truth, which she often confessed with penitence upon her knees, on the whole she felt happier, or at any rate more comfortable, during his occasional absences to which allusion has been made, when she could have her friends to tea and indulge in human gossip without being called "worldly."

It only remains to add that her little girl Tabitha, a name she shortened into Tabbie, was her constant joy, especially as she had no other children. Tabbie was a bright, fair-haired little thing, clever, too, with resource and a will of her own, an improved edition of herself, but in every way utterly unlike her father, a fact that secretly annoyed him. Everybody loved Tabitha, and Tabitha loved everybody, not excepting the natives, who adored her. Between the Kaffirs and Tabitha there was some strong natural bond of sympathy. They understood one another.

At length came the blow.

It happened thus. Not far from the borders of Zululand but in the country that is vaguely known as Portuguese Territory, was a certain tribe of mixed Zulu and Basuto blood who were called the Ama-Sisa, that is, the People of the Sisa. Now "Sisa" in the Zulu tongue has a peculiar meaning which may be translated as "Sent Away." It is said that they acquired this name because the Zulu kings when they exercised dominion over all that district were in the habit of despatching large herds of the royal cattle to be looked after by these people, or in their own idiom to be *sisa'd*, i.e. agisted, as we say in English of stock that are entrusted to another to graze at a distance from the owner's home.

Some, however, gave another reason. In the territory of this tribe was a certain spot of which we shall hear more later, where these same Zulu kings were in the habit of causing offenders against their law or customs to be executed. Such also, like the cattle, were "sent away," and from one of these two causes, whichever it may have been, or perhaps from both, the tribe originally derived its name.

It was not a large tribe, perhaps there were three hundred and fifty heads of families in it, or say something under two thousand souls in all, descendants, probably, of a mild, peace-loving, industrious Basuto stock on to which had been grafted a certain number of the dominant, warlike Zulus who perhaps had killed out the men and possessed themselves of the Basuto women and their cattle. The result was that among this small people there were two strains, one of the bellicose type, who practically remained Zulus, and the other of the milder and more progressive Basuto stamp, who were in the majority.

Among these Sisas missionaries had been at work for a number of years, with results that on the whole were satisfactory. More than half of them had been baptised and were Christians of a sort; a church had been built; a more or less modern system of agriculture had been introduced, and the most of the population wore trousers or skirts, according to sex. Recently, however, trouble had arisen over the old question of polygamy. The missionaries would not tolerate more than one wife, while the Zulu section of the tribe insisted upon the old prerogative of plural marriage.

The dispute had ended in something like actual fighting, in the course of which the church and the school were burnt, also the missionary's house. Because of these troubles this excellent man was forced to camp out in the wet, for it was the rainy season, and catching a chill, died suddenly of heart-failure following rheumatic fever just after he had moved into his new habitation, which consisted of some rather glorified native huts.

Subsequently to these events there came a petition from the chief of the tribe, a man called Kosa, whose name probably derived from the Zulu word Koos, which means chief or captain, addressed to the Church authorities and asking that a new Teacher might be sent to take the place of him who had died, also to rebuild the church and the school. If this were not done, said the messengers, the tribe would relapse into heathenism, since the Zulu and anti-Christian party headed by an old witch-doctor, named Menzi, was strong and gaining ground.

This was an appeal that could not be neglected, since hitherto the Sisa had been a spot of light in a dark place, as most of the surrounding peoples, who were of the old Zulu stock, remained heathen. If that light went out the chances were that they would continue to be so, whereas if it went on burning another result might be hoped, since from a spark a great fire may come. Therefore earnest search was made for a suitable person to deal with so difficult and delicate a situation, with the result that the lot fell upon the Rev. Thomas Bull.

Once his name was mentioned, it was acclaimed by all. He was the very man, they said, bold, determined, filled with a Jesuit's fiery zeal (although it need scarcely be explained that he hated Jesuits as a cat does mustard), one whom no witch-doctors would daunt, one, moreover, who being blessed with this world's goods would ask no pay, but on the contrary would perhaps contribute a handsome sum towards the re-building of the church. This, it may be explained, as the Mission itself scarcely possessed a spare penny with which to bless itself, was a point that could not be overlooked.

So Thomas was sent for and offered the post, after its difficulties and drawbacks had been fairly but diplomatically explained to him. He did not hesitate a minute, or at any rate five minutes; he took it at once, feeling that his call had come; also that it was the very thing for which he had been seeking. Up in that secluded spot in Portuguese Territory he would, he reflected, be entirely on his own, a sort of little bishop with no one to interfere with him, and able to have his own way about everything, which in more civilised regions he found he could not do. Here a set of older gentlemen, who were always appealing to their experience of natives, continually put a spoke into his wheel, bringing his boldest plans to naught. There it would be different. He would fashion his own wheel and grind the witch-doctor with his following to dust beneath its iron rim. He said that he would go at once, and what is more, he promised a donation of 1,000 pounds towards the rebuilding of the church and other burnt-out edifices.

"That is very generous of Bull," remarked the Dean when he had left the room.

"Yes," said another dignitary, "only I think that the undertaking must be looked upon as conditional. I understand, well, that the money belongs to Mrs. Bull."

"Probably she will endorse the bond as she is a liberal little woman," said the Dean, "and in any case our brother Bull, if I may be pardoned a vulgarism, will knock the stuffing out of that pestilent Menzi and his crowd."

"Do you think so?" asked the other. "I am not so certain. I have met old Menzi, and he is a tough nut to crack. He may 'knock the stuffing' out of him. Bull, sound as he is, and splendid as he is in many ways, does not, it seems to me, quite understand natives, or that it is easier to lead them than to drive them."

"Perhaps not," said the Dean, "but in the case of these Sisas it is rather a matter of Hobson's choice, isn't it?"

So this affair was settled, and in due course Thomas received his letter of appointment as priest-in-charge of the Sisa station.

On his arrival home a few days later, where he was not expected till the following week, Thomas was so pre-occupied that he scarcely seemed to notice his wife's affectionate greeting; even the fact that both she and Tabitha were arrayed in smart and unmissionary-like garments escaped him. Dorcas also looked pre-occupied, the truth being that she had asked a few young people, officers and maidens of the place (alas! as it chanced, among them were no clergy or their wives and daughters), to play tennis that afternoon and some of them to stop to supper. Now she was wondering how her austere spouse would take the news. He might be cross and lecture her; when he was both cross and lectured the combination was not agreeable.

A few formal enquiries as to health and a certain sick person were made and answered. Dorcas assured him that they were both quite well, Tabitha especially, and that she had visited the afflicted woman as directed.

"And how was she, dear?" he asked.

"I don't know, dear," she answered. "You see, when I got to the house I met Mrs. Tomley, the Rector's wife, at the door, and she said, rather pointedly I thought, that she and her husband were looking after the case, and though grateful for the kind assistance you had rendered, felt that they need not trouble us any more, as the patient was a parishioner of theirs."

"Did they?" said Thomas with a frown. "Considering all things—well, let it be."

Dorcas was quite content to do so, for she was aware that her husband's good-heartedness was apt to be interpreted as poaching by some who should have known better, and that in fact the ground was dangerous.

"I have something to tell you," she began nervously, "about an arrangement I have made for this afternoon."

Mr. Bull, who was drinking a tumbler of water—he was a tee-totaller and non-smoker, and one of his grievances was that his wife found it desirable to take a little wine for the Pauline reason—set it down and said:

"Never mind your afternoon arrangements, my dear; they are generally of a sort that can be altered, for *I* have something to tell *you*, something very important. My call has come."

"Your call, dear. What call? I did not know that you expected anyone—and, by the way——"

She got no further, for her husband interrupted.

"Do not be ridiculous, Dorcas. I said call—not caller, and I use the word in its higher sense."

"Oh! I understand, forgive me for being so stupid. Have they made you a bishop?"

"A bishop——"

"I mean a dean, or an archdeacon, or something!" she went on confusedly.

"No, Dorcas, they have not. I could scarcely expect promotion as yet, though it is true that I thought—but never mind, others no doubt have better claims and longer service. I have, however, been honoured with a most responsible duty."

"Indeed, dear. What duty?"

"I have been nominated priest-in-charge of the Sisa Station."

"O-oh! and where is that? Is it anywhere near Durban, or perhaps Maritzburg?"

"I don't exactly know at present, though I understand that it is about six days' trek from Eshowe in Zululand, but over the border in Portuguese territory. Indeed, I am not sure that one can trek all the way, at least when the rivers are in flood. Then it is necessary to cross one of them in a basket slung upon a rope, or if the river is not too full, in a punt. At this season the basket is most used."

"Great Heavens, Thomas! do you propose to put me and Tabbie in a basket, like St. Paul, and did you remember that we have just taken on this house for another year?"

"Of course I do. The families of missionaries must expect to face hardships, from which it is true circumstances have relieved you up to the present. It is therefore only right that they should begin now, when Tabitha has become as strong as any child of her age that I know. As for the house, I had forgotten all about it. It must be relet, or failing that we must bear the loss, which fortunately we can well afford."

Dorcas looked at him and said nothing because words failed her, so he went on hurriedly.

"By the way, love, I have taken a slight liberty with your name. It appears that the church at Sisa, which I understand was quite a nice one built with subscriptions obtained in England by one of my predecessors who chanced to have influence or connections at home, has been recently burnt down together with the mission-house. Now the house can wait, since, of course, we can make shift for a year or two in some native huts, but obviously we must have a church, and as the Society is overdrawn it cannot help in the matter. Under these circumstances I ventured to promise a gift of 1,000 pounds, which it is estimated will cover the re-erection of both church and house."

He paused awaiting a reply, but as Dorcas still said nothing, continued.

"You will remember that you told me quite recently that you found you had 1,500 pounds to your credit, therefore I felt quite sure that you would not grudge 1,000 pounds of it to enable me to fulfil this duty—this semi-divine duty."

"Oh!" said Dorcas. "As a matter of fact I intended to spend that 1,000 pounds, or much of it, otherwise. There are some people here whom I wanted to help, but fortunately I had not mentioned this to them, so they will have to do without the money and their holiday; also the children cannot be sent to school. And, by the way, how is Tabbie to be educated in this far-away place?"

"I am sorry, dear, but after all private luxuries, including that of benevolence, must give way to sacred needs, so I will write to the Dean that the money will be forthcoming when it is needed. As for Tabitha's education, of course we will undertake it between us, at any rate for the next few years."

"Yes, Thomas, since you have passed your word, or rather my word, the money will be forthcoming. But meanwhile, if you can spare me the odd 500 pounds, I suggest that I should stay here with Tabbie, who could continue to attend the college as a day-scholar, while you get us some place ready to live in among these savages, the Sneezers, or whatever they are called."

"My dear," answered Thomas, "consider what you ask. You are in perfect health and so is our child. Would it not, then, be a downright scandal that you should stop here in luxury while your husband went out to confront grave difficulties among the Sisas—not the Sneezers—for I may tell you at once that the difficulties are very grave? There is a noted witch-doctor amongst this people named Menzi, who, I understand, is suspected of having burned down the mission-house, and probably the church also, because he said that it was ridiculous that an unmarried man like the late priest should have so large a dwelling to live alone. This, of course, was but a cunning excuse for his savage malevolence, but if another apparent celibate arrives, he might repeat the argument and its application. Also often these barbarians consider that a man who is not married *must* be insane! Therefore it is absolutely necessary that you and the child should be present with me from the first."

"Oh! is it?" said Dorcas, turning very pink. "Well, I am sorry to say that just now it is absolutely necessary that I should be absent from you, since I have a tennis party this afternoon—the officers of the garrison are coming and about half a dozen girls—and I must go to arrange about the tea."

"A tennis party! A tennis party to those godless officers and probably equally godless girls," exclaimed her husband. "I am ashamed of you, Dorcas, you should be occupied with higher things."

Then at last the worm turned.

"Do you know, Thomas," she answered, springing up, "that I am inclined to be ashamed of you too, who I think should be occupied in keeping your temper. You have accepted some strange mission without consulting me, you have promised 1,000 pounds of my money without consulting me, and now you scold me because I have a few young people to play tennis and stop to supper. It is unchristian, it is uncharitable, it is—too bad!" and sitting down again she burst into tears.

The Rev. Thomas who by now was in a really regal rage, not knowing what to say or do, glared about him. By ill-luck his eye fell upon a box of cigarettes that stood upon the mantelpiece.

"What are those things doing here?" he asked. "I do not smoke, so they cannot be for me. Is our money—I beg pardon—your money which is so much needed in other directions to be wasted in providing such unnecessaries—for officers and—idle girls? Oh—bless it all," and seizing the offending cigarettes he hurled them through the open window, a scattered shower of white tubes which some Kaffirs outside instantly proceeded to collect.

Then he rushed from the house, and Dorcas went to get ready for her party. But first she sent a servant to buy another box of cigarettes. It was her first act of rebellion against the iron rule of the Rev. Thomas Bull.

CHAPTER III

In the end, as may be guessed, Dorcas, who was a good and faithful little soul, accompanied her husband to the Sisa country. Tabitha went also, rejoicing, having learned that in this happy land there was no school. Dorcas found the journey awful, but really, had she but known it, it was most fortunate, indeed ideal. Her husband, who was a little anxious on the point, had made the best arrangements that were possible on such an expedition.

The wagon in which they trekked was good and comfortable, and although it was still the rainy season, fortune favoured them in the matter of weather, so that when they came to the formidable river, they were actually able to trek across it with the help of some oxen borrowed from a missionary in that neighbourhood, without having recourse to the dreaded rope-slung basket, or even to the punt.

Beyond the river they were met by some Christian Kaffirs of the Sisa tribe, who were sent by the Chief Kosa to guide them through the hundred miles or so of difficult country which still lay between them and their goal. These men were pleasant-spoken but rather depressed folk, clad in much-worn European clothes that somehow became them very ill. They gave a melancholy account of the spiritual condition of the Sisas, who since the death of their last pastor, they said, were relapsing rapidly into heathenism under the pernicious influence of Menzi, the witch-doctor. Therefore Kosa sent his greetings and prayed the new Teacher to hurry to their aid and put a stop to this state of things.

"Fear nothing," said Thomas in a loud voice, speaking in Zulu, which by now he knew very well. "I *will* put a stop to it."

Then they asked him his name. He replied that it was Thomas Bull, which after the native fashion, having found out what bull meant in English, they translated into a long appellation which, strictly rendered, meant *Roaring-Leader-of-the-holy-Herd*. When he found this out, Thomas flatly declined any such unchristian title, with the result that, anxious to oblige, they christened him "Tombool," and as "Tombool" thenceforward he was known. (Dorcas objected to this name, but Tabitha remarked sagely that at any rate it was better than "Tomfool.")

This was to his face, but behind his back they called him *Inkunzi*, which means bull, and in order to keep up the idea, designated poor Dorcas *Isidanda*, that being interpreted signified a gentle-natured cow. To Tabitha they gave a prettier name, calling her *Imba* or Little Flower.

At first Dorcas was quite pleased with her title, which sounded nice, but when she came to learn what it meant it was otherwise.

"How can you expect me, Thomas, to live among a people who call me 'a mild cow'?" she asked indignantly.

"Never mind, my dear," he answered. "In their symbolical way they are only signifying that you will feed them with the milk of human kindness," a reply which did not soothe her at all. In fact, of the three the child alone was pleased, because she said that "Opening Flower" was a prettier name than Tabbie, which reminded her of cats.

Thenceforward, following a track, for it could not be called a road, they advanced slowly, first over a mountain pass on the farther side of which the wagon nearly upset, and then across a great bush-clad plain where there was much game and the lions roared round them at night, necessitating great fires to frighten them away. These lions terrified Dorcas, a town-bred woman who had never seen one of them except in the Zoo, so much that she could scarcely sleep, but oddly enough Tabitha was not disturbed by them.

"God will not let us be eaten by a lion, will He, Father?" she asked in her simple faith.

"Certainly not," he answered, "and if the brute tries to do so I shall shoot it."

"I'd rather trust to God, Father, because you know you can never hit anything," replied Tabitha.

Fortunately, however, it never became necessary for Thomas to show his skill as a marksman, for when they got through the bushveld there were no more lions.

On the fourth day after they left the river they found themselves upon gentle sloping veld that by degrees led them upwards to high land where it was cold and healthy and there were no mosquitoes. For two days they trekked over these high lands, which seemed to be quite uninhabited save by herds of feeding buck, till at length they attained their crest, and below them saw a beautiful mimosa-clad plain which the guides told them was the Sisa Country.

"The Promised Land at last! It makes me feel like another Moses," said Thomas, waving his arm.

"Oh, isn't it lovely!" exclaimed Tabitha.

"Yes, dear," answered her mother, "but—but I don't see any town."

This indeed was the case because there was none, the Sisa kraal, for it could not be dignified by any other name, being round a projecting ridge and out of sight. For the rest the prospect was very fair, being park-like in character, with dotted clumps of trees among which ran, or rather wound, a silver stream that seemed to issue from between two rocky koppies in the distance.

These koppies, the guides told them, were the gates of Sisa Town. They neglected to add that it lay in a hot and unhealthy hill-ringed hollow beyond them, the site having originally been chosen because it was difficult to attack, being only approachable through certain passes. Therefore it was a very suitable place in which to kraal the cattle of the Zulu kings in times of danger. That day they travelled down the declivity into the plain, where they camped. By the following afternoon they came to the koppies through which the river ran, and asked its name. The answer was *Ukufa*.

"*Ukufa?*" said Thomas. "Why, that means Death."

"Yes," was the reply, "because in the old days this river was the River of Death where evil-doers were sent to be slain."

"How horrible!" said Dorcas, for unfortunately she had overheard and understood this conversation.

By the side of the river was a kind of shelf of rock that was used as a road, and over this they bumped in their wagon, till presently they were past the koppies and could see their future home beyond. It was a plain some miles across, and entirely surrounded by precipitous hills, the river entering it through a gorge to the north. In the centre of this plain was another large koppie of which the river *Ukufa*, or Death, washed one side. Around this koppie, amid a certain area of cultivated land, stood the "town" of the Christian branch of the Sisa. It consisted of groups of huts, ten or a dozen groups in all, set on low ground near the river, which suggested that the population might number anything between seven hundred and a thousand souls.

At the time that our party first saw it the sun was sinking, and had disappeared behind the western portion of the barricade of hills. Therefore the valley, if it may be so called, was plunged in a gloom that seemed almost unnatural when compared with the brilliant sky above, across which the radiant lights of an African sunset already sped like arrows, or rather like red and ominous spears of flame.

"What a dreadful place!" exclaimed Dorcas. "Is our home to be here?"

"I suppose so," answered Thomas, who to tell the truth for once was himself somewhat dismayed. "It does look a little gloomy, but after all it is very sheltered, and home is what one makes it," he added sententiously.

Here the conversation was interrupted by the arrival of the Chief and some of the Christian portion of the Sisa tribe, who having been warned of its approach by messenger, to the number of a hundred and fifty or so had advanced to meet the party.

They were a motley crowd clad in every kind of garment, ranging from a moth-eaten General's tunic to practically nothing at all. Indeed, one tall, thin fellow sported only a battered helmet of rusty steel that had drifted here from some European army, a *moocha* or waistbelt of catskins, and a pair of decayed tennis-shoes through which his toes appeared. With them came what were evidently the remains of the church choir, when there was a church, for they wore dirty fragments of surplices and sang what seemed to be a hymn tune to the strains of a decadent accordion.

The tune was long and ended in a kind of howl like to that of a disappointed jackal. When at length it was finished the Chief Kosa appeared. He was a middle-aged man, become prematurely old because he had lived too fast in his pre-Christian days, or so report said. Now he had a somewhat imbecile appearance, for his fingers twitched and when he spoke his mouth jerked up at the corners; also he kept looking over his shoulder as though he were afraid of something behind him. Altogether he inspired Thomas with no confidence. Whatever else he might be, clearly he was not a staff for a crusader to lean upon.

Still he came forward and made a very nice speech, as a high-bred native noble, such as he was, can almost invariably do. With many pious expressions he welcomed the new Teacher, saying that he and his people, that is those of them who were Christians, would do their best to make him happy.

Thomas thanked him in appropriate language, adding that he on his part would do his best to promote their welfare and to save their souls.

Kosa replied that he was glad to hear it, because these needed saving, since most of the Sisa people were now servants of the devil. Since the last *Umfundisi*, or Teacher died, they had been walking the road to hell at a very great pace, marrying many wives, drinking gin and practising all kinds of witchcraft under the guidance of the *Isanusi* or doctor, Menzi. This man, he added, had burned down the church and the mission-house by his magic, though these had seemed to be destroyed by lightning.

With a proud gesture Thomas announced that he would soon settle Menzi and all his works, and that meanwhile, as the darkness was coming on, he would be glad if Kosa would lead them to the place where they were to sleep.

So they started, the accordion-man, playing execrably, leading the way, and trekked for about a mile and a half till they came to the koppie in the centre of the plain, reaching it by following the left bank of the river that washed its western face.

Passing between a number of tumbled walls built of loose stones, that once in bygone generations had sheltered the cattle of Chaka and other Zulu kings, they reached a bay in the side of the koppie that may have covered four acres of ground. Here by the edge of the river, but standing a little above it, were the burnt-out ruins of a building that by its shape had evidently been a church, and near to it other ruins of a school and of a house which once was the mission-station.

As they approached they heard swelling from within those cracked and melancholy walls the sound of a fierce, defiant chant which Thomas guessed must be some ancient Zulu war-song, as indeed it was. It was a very impressive song, chanted by many people, which informed the listeners that those who sung it were the King's oxen, born to kill the King's enemies, and to be killed for the King, and so forth; a deep-noted, savage song that thrilled the blood, at the first sound of which the accordion gave a feeble wail and metaphorically expired.

"Isn't that beautiful music, Father. I never heard anything like that before," exclaimed Tabitha.

Before Thomas could answer, out from the ruined doorway of the Church issued a band of men—there might have been a hundred of them—clad in all the magnificent panoply of old-time Zulu warriors, with tall plumes upon their heads, large shields upon their arms, kilts about their middles, and fringes of oxtails hanging from their knees and elbows. They formed into a double line and advanced, waving broad-bladed assegais. Then at a signal they halted by the wagon and uttered a deep-throated salute.

In front of their lines was a little withered old fellow who carried neither shield nor spear, but only a black rod to which was bound the tail of a *wildebeeste*. Except for his *moocha* he was almost naked, and into his grey hair was woven a polished ring of black gum, from which hung several little bladders. Upon his scraggy neck was a necklace of baboon's teeth and amulets, whilst above the *moocha* was twisted a snake that might have been either alive or stuffed.

His face, though aged and shrunken, was fine-featured and full of breeding, while his hands and feet were very small; his eyes were brooding, the eyes of a mystic, but when his interest was excited their glance was as sharp as a bradawl. Just now it was fixed on Thomas, who felt as if it were piercing him through and through. The owner of the eyes, as Thomas guessed at once, was Menzi, a witch-doctor very famous in those parts.

"Why are these men armed with spears? It is against the law for Kaffirs to carry spears," he said to the Chief.

"This is Portuguese Territory; there is no law in Portuguese Territory," answered Kosa with a vacant stare.

"Then we might be all murdered here and no notice taken," exclaimed Thomas.

"Yes, Teacher. Many people have been murdered here: my father was murdered, and I dare say I shall be."

"Who by?"

Kosa made no answer, but his vacant eyes rested for a little while on Menzi.

"Good God! what a country," said Thomas to himself, looking at Dorcas who was frightened. Then he turned to meet Menzi, who was advancing towards them.

Casting a glance of contempt at Kosa, of whom he took no further notice, Menzi saluted the new-comers by lifting his hand above his head. Then with the utmost politeness he drew a snuff-box fashioned from the tip of a buffalo-horn out of a slit in the lobe of his left ear, extracted the wooden stopper and offered Thomas some snuff.

"Thank you, but I do not take that nastiness," said Thomas.

Menzi sighed as though in disappointment, and having helped himself to a little, re-stoppered the horn and thrust it back into the lobe of his ear. Next he said, speaking in a gentle and refined voice:

"Greeting, Teacher, who, the messengers tell us, are called Tombool in your own language and in ours *Inkunzi*. A good name, for in truth you look like a bull. I am glad to see that you are made much more robust than was the last Teacher, and therefore will live longer in this place than he did. Though as for the lady-teacher——" and he glanced at the delicate-looking Dorcas.

Thomas stared at this man, to whom already he had taken a strong dislike. Then moved thereto either by a very natural outburst of temper, or perchance by a flash of inspiration, he replied:

"Yes, I shall live longer than did my brother, who died here and has gone to Heaven, and longer I think than you will."

This personal remark seemed to take Menzi aback; indeed for a moment he looked frightened. Recovering himself, however, he said:

"I perceive, Teacher Tombool, that like myself you are a witch-doctor and a prophet. At present I do not know which of us will live the longer, but I will consult my Spirits and tell you afterwards."

"Pray do not trouble to do so on my account, for I do not believe in your Spirits."

"Of course you do not, Teacher. No doctor believes in another doctor's Spirits, since each has his own, and there are more Spirits than there are doctors. Teacher Tombool, I greet you and tell you at once that we are at war over this matter of Spirits. This tribe, Teacher, is a cleft log, yes, it is split into two. The Chief there, Kosa, sits on one half of the log with his Christians; I sit on the other half with the rest, who are as our fathers were. So if you wish to fight I shall fight with such weapons as I have. No, do not look at the spears—not with spears. But, if you leave me and my following alone, we shall leave you alone. If you are wise I think that you will do well to walk your own road and suffer us to walk ours."

"On the contrary," answered Thomas, "I intend that all the Sisa people shall walk one road, the road that leads to Heaven."

"Is it so, Teacher?" Menzi replied with a mysterious smile.

Then he turned his head and looked at the darkling river that just here, where it ran beneath an overhanging ledge of the koppie, was very deep and still. Thomas felt that there was a world of meaning in his look, though what it might be he did not know. Suddenly he remembered that this river was named Death.

After Menzi had looked quite a long while, once more he saluted as though in farewell, searching the faces of the three white people, especially Tabitha's, with his dreamy eyes and, letting them fall, searching the ground also. Near to where he stood grew a number of veld flowers, such as appear in their glory after the rains in Africa. Among these was a rare and beautiful white lily. This lily Menzi plucked, and stepping forward, presented it to Tabitha, saying:

"A flower for the Flower! A gift to a child from one who is childless!"

Her father saw and meditated interference. But he was too late; Tabitha had already taken the lily and was thanking Menzi in his own tongue, which she knew well enough, having been brought up by Zulu nurses. He smiled at her, saying:

"All Spirits, black or white, love flowers."

Then for a third time he saluted, not the others, but Tabitha, with more heartiness than before, and turning, departed, followed by his spearmen, who also saluted Tabitha as they filed in front of her.

It was a strange sight to see these great plumed men lifting their broad spears to the beautiful bright-haired child who stood there holding the tall white lily in her hand as though it were a sceptre.

CHAPTER IV

When Menzi and his company had departed, vanishing round the corner of the koppie, Thomas again asked the Chief where they were to sleep, an urgent matter as darkness was now approaching.

Kosa answered with his usual vagueness that he supposed in the hut where the late Teacher had died after the mission-house was burnt down. So they trekked on a little way, passing beneath the shelf of rock that has been mentioned as projecting from that side of the koppie which overhung the stream, where there was just room for a wagon to travel between the cliff and the water.

"What a dark road," said Dorcas, and one of the Christian natives who understood some English, having been the body-servant of the late missionary—it was he with the accordion—replied in Zulu:

"Yes, Lady; this rock is called the Rock of Evildoers, because once those accused of witchcraft and others were thrown from it by the order of the King, to be eaten by the crocodiles in that pool. But," he added, brightening up, "do not be afraid, for there are no more Zulu kings and we have hunted away the crocodiles, though it is true that there are still plenty of wizards who ought to be thrown from the rock," and he looked over his shoulder in the direction Menzi had taken, adding in a low voice, "You have just seen the greatest of them, Lady."

"How horrible!" said Dorcas for the second time.

A few yards farther on they emerged from this tunnel-like roadway and found themselves travelling along the northern face of the koppie. Here, surrounded by a fence, stood the Chief's kraal, and just outside of it a large, thatched hut with one or two smaller huts at its back. It was a good hut of its sort, being built after the Basuto fashion with a projecting roof and a doorway, and having a kind of verandah floored with beaten lime.

"This was the Teacher's house," said Kosa as the wagon halted.

"I should like to look inside it at once," remarked Dorcas doubtfully, adding, "Why, what's that?" and she pointed to a suspicious-looking, oblong mound that was covered with weeds, over which she had almost stumbled.

"That is the grave of the late Teacher, Lady. We buried him here because Menzi's people took up the bones of those who were in the churchyard and threw them into the river," explained Kosa.

Dorcas looked as though she were going to faint, but Thomas, rising to the occasion, remarked:

"Come on, dear. The dead are always with us, and what better company could we have than the dust of our sainted predecessor."

"I would rather have his room," murmured Dorcas, and gathering herself together, proceeded to the hut.

Somebody opened the door with difficulty, and as it seemed to be very dark within Thomas struck a match, by the light of which Dorcas peered into the interior. Next second she fell back into his arms with a little scream.

"Take me away!" she said. "The place is full of rats."

He stared; it was quite true. There, sitting up upon the dead missionary's bed, was a singularly large rat that did not seem in the least frightened by their appearance, whilst other creatures of the same tribe scuttled about the floor and up the walls.

Dorcas slept, or did not sleep, that night in the wagon with Tabitha, while Thomas took his rest beneath it as well as a drizzling rain that was falling would allow.

Such was the beginning of the life of the Bull family in Sisa-Land, not an encouraging beginning, it will be admitted, though no worse and perhaps much better than that which many missionaries and their families are called upon to face in various regions of the earth. What horror is there that missionaries have not been called upon to endure? St. Paul tells us of his trials, but they are paralleled, if not surpassed, even in the present day.

Missionaries, however good, may not always be wise folk; the reader might even think the Rev. Thomas Bull to be no perfect embodiment of wisdom, sympathy or perhaps manners, but taking them as a class they are certainly heroic folks, who endure many things for small reward, as we reckon reward. In nothing perhaps do they show their heroism and faith more greatly than in their persistent habit of conveying women and young children into the most impossible places of the earth, there to suffer many things, not exclusive, occasionally, of martyrdom. At least the Protestant section of their calling does this; the Roman Catholics are wiser. In renouncing marriage these save themselves from many agonies, and having only their own lives and health at stake, are perhaps better fitted to face rough work in rough places.

Even Thomas Bull, not a particularly sensitive person, was tempted more than once to arrive at similar conclusions during his period of service in Sisa-land, although neither he nor his wife or child was called upon to face the awful extremities that have confronted others of his cloth; for instance, another Thomas, one Owen, who was a missionary in Zululand at the time when Dingaan, the King, massacred Retief and his Boers beneath his eyes.

On the following morning Thomas crept out from beneath his wagon, not refreshed, it is true, but filled with a renewed and even more fiery zeal. During those damp hours of unrest he had reflected much and brought the whole position into perspective, a clear if a narrow perspective. The Chief with whom he had to deal evidently was a fool, if not an imbecile, and the Christians who remained after a generation of teaching were for the most part poor creatures, the weak-kneed amongst this mixed-blood tribe, probably those of the milder Basuto origin.

Such strength as remained in the people, who were, after all, but a dwindling handful marooned in a distant spot, was to be found among those of the old Zulu stock. They were descendants of the men sent by the Kings Chaka and Dingaan to keep an eye upon the humble Basuto slaves, whose duty it was to herd the royal cattle, the men, too, to whom was entrusted the proud but hateful business of carrying out the execution of persons that, for one reason or another, it was not desirable to kill at home.

The individuals detailed for these duties were for the most part of high blood, inconvenient persons, perhaps, whom it was desired to move to a distance. Thus, as Thomas Bull soon learned, Menzi was said to be no less a man than the grandson of the King Dingaan himself, one whose father had developed troublesome ambitions, but whose life had been spared because his mother was a favourite with the King.

Hence some of the grandson's pride, which was enhanced by the fact that in his youth he had been trained in medicine and magic by a certain Zikali, alias "Opener-of-Roads," who was said to have been the greatest witch-doctor that ever lived in Zululand, and through him had acquired, or perhaps developed inherent psychic gifts, that were in any case considerable.

In the end, however, he had returned to his petty tribe, neglecting larger opportunities, as Thomas learned, because of some woman to whom he was attached at home. It seemed, however, that he might as well have stayed away, since on his arrival he found that this woman had become one of the Chief's wives, for which reason he afterwards killed that Chief, Kosa's father, and possessed himself of the woman, who died immediately afterwards, as Menzi suspected by poisoning. It was principally for this reason that he hated Kosa, his enemy's son, and all who clung to him; and partly because of that hatred and the fear that it engendered Kosa and his people had turned Christian, hoping to protect themselves thus against Menzi and his wizardries. Also for this dead woman's sake, Menzi had never married again.

Thomas did not learn all these details, and others that need not be mentioned, at once, but by the time he crept out from under that wagon he had guessed enough to show that he was face to face with a very tough proposition, and being the man he was, he girded his loins to meet it, vowing that he would conquer Menzi or die in the attempt.

That very morning he called a council of the Christians and set to work with a will. The first thing to do was to make the late missionary's huts habitable, which did not take long, and the next to commence the rebuilding of the church. Thomas, true to his principles, insisted on beginning with the church and letting the mission-house stand over, although Dorcas, small blame to her, complained at being obliged to live for an indefinite time in a hut like a Kaffir woman. However, as usual, she was obliged to give way.

As it chanced, here there was little difficulty about building operations, for stone and wood and *tambuki* grass for thatching were all at hand in plenty. Also the Basuto section of the Sisa, as is common among that race, were clever masons and carpenters, some of them having followed those trades in Natal and the more settled places in Zululand, where dwellings had to be erected. Moreover, they possessed wagons, and now that the dry season was approaching were able to fetch stores of every kind from the borders of Natal. Lastly, thanks to Dorcas's banking account, money was by comparison no object, an unusual circumstance where missionaries are concerned.

So all the week Thomas laboured at these matters and at making himself acquainted with his congregation, and all Sunday he held open-air services or taught in the ruins of the old church.

Thus in the midst of so many new interests matters went on not uncomfortably, and Dorcas became more or less reconciled to her life. Still she could never get over her loathing of the place which she believed to be ill-omened, perhaps because of its gloomy aspect, coupled with the name of the river and the uses to which it had been put, after all not so very long ago. Naturally, also, this distaste was accentuated by the unlucky circumstances of their arrival.

Tabitha, too, was really happy, since she loved this wild free life, and having been brought up amongst Kaffirs and talking their language almost as well as she did her own, soon she made many friends.

Perhaps it was a sense that the information would not be well received by her father that prevented her from mentioning that the greatest of those friends was the old witch-doctor, Menzi, whom she often met when she was rambling about the place. Or it may have been pure accident, since Thomas was too busy to bother about such trifles, while her mother, who of course knew, kept her own counsel. The truth is that though he was a heathen witch-doctor, Dorcas liked old Menzi better than any other native in the district, because she said, quite truly, that he was a gentleman, however sinful and hardhearted he might be. Moreover, with a woman's perception she felt that if only he were a friend, at a pinch he might be worth all the others put together, while if he were an enemy, conversely the same applied.

So it came about that in the end there arose a very strange state of affairs. Menzi hated Thomas and did all he could to thwart him. He liked Dorcas and did all he could to help her, while the child Tabitha he came to worship, for some reason he never revealed, which was hidden in the depths of his secret soul; indeed ere long had she been his own daughter he could not have loved her more. It was he who amongst many other things gave her the pretty carved walking-stick of black and white *umzimbeet* wood, also the two young blue cranes and the kid that afterwards were such pets of hers, and with them the beautiful white feathers of a cock ostrich that had been killed on the veld. In the same way it was he who sent milk and eggs to Dorcas when she was at her wits' end for both, which more than once were found mysteriously at the door of their hut, and not any of his Christian flock, as Thomas fondly imagined.

Thus things went on for a while.

Meanwhile Thomas found this same Menzi a stumbling-block and a rock of offence. Whenever he tried to convert man, woman, or child he was confronted with Menzi or the shadow of Menzi. Thus those with whom he was arguing would ask him why he could not work miracles like Menzi. Let him show them pictures in the fire, or tell them who had stolen their goods or where they would find their strayed cattle, and perhaps they would believe him. And so forth.

At length Thomas grew exasperated and announced publicly that he credited nothing of this magic, and that Menzi was only a common cheat who threw dust into their eyes. If Menzi could perform marvels, let him show these marvels to him, Thomas, and to his wife, that they might judge of them for themselves.

Apparently this challenge was repeated to the witch-doctor. At least one morning a few days later, when Thomas went out accompanied by Dorcas and Tabitha, to meet the Chief Kosa and others and to discuss with them whether ultimately the mission-house should be rebuilt upon the old site or elsewhere, he found a great concourse of people, all or nearly all the tribe indeed, assembled on a level place where in the old days stood one of the great kraals designed to hold the king's cattle. Out of the crowd emerged Kosa, looking rather sillier than usual, and of him Thomas inquired why it was gathered. Was it to consult with him about the mission-house?

"No, Teacher," answered the Chief, "Menzi has heard that you call him a cheat, and has come to show that he is none, assembling all the people that they may judge between you and him."

"I do not want to see his tricks," said Thomas angrily. "Tell him to go away."

"Oh, Teacher!" replied Kosa, "that would not be wise, for then everyone would believe that Menzi's magic is so great that you are afraid even to look upon it. It is better to let him try. Perhaps if you pray hard he will fail, for his spirits will not always come when he calls them."

Thomas hesitated, then, being bold by nature, determined that he would see the thing through. After all, Menzi was an impostor and nothing else, and could work no more magic than he could himself. Here was a providential opportunity to expose him. So followed by the others he advanced into the crowd, which made way for him.

In an open space in its centre, sat Menzi wearing all his witch-doctor's trappings, bladders in his hair, snakeskins tied about him, and the rest, but even in this grotesque attire still managing to look dignified. With him were several acolytes or attendants, one of them an old woman, also peculiarly arrayed and carrying hide bags that contained their master's medicines. He rose as they came, saluted Thomas and smiled at Dorcas and Tabitha, very sweetly at the latter.

"O Teacher," he said, "my ears hear that you say that I am a liar and a cheat who have no wonders at my command; to whom the Spirits never speak and who deceives the people. Now, Teacher, I have come here that it may be seen whether you are right or I am right. If your magic is greater than mine, then I can do nothing and I will eat the dust before you. But if mine prevails, then perhaps all these will say that you are the cheat, not I. Also it is true that I am not a great magician as was my master, Zikali, the Opener-of-Roads, and cannot show you things worthy to be seen. Nor will I smell out evildoers, witches and wizards, since then the people might kill them, and I think that there are some here who deserve to die in the ancient fashion. No, I will not do this, since it is not right that those with you," here he glanced at Dorcas and Tabitha, "should look upon the sight of blood, even in this land where the White-man's law has no power. Still there are little things that may serve to amuse you for an hour and hurt no one. Have any of you lost anything, for instance?"

"Yes, I have," said Tabitha with a laugh.

"Is it so, Little Flower? Then be silent and do not say what you have lost. Have you told any what you have lost?"

"No," answered Tabitha, "because I was afraid I should be scolded."

"There, *Imba*, there, Little Flower, even that is too much, because you see the old cheat might guess something from your words. Yes, he might guess that it is something of value that you have lost, such as a bracelet of gold, or the thing that ticks, on which you white people read the time. Nay, be silent and do not let your face move lest I should read it. Now let us see what it is that you have lost."

Then he turned to his confederates, as Thomas called them, and began to ask them questions which need not be set out in detail. Was it an animal that the Little Flower had lost? No, it was not an animal, the Spirits told him that it was not. Was it an article of dress? No, they did not think it was an article of dress, yet the Spirits seemed to suggest that it had something to do with dress. Was it a shoe? Was it scissors? Was it a comb? Was it a needle? No, but it was something that had to do with needles. What had to do with needles? Thread. Was it thread? No, but something that had to do with thread. Was it a silver shield which pushed the needle that drew the thread?

Here Tabitha could contain herself no longer, but clapped her hands and cried out delightedly:

"Yes, that's it. It's my thimble."

"Oh! very well," said Menzi, "but it is easy to discover what is lost and hard to find it."

Then followed another long examination of the assessors or acolytes, or witch-doctor's chorus, by which it was established at length that the thimble had been lost three days before, when Tabitha was sitting on a stone sewing, that she believed it had fallen into a crevice of rocks, and so forth.

After this the chorus was silent and Menzi himself took up the game, apparently asking questions of the sky and putting his ear to the ground for an answer.

At length he announced: (1) That the thimble was not among the rocks; (2) That it was not lost at all.

"But it is, it is, you silly old man," cried Tabitha excitedly. "I have hunted everywhere, and I cried about it because I haven't got another, and can't buy one here, and the needle hurts my finger."

Menzi contemplated her gravely as though he were looking her through and through.

"It is *not* lost, Little Flower. I see it; you have it now. Put your hand into the pocket of your dress. What do you find there?"

"Nothing," said Tabitha. "That is, nothing except a hole."

"Feel at the bottom of your dress, there on the right. No, a little more to the front. What do you feel there?"

"Something hard," said Tabitha.

"Take this knife and cut the lining of your dress where you feel the hard thing. Ah! there is the silver shield which you have been carrying about with you all these days."

The crowd murmured approval. Dorcas exclaimed: "Well, I never!" and Thomas looked first puzzled, then angry, then suspicious.

"Does the Teacher think that the Floweret and the old doctor have made a plot together?" asked Menzi. "Can a sweet Flower make plots and tell lies like the old doctor? Well, well, it is nothing. Now let us try something better. My bags, my bags."

Thomas made as though he would go away, but Menzi stopped him, saying:

"No, doubters must stay to see the end of their doubts. What shall I do? Ah! I have it."

Then from one of the bags he drew out a number of crooked black sticks that looked like bent ebony rulers, and built them up criss-cross in a little pile upon the ground. Next he found some bundles of fine dried grass, which he thrust into the interstices between the sticks, as he did so bidding one of his servants to run to the nearest hut and bring a coal of fire upon a sherd.

"A match will not do," he said. "White men have touched it."

Presently the burning ember arrived, and muttering something, Menzi blew upon it as though to keep it alight.

"Now, White Teacher," he said in a voice that had suddenly become commanding, "think of something. Think of what you will, and I will show it to you."

"Indeed," said Thomas with a smile. "I have thought of something; now make good your words."

Menzi thrust the ember into the haylike fibres and blew. They caught and blazed up fiercely, making an extraordinarily large flame considering the small amount of the kindling. The ebony-like sticks also began to blaze. Menzi grew excited.

"My Spirit, come to me; my Spirit, come to me!" he cried. "O my Spirit, show this White Teacher Tombool that I am not a cheat!"

He ran round and round the fire; he leapt into the air, then suddenly shouted: "My Spirit has entered into me; my Snake is in my breast!"

All his excitement went; he grew quite calm, almost cataleptic. Holding his thin hands over the fire, slowly he let them fall, and as he did so the fierce flames died down.

"It's going out," said Tabitha.

Menzi smiled at her and lifted his hands again. Lo! the fire that seemed to be dead leapt up after them in a fierce blaze. Again he dropped his hands and the fire died away. Then he moved his arms to and fro and it came back, following the motions of his arms as though he drew it by a string.

"Have you thought, White Teacher? Have you thought?" he asked. "Good! Arise, smoke!"

Behold, instead of the clear flame appeared a fan-shaped column of dense white smoke, behind which Menzi vanished, all except his outstretched hands.

"Look on to the smoke, White people, and do you, Little Flower, tell me what you see there," he called from behind this vaporous veil.

Tabitha stared, they all stared. Then she cried out:

"I see a room, I see an old man in a clergyman's coat reading a letter. Why, it is the Dean whom we used to know in Natal. There's the wart on his nose and the tuft of hair that hangs down over his eye, and he's reading a letter written by Father. I know the writing. It begins, 'My dear Dean, Providence has appointed me to a strange place'——"

"Is that what you see also, Teacher?" asked Menzi. "And if so, is it what you pictured in your thought?"

Thomas turned away and uttered something like a groan, for indeed he had thought of the Dean and of the letter he had written to him a month before.

"The Teacher is not satisfied," said Menzi. "If he had seen all he thought of, being so good and honest, he would tell us. There is some mistake. My Spirit must have deceived me. Think of something else, Teacher, and tell the lady, and the child Imba, and Kosa, and another, what it is you are thinking of. Go aside and tell them where I cannot hear."

Thomas did so—in some way he felt compelled to do so.

"I am going to think of the church as I propose it shall be when finished according to the plans I have made," he said hoarsely. "I am going to think of it with a belfry spire roofed with red tiles and a clock in the tower, and I am going to think of the clock as pointing to the exact hour of noon. Do you all understand? It is impossible that this man should know of how I mean to build that spire and about the clock, because until this moment no one knew except myself. If he can show me that, I shall begin to believe that he is inspired by his master, the devil. Do you all understand?"

They said they did, and Menzi called out:

"Be quick, White Teacher. Be quick, I grow tired. My Spirit grows tired. The smoke grows tired. Come, come, come!"

They returned and stood in front of the fire, and in obedience to Menzi's motions once more the fan of smoke arose. On it grew something nebulous, something uncertain that by degrees took the form of a church. It was not very clear, perhaps because Thomas found it difficult to conceive the exact shape of the church as it would be when it was finished, or only conceived it bit by bit. One thing, however, was very distinct in his mind, and that was the proposed spire and the clock. As a result, there was the spire standing at the end of the shadowy church vivid and distinct. And there was the clock with its two copper hands exactly on the stroke of noon!

"Tell me what you see, Little Flower," said Menzi in a hollow voice.

"I see what Father told me he would think of, a church and the spire of the church, and the clock pointing to twelve."

"Do you all see that," asked Menzi, "and is it what the Teacher said he would think about?"

"Yes, Doctor," they answered.

"Then look once more, for *I* will think of something. I will think of that church falling. Look once more."

They looked, and behold the shadowy fabric began to totter, then it seemed to collapse, and last of all down went the spire and vanished in the smoke.

"Have you seen anything, O people?" said Menzi, "for standing behind this smoke I can see nothing. Mark that it is thick, since through it I am invisible to you."

This was true, since they could only perceive the tips of his outstretched fingers appearing upon each side of the smoke-fan.

"Yes," they answered, "we have seen a church fall down and vanish."

"That was my thought," said Menzi; "have I not told you that was the thought my Spirit gave me?"

"This is black magic, and you are a fiend!" shouted Thomas, and was silent.

"Not so, Tombool, though it is true that I have gifts which you clever White people do not understand," answered Menzi.

By degrees the smoke melted away, and there on the ground were the ten or twelve crooked pieces of ebony that they had seen consumed, now to all appearance quite untouched by the flame. There too on their farther side lay Menzi, shining with perspiration, and in a swoon or sleeping.

"Come away," said Thomas shortly, and they turned to go, but at this moment something happened.

Menzi, it will be remembered, had given Tabitha a kid of a long-haired variety of goat peculiar to these parts. This little creature had already grown attached to its mistress and walked about after her, in the way which pet goats have. It had followed her that morning, but not being interested in tricks or magic, engaged itself in devouring herbs that grew amongst the tumbled stones of the old kraal.

Suddenly Menzi recovered from his faint or seizure and, looking up, directed his attendants to return the magical ebony rods which burned without being consumed to one of the hide bags that contained his medicines. The assembly began to break up amidst a babel of excited talk.

Tabitha looked round for her goat, and perceiving it at a little distance, ran to fetch it, since the creature, being engaged in eating something to its taste, would not come at her call. She seized it by the neck to drag it away, with the result that its fore-feet, obstinately set upon the wall, overturned a large stone, revealing a great puff adder that was sleeping there.

The reptile thus disturbed instantly struck backwards after the fashion of its species, so that its fangs, just missing Tabitha's hands, sank deep into the kid's neck. She screamed and there was a great disturbance. A native ran forward and pinned down the puff-adder with his walking-stick of which the top was forked. The kid immediately fell on to its side, and lay there bleeding and bleating. Tabitha began to weep, calling out, "My goat is killed," between her sobs.

Menzi, distinguishing her voice amid the tumult, asked what was the matter. Someone told him, whereon he commanded that the kid should be brought to him and the snake also. This was done, Tabitha following her dying pet with her mother, for by now Thomas had departed, taking no heed of these events, which perhaps he was too disturbed to notice.

"Save my goat! Save my goat, O Menzi!" implored Tabitha.

The old witch-doctor looked at the animal, also at the hideous puff-adder that had been dragged along the ground in the fork of the stick.

"It will be hard, Little Flower," he said, "seeing that the goat is bitten in the neck and this snake is very poisonous. Still for your sake I will try, although I fear that it may prove but a waste of good medicine."

Then he took one of his bags and from it selected a certain packet wrapped in a dried leaf, out of which he shook some grey powder. Seizing the kid, which seemed to be almost dead, he made an incision in its throat over the wound, and into it rubbed some of this powder. Next he spat upon more of the powder, thus turning it into a paste, and opening the kid's mouth, thrust it down its throat, at the same time muttering an invocation or spell.

"Now we must wait," he said, letting the kid fall upon the ground, where it lay to all appearance dead.

"Is that powder any good?" asked Dorcas rather aimlessly.

"Yes, it is very good, Lady; a medicine of power of which I alone have the secret, a magic medicine. See, I will show you. Except the *immamba*, the ring-snake that puffs out its head, this one is the most deadly in our country. Yet I do not fear it. Look!"

Leaning forward, he seized the puff-adder, and drawing it from beneath the fork, suffered it to strike him upon the breast, after which he deliberately killed it with a stone. Then he took some of the grey powder and rubbed it into the punctures; also put more of it into his mouth, which he swallowed.

"Oh!" exclaimed Dorcas, "he will die," and some of the Christian Kaffirs echoed her remark.

But Menzi did not die at all. On the contrary, after shivering a few times he was quite himself, and, indeed, seemed rather brighter than before, like a jaded business man who has drunk a cocktail.

"No, Wife of Tombool," he said, "I shall not die; every year I doctor myself with this magic medicine that is called *Dawa*, after which all the snakes in Sisa-Land—remember that they are many, Little Flower—may bite me if they like."

"Is it your magic or is it the medicine that protects you?" asked Dorcas.

"Both, Lady. The medicine *Dawa* is of no use without the magic words, and the magic words are of no use without the medicine. Therefore alone in all the land I can cure snake bites, who have both medicine and magic. Look at your goat, Little Flower. Look at your goat!"

Tabitha looked, as did everyone else. The kid was rising to its feet. It rose, it baa'd and presently began to frisk about its mistress, like Menzi apparently rather brighter than before.

CHAPTER V

A year had gone by, during which time, by the most heroic exertions, Thomas Bull had at length succeeded in rebuilding the church. There it stood, a very nice mission-church, constructed of sun-dried bricks neatly plastered over, cool and spacious within, for the thatched roof was lofty, beautifully furnished (the font and the pulpit had been imported from England), and finished off with the spire and clock of his dreams, the latter also imported from England and especially adjusted for a hot climate.

Moreover, there was a sweet and loud-throated bell upon which the clock struck, with space allowed for the addition of others that must wait till Thomas could make up his mind to approach Dorcas as to the provision of the necessary funds. Yes, the church was finished, and the Bishop of those parts had made a special journey to consecrate it at the hottest season of the year, and as a reward for his energy had contracted fever and nearly been washed away in a flooded river.

Only one thing was lacking, a sufficient congregation to fill this fine church, which secretly the Bishop, who was a sensible man, thought would have been of greater value had it been erected in any of several other localities that he could have suggested. For alas! the Christian community of Sisa-Land did not increase. Occasionally Thomas succeeded in converting one of Menzi's followers, and occasionally Menzi snatched a lamb from the flock of Thomas, with the result that the scales remained even neither going up nor down.

The truth was, of course, that the matter was chiefly one of race; those of the Sisas in whom the Basuto blood preponderated became Christian, while those who were of the stubborn Zulu stock, strengthened and inspired by their prophet Menzi, remained unblushingly heathen.

Still Thomas did not despair. One day, he told himself, there would be a great change, a veritable landslide, and he would see that church filled with every Zulu in the district. Needless to say, he wished him no ill, but Menzi was an old man, and before long it might please Providence to gather that accursed wizard to his fathers. For that he was a wizard of some sort Thomas no longer doubted, a person directly descended from the Witch of Endor, or from some others of her company who were mentioned in the Bible. There was ample authority for wizards, and if they existed then why should they they not continue to do so? Since he could not explain it, Thomas swallowed the magic, much as in his boyhood he used to swallow the pills.

Yes, if only Menzi were removed by the will of Heaven, which really, thought Thomas, must be outraged by such proceedings, his opportunity would come, and "Menzi's herd," as the heathens were called in Sisa-land, would be added to his own. The Bishop, it is true, was not equally sanguine, but said nothing to discourage zeal so laudable and so uncommon.

It was while his Lordship was recovering from the sharp bout of fever which he had developed in a new and mosquito-haunted hut with a damp floor that had been especially erected for his accommodation, that at last the question of the re-building of the mission-house came to a head, which it could not do while all the available local labour, to say nothing of some hired from afar, was employed upon the church.

Thomas, it was true, wished to postpone it further, pointing out that a school was most necessary, and that after all they had grown quite accustomed to the huts and were fairly comfortable in them.

On this point, however, Dorcas was firm; indeed, it would not be too much to say that, having already been disappointed once, she struck with all the vigour of a trade-unionist. She explained that the situation of the huts on the brink of the river was low and most unhealthy, and that in them she was becoming a victim to recurrent attacks of fever. He, Thomas, might be fever-proof, as indeed she thought he was. It was true also that Tabitha had been extraordinarily well and grown much ever since she came to Sisa-Land, which puzzled her, inasmuch as the place was notoriously unhealthy for children, even if they were of native blood. Indeed, in her agitation she added an unwise remark to the effect that she could only explain their daughter's peculiar health by supposing that Menzi had laid a "good charm" upon her, as all the natives believed, and he announced publicly that he had done.

This made Thomas very angry, admittedly not without cause. Forgetting his conversion to a belief in the reality of Menzi's magic, he talked in a loud voice about the disgrace of being infected with vile, heathen superstitions, such as he had never thought to hear uttered by his wife's Christian lips. Dorcas, however, stuck to her point, and enforced it by a domestic example, adding that the creatures which in polite society are called "bed-pests," that haunted the straw of the huts, tormented her while Tabitha never had so much as a single bite.

The end of it was that the matter of mission-house *versus* huts was referred to the Bishop for his opinion. As the teeth of his Lordship were chattering with ague resulting, he knew full well, from the fever he had contracted in the said huts, Dorcas found in him a most valuable ally. He agreed that a mission-house ought to be built before the school or anything else, and suggested that it should be placed in a higher and better situation, above the mists that rose from the river and the height to which mosquitoes fly.

Bowing to the judgment of his superior, which really he heard with gratitude, although in his zeal and unselfishness he would have postponed his own comfort and that of his family till other duties had been fulfilled, Thomas replied that he knew only one such place which would be near enough to the Chief's town. It was on the koppie itself, about fifty feet above the level of and overhanging the river, where he had noted there was always a breeze, even on the hottest day, since the conformation of this hill seemed to induce an unceasing draught of air. He added that if his Lordship were well enough, they might go to look at the site.

So they went, all of them. Ascending a sloping, ancient path that was never precipitous, they came to the place, a flat tableland that perhaps measured an acre and a half, which by some freak of nature had been scooped out of the side of the koppie, and was backed by a precipitous cliff in which were caves. The front part of this plateau, that which approached to and overhung the river, was of virgin rock, but the acre or so behind was filled with very rich soil that in the course of centuries had been washed down from the sides of the koppie, or resulted from the decomposition of its material.

"The very place," said the Bishop. "The access is easy. The house would stand here—no need to dig deep foundations in this stone, and behind, when those trees have been cleared away, you could have a beautiful and fertile garden where anything will grow. Also, look, there is a stream of pure water running from some spring above. It is an ideal site for a house, not more than three minutes' walk from the church below, the best I should say in the whole valley. And then, consider the view."

Everyone agreed, and they were leaving the place in high spirits, Dorcas, who had household matters to attend, having already departed, when whom should they encounter but Menzi seated on a stone just where the path began to descend. Thomas would have passed him without notice as one with whom he was not on speaking terms, but the Bishop, having been informed by Tabitha who he was, was moved by curiosity to stop and interchange some words with him, as knowing his tongue perfectly, he could do.

"*Sakubona*" (that is, "good day"), he said politely.

Menzi rose and saluted with his habitual courtesy, first the Bishop, then the others, as usual reserving his sweetest smile for Tabitha.

"Great Priest," he said at once, "I understand that the Teacher Tombool intends to build his house upon this place."

The Bishop wondered how on earth the man knew that, since the matter had only just been decided by people talking in English, but answered that perhaps he might do so.

"Great Priest," went on Menzi in an earnest voice, "I pray you to forbid the Teacher Tombool from doing anything of the sort."

"Why, friend?" asked the Bishop.

"Because, Great Priest, this place is haunted by the spirits of the dead, and those who live here will be haunted also. Hearken. I myself when I was young have seen evil-doers brought from Zululand and hurled from that rock, blinded and broken-armed, by order of the King. I say that scores have been thrown thence to be devoured by the crocodiles in the pool below. Will such a sight as this be pleasant for white eyes to look upon, and will such cries as those of the evil-doers who have 'gone down' be nice for white ears to hear in the silence of the night?"

"But, my good man," said the Bishop, "what you say is nonsense. These poor creatures are dead, 'gone down' as you say, and do not return. We Christians have no belief in ghosts, or if they exist we are protected from them."

"None at all," interposed Thomas boldly and speaking in Zulu. "This man, my Lord, is at his old tricks. For reasons of his own he is trying to frighten us; for my part I will not be frightened by a native witch-doctor and his rubbish, even if he does deal with Satan. With your permission I shall certainly build the mission-house here."

"Quite right, of course, quite right," said the Bishop, though within himself he reflected that evidently the associations of the spot were disagreeable, and that were he personally concerned, perhaps he should be inclined to consider an alternative site. However, it was a matter for Mr. Bull to decide.

"I hear that Tombool will not be turned from his purpose. I hear that he will still build his house upon this rock. So be it. Let him do so and see. But this I say, that Imba, the Floweret, shall not be haunted by the *Isitunzi* (the ghosts of the dead) who wail in the night," said Menzi.

He advanced to Tabitha, and holding his hands over her he cried out:

"Sweet eyes, be blind to the *Isitunzi*. Little ears, do not hear their groans. Spirits, build a garden fence about this flower and keep her safe from all night-prowling evil things. Imba, little Flower, sleep softly while others lie awake and tremble."

Then he turned and departed swiftly.

"Dear me!" said the Bishop. "A strange man, a very strange man. I don't know quite what to make of him."

"I do," answered Thomas, "he is a black-hearted villain who is in league with the devil."

"Yes, I dare say—I mean as to his being a villain, that is according to our standards—but does your daughter—a clever and most attractive little girl, by the way—think so? She seemed to look on him with affection—one learns to read children's eyes, you know. A very strange man, I repeat. If we could see all his heart we should know lots of things and understand more about these people than we do at present. Has it ever struck you, Mr. Bull, how little we white people *do* understand of the black man's soul? Perhaps a child can see farther into it than we can. What is the saying—'a little child shall lead them,' is it not? Perhaps we do not make enough allowances. 'Faith, Hope and Charity, these three, but the greatest of these is charity'—or love, which is the same thing. However, of course you are quite right not to have been frightened by his silly talk about the *Isitunzi*, it would never do to show fear or hesitation. Still, I am glad that Mrs. Bull did not hear it; you may have noticed that she had gone on ahead, and if I were you I should not repeat it to her, since ladies are so nervous. Tabitha, my dear, don't tell your mother anything of all this."

"No, Bishop," answered Tabitha, "I never tell her all the queer things that Menzi says to me when I meet him, or at least not many of them."

"I wish I had asked him if he had a cure for your local fever," said the Bishop with a laugh, "for against it, although I have taken so much that my ears buzz, quinine cannot prevail."

"He has given me one in a gourd, Bishop," replied Tabitha confidentially, "but I have never taken any, because you see I have had no fever, and I haven't told mother, for if I did she would tell father" (Thomas had stridden ahead, and was out of hearing), "and he might be angry because he doesn't like Menzi, though I do. Will you have some, Bishop? It is well corked up with clay, and Menzi said it would keep for years."

"Well, my dear," answered the Bishop, "I don't quite know. There may be all sorts of queer things in Mr. Menzi's medicine. Still, he told you to drink it if necessary, and I am absolutely certain that he does not wish to poison *you*. So perhaps I might have a try, for really I feel uncommonly ill."

So later on, with much secrecy, the gourd was produced, and the Bishop had "a try." By some strange coincidence he felt so much better after it that he begged for the rest of the stuff to comfort him on his homeward journey, which ultimately he accomplished in the best of health.

That most admirable and wide-minded prelate departed, and so far as history records was no more seen in Sisa-Land. But Thomas remained, and set about the building of the house with his usual vigour. Upon the Death Rock, as it was called, in course of time he erected an excellent and most serviceable dwelling, not too large but large enough, having every comfort and convenience that his local experience could suggest and money could supply, since in this matter the cheque-book of the suffering Dorcas was entirely at his service.

At length the house was finished, and with much rejoicing the Bull family, deserting their squalid huts, moved into it at the commencement of the hot season. After the first agitations of the change and of the arrangement of the furniture newly-arrived by wagon, they settled down very comfortably, directing all their energies towards the development of the garden, which had already been brought into some rough order during the building of the house.

One difficulty, however, arose at once. For some mysterious reason they found that not a single native servant would sleep in the place, no, not even Tabitha's personal attendant, who adored her. Every soul of them suddenly developed a sick mother or other relative who would instantly expire if deprived of the comfort of their society after dark. Or else they themselves became ailing at that hour, saying they could not sleep upon a cliff like a rock-rabbit.

At any rate, for one cause or another off they went the very moment that the sun vanished behind the western hills, nor did they reappear until it was well up above those that faced towards the east.

At least this happened for one night. On the following day, however, a pleasant-looking woman named Ivana, whom they knew to be of good repute, though of doubtful religion, as sometimes she came to church and sometimes she did not, appeared and offered her services as "night-dog"—that is what she called it—to Tabitha, saying that she did not mind sleeping on a height. Since it was inconvenient to have no one about the place from dark to dawn, and Dorcas did not approve of Tabitha being left to sleep alone, the woman, whose character was guaranteed by the Chief Kosa and the elders of the church, was taken on at an indefinite wage. To the matter of pecuniary reward, indeed, she seemed to be entirely indifferent.

For the rest she rolled herself in blankets, native fashion, and slept across Tabitha's door, keeping so good a watch that once when her father wished to enter the room to fetch something after the child was asleep, she would not allow even him to do so. When he tried to force a way past her, suddenly Ivana became so threatening that he thought she was about to spring at him. After this he wanted to dismiss her, but Dorcas said it only showed that she was faithful, and that she had better be left where she was, especially as there was no one to take her place.

So things went on till the day of full moon. On that night Ivana appeared to be much agitated, and insisted that Tabitha should go to bed earlier than was usual. Also after she was asleep Dorcas noticed that Ivana walked continually to and fro in front of the door of the child's room and up and down the veranda on to which its windows opened, droning some strange song and waving a wand.

However, at the appointed hour, having said their prayers, Dorcas and her husband went to bed.

"I wonder if there is anything strange about this place," remarked Dorcas. "It is so very odd that no native will stop here at night except that half-wild Ivana."

"Oh! I don't know," replied Thomas with a yawn, real or feigned. "These people get all sorts of ideas into their silly heads. Do stop twisting about and go to sleep."

At last Dorcas did go to sleep, only to wake up again suddenly and with great completeness just as the church clock below struck three, the sound of which she supposed must have roused her. The brilliant moonlight flooded the room, and as for some reason she felt creepy and disturbed, Dorcas tried to occupy her mind by reflecting how comfortable it looked with its new, imported furnishings, very different from that horrible hut in which they had lived so long.

Then her thoughts drifted to more general matters. She was heartily tired of Sisa-Land, and wished earnestly that her husband could get a change of station, which the Bishop had hinted to her would not be impossible—somewhere nearer to civilisation. Alas! he was so obstinate that she feared nothing would move him, at any rate until he had converted "Menzi's herd," who were also obstinate, and remained as heathen as ever. Indeed why, with their ample means, should they be condemned to perpetual exile in these barbarous places? Was there not plenty of work to be done at home, where they might make friends and live decently?

Putting herself and her own wishes aside, this existence was not fair to Tabitha, who, as she saw, watching her with a mother's eye, was becoming impregnated with the native atmosphere. She who ought to be at a Christian school now talked more Zulu than she did English, and was beginning to look at things from the Zulu point of view and to use their idioms and metaphors even when speaking her own tongue. She had become a kind of little chieftainess among these folk, also, Christian and heathen alike. Indeed, now most of them spoke of her as the Maiden *Inkosikazi*, or Chieftainess, and accepted her slightest wish or order as law, which was by no means the case where Dorcas herself and even Thomas were concerned.

In fact, one or twice they had been driven to make a request through the child, notably upon an important occasion that had to do with the transport-riding of their furniture, to avoid its being left for a couple of months on the farther side of a flooded river. The details do not matter, but what happened was that when Tabitha intervened that which had been declared to be impossible proved possible, and the furniture arrived with wonderful celerity. Moreover, Tabitha made no request; as Dorcas knew, though she hid it from Thomas, she sent for the headmen, and when they were seated on the ground before her after their fashion, Menzi among them, issued an order, saying:

"What! Are my parents and I to live like dogs without a kennel or cattle that lack a winter kraal, because you are idle? Inspan the wagons and fetch the things or I shall be angry. *Hamba*—Go!"

Thereon they rose and went without argument, only lifting their right hands above their heads and murmuring, "*Ikosikaas! Umame!* (Chieftainess! Mother!) we hear you." Yes, they called Tabitha "Mother!"

It was all very wrong, thought Dorcas, but she supposed, being a pious little person, that she must bear her burden and trust to Providence to free her from it, and she closed her eyes to wipe away a tear.

When Dorcas opened them again something very strange seemed to have happened. She felt wide awake, and yet knew that she must be dreaming because the room had disappeared. There was nothing in sight except the bare rock upon which the house stood. For instance, she could see the gorge behind as it used to be before they made it into a garden, for she recognised some of the very trees that they had cut down. Moreover, from one of the caves at the end of it issued a procession, a horrible procession of fierce-looking, savage warriors, with spears and knobkerries, who between them half dragged, half carried a young woman and an elderly man.

They advanced. They passed within a few feet of her, and observing the condition of the woman and the man, she saw that these must be led because for a certain reason they could not see where to go,—oh! never mind what she saw.

The procession reached the edge of the rock where the railing was, only now the railing had gone like the house. Then for the first time Dorcas heard, for hitherto all had seemed to happen in silence.

"Die, *Umtakati!* Die, you wizard, as the King commands, and feed the river-dwellers," said a deep voice.

There followed a struggle, a horrible twisting of shapes, and the elderly man vanished over the cliff, while a moment later from below came the noise of a great splash.

Next the girl was haled forward, and the words of doom were repeated. She seemed to break from her murderers and stagger to the edge of the precipice, crying out:

"O Father, I come!"

Then, with one blood-curdling shriek, she vanished also, and again there followed the sound of a great splash that slowly echoed itself to silence.

All had passed away, leaving Dorcas paralysed with terror, and wet with its dew, so that her night-gear clung to her body. The room was just as it had been, filled with the soft moonlight and looking very comfortable.

"Thomas!" gasped his wife, "wake up."

"I *am* awake," he answered in his deep voice, which shook a little. "I have had a bad dream."

"What did you dream? Did you see two people thrown from the cliff?"

"Something of that sort."

"Oh! Thomas, Thomas, I have been in hell. This place is haunted. Don't talk to me of dreams. Tabitha will have seen and heard too. She will be driven mad. Come to her."

"I think not," answered Thomas.

Still he came.

At the door of Tabitha's room they found the woman Ivana, wide-eyed, solemn, silent.

"Have you seen or heard anything, Ivana?" asked Thomas.

"Yes, Teacher," she answered, "I have seen what I expected to see and heard what I expected to hear on this night of full moon, but I am guarded and do not fear."

"The child! The child!" said Dorcas.

"The *Inkosikazi* Imba sleeps. Disturb her not."

Taking no heed, they thrust past her into the room. There on her little white bed lay Tabitha fast asleep, and looking like an angel in her sleep, for a sweet smile played about her mouth, and while they watched she laughed in her dreams. Then they looked at each other and went back to their own chamber to spend the rest of the night as may be imagined.

Next morning when they emerged, very shaken and upset, the first person they met was Ivana, who was waiting for them with their coffee.

"I have a message for you, Teacher and Lady. Never mind who sends it, I have a message for you to which you will do well to give heed. Sleep no more in this house on the night of full moon, though all other nights will be good for you. Only the little Chieftainess Imba ought to sleep in this house on the night of full moon."

So indeed it proved to be. No suburban villa could have been more commonplace and less disturbed than was their dwelling for twenty-seven nights of every month, but on the twenty-eighth they found a change of air desirable. Once it is true the stalwart Thomas, like Ajax, defied the lightning, or rather other things that come from above—or from below. But before morning he appeared at the hut beneath the koppie announcing that he had come to see how they were getting on, and shaking as though he had a bout of fever.

Dorcas asked him no questions (afterwards she gathered that he had been favoured with quite a new and very varied midnight programme); but Tabitha smiled in her slow way. For Tabitha knew all about this business as she knew everything that passed in Sisa-Land. Moreover, she laughed at them a little, and said that *she* was not afraid to sleep in the mission-house on the night of full moon.

What is more, she did so, which was naughty of her, for on one such occasion she slipped back to the house when her parents were asleep, followed only by her "night-dog," the watchful Ivana, and returned at dawn just as they had discovered that she was missing, singing and laughing and jumping from stone to stone with the agility of her own pet goat.

"I slept beautifully," she cried, "and dreamed I was in heaven all night."

Thomas was furious and rated her till she wept. Then suddenly Ivana became furious too and rated him.

Should he be wrath with the Little Chieftainess Imba, she asked him, because the *Isitunzis*, the spirits of the dead, loved her as did everything else? Did they not understand that the Floweret was unlike them, one adored of dead and living, one to be cherished even in her dreams, one whom "Heaven Above," together with those who had "gone below," built round with a wall of spells?—and more of such talk, which Thomas thought so horrible and blasphemous that he fled before its torrent.

But when he came back calmer he said no more to Tabitha about her escapade.

It was a long while afterwards, at the beginning of the great drought, that another terrible thing happened. On a certain calm and beautiful day Tabitha, who still grew and flourished, had taken some of the Christian children to a spot on the farther side of the koppie, where stood an old fortification originally built for purposes of defence. Here, among the ancient walls, with the assistance of the natives, she had made a kind of summer-house as children love to do, and in this house, like some learned eastern pundit in a cell, a very pretty pundit crowned with a wreath of flowers, she sat upon the ground and instructed the infant mind of Sisa-Land.

She was supposed to be telling them Bible stories to prepare them for their Sunday School examination, which, indeed, she did with embellishments and in their own poetic and metaphorical fashion. The particular tale upon which she was engaged, by a strange coincidence, was that from the Acts which narrates how St. Paul was bitten by a viper upon the Island of Melita, and how he shook it off into the fire and took no hurt.

"He must have been like Menzi," said Ivana, who was present, whereon Tabitha's other attendant, who was also with her as it was daytime, started an argument, for being a Christian she was no friend to Menzi, whom she called a "dirty old witch-doctor."

Tabitha, who was used to these disputations, listened smiling, and while she listened amused herself by trying to thrust a stone into a hole in the side of her summer-house, which was formed by one of the original walls of the old kraal.

Presently she uttered a scream, and snatched her arm out of the hole. To it, or rather to her hand, was hanging a great hooded snake of the cobra variety such as the Boers call *ringhals*. She shook it off, and the reptile, after sitting up, spitting, hissing and expanding its hood, glided back into the wall. Tabitha sat still, staring at her lacerated finger, which Ivana seized and sucked.

Then, bidding one of the oldest of the children to take her place and continue sucking, Ivana ran to a high rock a few yards away which overlooked Menzi's kraal, that lay upon a plain at a distance of about a quarter of a mile, and called out in the low, ringing voice that Kaffirs can command, which carries to an enormous distance.

"Awake, O Menzi! Come, O Doctor, and bring with you your *Dawa*. The little Chieftainess is bitten in the finger by a hooded snake. The Floweret withers! Imba dies!"

Almost instantly there was a disturbance in the kraal and Menzi appeared, following by a man carrying a bag. He cried back in the same strange voice:

"I hear. I come. Tie string or grass round the lady Imba's finger below the bite. Tie it hard till she screams with pain."

Meanwhile the Christian nurse had rushed off over the crest of the koppie to fetch Thomas and Dorcas, or either of them. As it chanced she met them both walking to join Tabitha in her bower, and thus it came about that they reached the place at the same moment as did old Menzi bounding up the rocks like a *klipspringer* buck, or a mountain sheep. Hearing him, Thomas turned in the narrow gateway of the kraal and asked wildly:

"What has happened, Witch-doctor?"

"This has happened, White-man," answered Menzi, "the Floweret has been bitten by a hooded snake and is about to die. Look at her," and he pointed to Tabitha, who notwithstanding the venom sucking and the grass tied round her blackened finger, sat huddled-up, shivering and half comatose.

"Let me pass, White-man, that I may save her if I can," he went on.

"Get back," said Thomas, "I will have none of your black magic practised on my daughter. If she is to live God will save her."

"What medicines have you, White-man?" asked Menzi.

"None, at least not here. Faith is my medicine."

Dorcas looked at Tabitha. She was turning blue and her teeth were chattering.

"Let the man do his best," she said to Thomas. "There is no other hope."

"He shan't touch her," replied her husband obstinately.

Then Dorcas fired up, meek-natured though she was and accustomed though she was to obey her husband's will.

"I say that he shall," she cried. "I know what he can do. Don't you remember the goat? I will not see my child die as a sacrifice to your pride."

"I have made up my mind," answered Thomas. "If she dies it is so decreed, and the spells and filth of a heathen cannot save her."

Dorcas tried to thrust him aside with her feeble strength, but big and burly, he stood in the path like a rock, blocking the way, with the stone entrance walls of the little pleasure-house on either side of him.

Suddenly the old Zulu, Menzi, became rather terrible; he drew himself up; he seemed to swell in size; his thin face grew set and fierce.

"Out of the path, White-man!" he said, "or by Chaka's head I will kill you," and from somewhere he produced a long, thin-bladed knife of native iron fixed on a buck's horn.

"Kill on, Wizard," shouted Thomas. "Kill if you can."

"Listen," said Dorcas. "If our daughter dies because of you, then I have done with you. We part for ever. Do you understand?"

"Yes, I understand," he answered heavily. "So be it."

Tabitha behind them made some convulsive noise. Thomas turned and looked at her; she was slowly sinking down upon her side. His face changed. All the rage and obstinacy went out of it.

"My child! Oh, my child!" he cried, "I cannot bear this. Love is stronger than all. When I come up for judgment, may it be remembered that love is stronger than all!"

Then he stepped out of the gateway, and sat down upon a stone hiding his eyes with his hand.

Menzi threw down the knife and leapt in, followed by his servant who bore his medicines, and the woman Ivana. He did his office; he uttered his spells and invocations, he rubbed *Dawa* into the wound, and prising open the child's clenched teeth, thrust more of it, a great deal more, down her throat, while all three of them rubbed her cold limbs.

About half an hour afterwards he came out of the place followed by Ivana, who carried Tabitha in her strong arms; Tabitha was very weak, but smiling, and with the colour returning to her cheeks. Of Thomas he took no notice, but to Dorcas he said:

"Lady, I give you back your daughter. She is saved. Let her drink milk and sleep."

Then Thomas, whose judgment and charity were shaken for a while, spoke, saying:

"As a man and a father I thank you, Witch-doctor, but know that as a priest I swear that I will never have more to do with you, who, I am sure, by your arts, can command these reptiles to work your will and have planned all this to shame me. No, not even if you lay dying would I come to visit you."

Thus stormed Thomas in his wrath and humiliation, believing that he had been the victim of a plot and not knowing that he would live bitterly to regret his words.

"I see that you hate me, Teacher," said Menzi, "and though here I do not find the gentleness you preach, I do not wonder; it is quite natural. Were I you I should do the same. But you are Little Flower's father—strange that she should have grown from such a seed—and though we fight, for that reason I cannot hate you. Be not disturbed. Perhaps it was the sucking of the wound and the grass tied round her finger which saved her, not my spells and medicine. No, no, I cannot hate you, although we fight for mastery, and you pelt me with vile words, saying that I charmed a deadly *immamba* to bite Little Flower whom I love, that I might cure her and make a mock of you. Yet I do hate that snake which bit the maiden Imba of its own wickedness, the hooded *immamba* that you believe to be my familiar, and it shall die. Man," here he turned to his servant, "and you, Ivana and the others, pull down that wall."

They leapt to do his bidding, and presently discovered the *ringhals* in its hole. Heedless of its fangs and writhings, Menzi sprang at it with a Zulu curse, and seizing it, proceeded to kill it in a very slow and cruel fashion.

CHAPTER VI

The great drought fell upon Sisa-Land like a curse from Heaven. For month after month the sun beat fiercely, the sky was as brass, and no rain fell. Even the dews seemed to depart. The springs dried up. The river Ukufa, the river called Death, ceased to flow, so that water could only be found in its deepest hollows. The pool beneath the Rock of Evildoers, the Death Rock, sank till the bones of those who had been murdered there many years before appeared as the crocodiles had left them. Cattle died because there was no grass; cows ceased to give their milk even where they could be partially fed and watered, so that the little children died also. Even in the dampest situations the crops withered, till at last it became certain that unless rain fell within a month, before another cold season had gone by there would be starvation everywhere. For the drought was widespread, and therefore corn could not be sent from other districts, even if there were cattle to draw it.

Every day Thomas put up prayers for rain in the church, and on two occasions held special services for this purpose. These were better attended than any others had ever been, because his congregation felt that the matter was extremely urgent, affecting them all, and that now was the time when, whatever happened to the heathen, good Christians like themselves should be rewarded.

However this did not chance, since the drought went on as fiercely as before.

Menzi was, of course, a rain-doctor, a "Heaven-herd" of the highest distinction; one who, it was reputed, could by his magic cause the most brazen sky to melt in tears. His services had been called in by neighbouring tribes, with the result, it was rumoured, that those tribes had been rewarded with partial showers. Also with great ceremony he had gone through his rites for the benefit of the heathen section of the Sisa people. Behold! by some curious accident on the following day a thunderstorm had come up, and with it a short deluge of rain which sufficed to make it certain that the crops in those fields on which it fell would keep alive, at any rate for a while.

But mark what happened. As is not uncommon in the case of thunder showers, this rain fell upon the lands which the heathen cultivated on one side of the koppie, whereas those that belonged to the Christian section upon the other side received not a single drop. The unjust were bedewed, the just were left dry as bones. All that they received was the lightning, which killed an old man, one of the best Christians in the place. The limits of the torrent might have been marked off with a line. When it had passed, to the heathen right stood pools of water; to the Christian left there was nothing but blowing dust.

Now these Christians, weak-kneed some of them, began to murmur, especially those who, having passed through a similar experience in their youth, remembered what starvation meant in that country. Religion, they reflected, was all very well, but without mealies they could not live, and without Kaffir corn there would be no beer. Indeed, metaphorically, before long they passed from murmurs to shouting, and their shouts said this: Menzi must be invited to celebrate a rain-service in his own fashion for the benefit of the entire tribe.

Thomas argued in vain. He grew angry; he called them names which doubtless they deserved; he said that they were spiritual outcasts. By this time, being frantic, his flock did not care what he said.

Either Menzi must come, they explained, or they would turn heathen. The Great One in the sky could work as well through Menzi as through him, Tombool or anybody else. Menzi *must* come.

Thomas threatened to excommunicate them all, a menace which did not amount to much as they were already excommunicating themselves, and when they remained obstinate, told them that he would have nothing to do with this rain-making business, which was unholy and repugnant to him. He told them, moreover, that he was certain that their wickedness would bring some judgment upon them, in which he proved to be right.

The end of it was that Menzi was summoned, and arrived with a triumphant smile, saying that he was certain he could put everything in order, and that soon they would have plenty of rain, that is, if they all attended his invocations and made him presents suitable to so great an occasion.

The result was that they did attend them, man, woman and child, seated in a circle in that same old kraal where the witch-doctor had so marvellously shown pictures upon the smoke. Each of them also brought his gift in his hand, or, if it were a living thing, drove it before him.

Thomas went down and addressed them in the midst of a sullen silence, calling them wicked and repeating his belief that they would bring a judgment on their own heads, they who were worshipping Baal and making offerings to his priest.

After he had talked himself hoarse, Menzi said mildly that if the Teacher Tombool had finished he would get to business. Why should the Teacher be angry because he, Menzi, offered to do what the Teacher could not—save the land from starving? And as for the gifts to himself, did not White Teachers also receive pay and offerings at certain feasts?

Then, making a gesture of despair, Thomas returned to his house, and with Dorcas and Tabitha watched the savage ceremony from the edge of the cliff that overhung the river, or rather what had been the river. He could not see much of it because they were too far away, but he perceived those apostate Christians prostrating themselves at Menzi's order, probably, he reflected, to make prayers to the devil. In fact they were not doing this, but only repeating Menzi's magical chants with appropriate gestures, as for countless ages their forefathers had done upon similar occasions.

Next an unfortunate black goat was dragged forward by the horns, a very thin black goat, and its throat was cut over a little fire, a sacrifice that suggested necromancy of the most Satanic sort.

After this Thomas and his family went back into the house and shut the windows, that they might not hear the unholy shoutings of the misguided mob. When they went out again Menzi had departed, and so had the others. The place was empty.

The following day was Sunday, and Thomas locked the church on the inner side, and read the service with Dorcas and Tabitha for sole congregation. It was a melancholy business, for some sense of evil seemed to hang over all three of them, also over everybody else, for the Christians went about with dejected looks and not one person spoke to them. Only Ivana came at night as usual to sleep with Tabitha, though even she said nothing.

Next morning they woke up to find the heavens black with clouds, heavy, ominous clouds; the truth being that the drought was drawing to its natural end. Thomas noted this, and reflected bitterly how hard it was that this end should not have come twenty-four hours earlier. But so events had been decreed and he was helpless.

By midday it began to rain, lightly at first, and from his rock he could see the people, looking unnatural and distorted in that strange gloom, for the clouds had descended almost to the earth, rushing about, holding out their hands as though to clasp the blessed moisture and talking excitedly one to the other. Soon they were driven into their huts, for the rain turned into a kind of waterspout. Never had such rain been known in Sisa-Land.

All that afternoon it poured, and all the night with ever-increasing violence; yes, and all the following morning, so that by noon Thomas's rain-gauge showed that over twelve inches had fallen in about twenty-four hours, and it was still raining. Water rushed down from the koppie; even their well-built house could not keep out the wet, and, to the despair of Dorcas, several of the rooms were flooded and some of the new furniture was spoiled. The river beneath had become a raging torrent, and was rising every hour. Already it was over its banks, and the water had got into the huts of the Chief's kraal and the village round it, so that their occupants were obliged to seek safety upon the lower rocks of the koppie, where they sat shivering in the wet.

Night came at last, and through the darkness they heard cries as of people in distress. The long hours wore away till dawn, a melancholy dawn, for still it rained, though more lightly now, and no sun could be seen.

"Father," cried Tabitha, who, clad in oilskins, had gone a little way down the road, "come here and look."

He went. The child pointed to the village below, or rather what had been the village, for now there was none. It had gone and with it Kosa's kraal; the site was a pool, the huts had vanished, all of them, and some of the roofs lay upon the sides of the koppie, looking like overturned coracles. Only the church and the graveyard remained, for those stood on slightly higher ground by the banks of the river.

A little while later a miserable and dejected crowd arrived at the mission-house, wrapped up in blankets or anything else that they had managed to save.

"What do you want?" asked Thomas.

"Teacher," replied the Chief Kosa, with twitching face and rolling eyes, "we want you to come down to the church and pray for us. Our houses are gone, our fields are washed away. We want you to come to pray for us, for more rain is gathering on the hills and we are afraid."

"You mean that you are cold and wish to take refuge in the church, of which I have the key. You have sought rain and now you have got rain, such rain as you deserve. Why do you complain? Go to your witch-doctor and ask him to save you."

"Teacher, come down to the church and pray for us," they wailed.

In the end Thomas went, for his heart was moved to pity, and Dorcas and Tabitha went with him.

They entered the church, wading to it through several inches of water, and the service of intercession began, attended by every Christian in the place—except a few who were drowned—a miserable and heartily repentant crowd.

While it was still in progress suddenly there was a commotion, and Menzi himself rushed into the church. It was the first time he had ever entered there.

"Come forth!" he cried. "Come forth if you would save your lives. The water has eaten away the ground underneath this Heaven-house. It falls! I say it falls!"

Then he peered about him in the shadowed place till he found Tabitha. Leaping at her, he threw his long thin arms round her and bore her from the church. The others began to follow swiftly, and as Menzi passed the door carrying Tabitha, there came a dreadful rending sound, and one of the walls opened, letting in the light.

All fled forth, Thomas still in his surplice and his soul filled with bitterness, for as he went it came into his mind that this must be a farewell to that cherished church reared with so much love, cost and labour.

Outside the building on a patch of higher land, an upthrown plateau of rock, where presently all gathered beyond the reach of the waters, stood Menzi and Tabitha. Thomas looked at him and said:

"Doubtless you think that your spells have worked well, Witch-doctor, for see the ruin about us. Yet I hold otherwise, and say, 'Wait till the end!' To set a rock rolling down a hill is easy for those who have the strength. But who knows on whom it will fall at last?"

"You speak foolishly, Teacher," answered Menzi. "I do not think that my spells have worked well, for something stronger than I am has spoiled them. Mayhap it is you, Teacher, or the *Great-Great* whom you serve in your own fashion. I do not know, but I pray you to remember that long since on the smoke of my magic fire I showed you what would come about if you re-built the Heaven-house upon this place. But you said I was a cheat and would not be warned. Therefore things have gone as the Spirits appointed that they should go. Your Christians made me gifts and asked me to bring rain and it has come in plenty, and with it other things, more than you asked. Look," and he pointed downwards.

The church was falling. Its last foundations were washed away. Down it came with a mighty crash, to melt into the flood that presently filled the place where it had been. Its collapse and the noise of it were terrible, so terrible that the Christians gathered on the rock uttered a heart-rending wail of woe. The spire, being built upon a deeper bed because of its weight, stood longer than the rest of the fabric, but presently it went also.

Thrice it seemed to bow towards them, then it fell like a child's castle. Reckoning its height with his eye, Thomas saw that it could not reach them where they stood, and so did the others, therefore no one stirred. As the tower collapsed the clock sounded the first stroke of the hour, then suddenly became silent for ever and vanished beneath the waters, a mass of broken metal.

But the bell on which it had struck was hurled forward by the sway of the fall like a stone from a sling. It sped towards them through the air, a great dark object. Men ran this way and that, so that it fell upon the rock where none stood. It fell; it flew to pieces like an exploding shell, and its fragments hurtled over them with a screaming sound. Yet as it chanced the tongue or clapper of it took a lower course, perhaps because it was heavier, and rushing onwards like a thrown spear, struck Menzi full upon the chest, crushing in his breast bone.

They bore him up to the mission-house, since there was nowhere else whither he could be taken. Here they laid him on a bed, leaving the woman, Ivana, to watch him, for they had no skill to deal with such injuries as his. Indeed, they thought him dead.

For a long while Menzi lay senseless, but after night had fallen his mind returned to him and he bade Ivana bring Tabitha to him, Tabitha and no one else. If she could not or would not come, then Ivana must bring no one else, for if she did he would curse her and die at once.

There were discussions and remonstrances, but in the end Tabitha was allowed to go, for after all a fellow-creature was dying, and this was his last wish. She came, and Menzi received her smiling. Yes, he smiled and saluted her with shaking but uplifted arm, naming her *Inkosikazi* and *Umame*, or Mother.

"Welcome, Maiden Imba. Welcome, Little Flower," he said. "I wish to say good-bye to you and to bless you; also to endow you with my Spirit, that it may guard you throughout your life till you are as I am. I have hated some of the others, but I have always loved you, Little Flower."

"And I have loved you too, Menzi," said Tabitha, with a sob.

"I know, I know! We witch-doctors read hearts. But do not weep, Little Flower. Why should you for such as I, a black man, a mere savage cheat, as your father named me? Yet I have not been altogether a cheat, O Imba, though sometimes I used tricks like other doctors, for I have a strength of my own which your white people will never understand, because they are too young to understand. It only comes to the old folk who have been since the beginning of the world, and remain as they were at the beginning. I have been wicked, Little Flower, according to your white law. I have killed men and done many other things that are according to the law of my own people, and by that law I look for judgment. Yet, O Imba, I will say this—that I believe your law to be higher and better than my law. Has it not been shown to-day, since of all that were gathered on the rock yonder I alone was struck down and in the hour of my victory? The strongest law must be the best law, is it not so? Tell me, Little Flower, would it please you if I died a Christian?"

"Yes, very much," said Tabitha, fixing upon this point at once and by instinct avoiding all the other very doubtful disputations. "I will bring my father."

"Nay, nay, Little Flower. Your father, the Teacher Tombool, swore in his wrath that he would not come to visit me even if I lay dying, and now that I am dying he shall keep his oath and repent of it day by day till he too is dying. If I am to die a Christian, you must make me one this moment; *you* and no other. Otherwise I go hence a heathen as I have lived. If you bring your father here I will die at once before he can touch me, as I have power to do."

Then Tabitha, who although so young had strength and understanding and knew, if she thwarted him, that Menzi would do as he threatened, took water and made a certain Sign upon the brow of that old witch-doctor, uttering also certain words that she had often heard used in church at baptisms.

Perhaps she was wrong; perhaps she transgressed and took too much upon her. Still, being by nature courageous, she ran the risk and did these things as afterwards Ivana testified to the followers of Menzi.

"Thank you, Little Flower," said Menzi. "I do not suppose that this Christian magic will do me any good, but that you wished it is enough. It will be a rope to tie us together, Little Flower. Also I have another thought. When it is known that I became a Christian at the last then, if *you* bid them, Little Flower, the 'heathen-herd' will follow where the bull Menzi went before them. They are but broken sherds and scorched sticks" (i.e. rubbish) "but they will follow and that will please you, Little Flower, and your father also."

Here Menzi's breath failed, but recovering it, he continued:

"Hearken! O Imba! I give my people into your hand; now let your hand bend the twig as you would have it grow. Make them Christian if you will, or leave them heathen if you will; I care nothing. They are yours to drive upon whatever path you choose to set their feet, *yours*, O Imba, not Tombool's. Also, I, who lack heirs, give you my cattle, all of them. Ivana, make known my words, and with them the curse of Menzi, the King's child, the *Umazisi*, the Seer, on any who dare to disobey. Say to those of my House and to my people that henceforth the Maiden Imba is their lady and their mother."

Again he paused a little, then went on:

"Now I charge my Spirit to watch over you, Little Flower, till you die and we come to talk over these matters otherwhere, and my Spirit as it departs tells me that it will watch well, and that you will be a very happy woman, Little Flower."

He shut his eyes and lay still a while. Then he opened them again and said:

"O Imba, tell your father, the Teacher Tombool, from me that he does not understand us black people, whom he thinks so common, as you understand us, Little Flower, and that he would be wise to go to minister to white ones."

After this, once more he smiled at Tabitha and then shut his eyes again for the last time, and that was the end of the witch-doctor Menzi.

It may be added that after he had rebuilt the church for the second time, and numbered all the "Menzi-herd" among his congregation, which he did now that "the bull of the herd" was dead, as Menzi had foretold that he would, if Tabitha, whom he had "wrapped with his blanket," decreed it, Thomas took the sage advice of his departed enemy.

Now, in the after years, he is the much respected if somewhat feared bishop of white settlers in a remote Dominion of the Crown.

Thomas to-day knows more than he used to know, but one thing he has never learned, namely that it was the hand of a maid, yes, the little hidden hand of Tabitha, that drove all "Menzi's herd" into the gates of the "Heavenly Kraal," as some of them named his church.

For Tabitha knew when to be silent. Perhaps the Kaffirs, whose minds she could read as an open book, taught her this; or perhaps it was one of the best gifts to her of old Menzi's "Spirit," into whose care he passed her with so much formality.

This is the story of the great fight between Thomas Bull the missionary and Menzi the witch-doctor, who was led by his love of a little child whither he never wished to go; not for his own soul's sake, but just because of that little child.

Menzi did not care about his soul, but, being so strange a man, for some reason that he never explained, for Tabitha, his "Little Flower," he cared very much indeed. That was why he became a Christian at the last, since in his darkened, spell-bound heart he believed that if he did not, when she too "went down" he would never find her again.

Only A Dream

Footprints—footprints—the footprints of one dead. How ghastly they look as they fall before me! Up and down the long hall they go, and I follow them. *Pit, pat* they fall, those unearthly steps, and beneath them starts up that awful impress. I can see it grow upon the marble, a damp and dreadful thing.

Tread them down; tread them out; follow after them with muddy shoes, and cover them up. In vain. See how they rise through the mire! Who can tread out the footprints of the dead?

And so on, up and down the dim vista of the past, following the sound of the dead feet that wander so restlessly, stamping upon the impress that will not be stamped out. Rave on, wild wind, eternal voice of human misery; fall, dead footsteps, eternal echo of human memory; stamp, miry feet; stamp into forgetfulness that which will not be forgotten.

And so on, on to the end.

Pretty ideas these for a man about to be married, especially when they float into his brain at night like ominous clouds into a summer sky, and he is going to be married to-morrow. There is no mistake about it—the wedding, I mean. To be plain and matter-of-fact, why there stand the presents, or some of them, and very handsome presents they are, ranged in solemn rows upon the long table. It is a remarkable thing to observe when one is about to make a really satisfactory marriage how scores of unsuspected or forgotten friends crop up and send little tokens of their esteem. It was very different when I married my first wife, I remember, but then that match was not satisfactory—just a love-match, no more.

There they stand in solemn rows, as I have said, and inspire me with beautiful thoughts about the innate kindness of human nature, especially the human nature of our distant cousins. It is possible to grow almost poetical over a silver teapot when one is going to be married to-morrow. On how many future mornings shall I be confronted with that tea-pot? Probably for all my life; and on the other side of the teapot will be the cream jug, and the electro-plated urn will hiss away behind them both. Also the chased sugar basin will be in front, full of sugar, and behind everything will be my second wife.

"My dear," she will say, "will you have another cup of tea?" and probably I shall have another cup.

Well, it is very curious to notice what ideas will come into a man's head sometimes. Sometimes something waves a magic wand over his being, and from the recesses of his soul dim things arise and walk. At unexpected moments they come, and he grows aware of the issues of his mysterious life, and his heart shakes and shivers like a lightning-shattered tree. In that drear light all earthly things seem far, and all unseen things draw near and take shape and awe him, and he knows not what is true and what is false, neither can he trace the edge that marks off the Spirit from the Life. Then it is that the footsteps echo, and the ghostly footprints will not be stamped out.

Pretty thoughts again! and how persistently they come! It is one o'clock and I will go to bed. The rain is falling in sheets outside. I can hear it lashing against the window panes, and the wind wails through the tall wet elms at the end of the garden. I could tell the voice of those elms anywhere; I know it as well as the voice of a friend. What a night it is; we sometimes get them in this part of England in October. It was just such a night when my first wife died, and that is three years ago. I remember how she sat up in her bed.

"Ah! those horrible elms," she said; "I wish you would have them cut down, Frank; they cry like a woman," and I said I would, and just after that she died, poor dear. And so the old elms stand, and I like their music. It is a strange thing; I was half broken-hearted, for I loved her dearly, and she loved me with all her life and strength, and now—I am going to be married again.

"Frank, Frank, don't forget me!" Those were my wife's last words; and, indeed, though I am going to be married again to-morrow, I have not forgotten her. Nor shall I forget how Annie Guthrie (whom I am going to marry now) came to see her the day before she died. I know that Annie always liked me more or less, and I think that my dear wife guessed it. After she had kissed Annie and bid her a last good-bye, and the door had closed, she spoke quite suddenly: "There goes your future wife, Frank," she said; "you should have married her at first instead of me; she is very handsome and very good, and she has two thousand a year; *she* would never have died of a nervous illness." And she laughed a little, and then added:

"Oh, Frank dear, I wonder if you will think of me before you marry Annie Guthrie. Wherever I am I shall be thinking of you."

And now that time which she foresaw has come, and Heaven knows that I have thought of her, poor dear. Ah! those footsteps of one dead that will echo through our lives, those woman's footprints on the marble flooring which will not be stamped out. Most of us have heard and seen them at some time or other, and I hear and see them very plainly to-night. Poor dead wife, I wonder if there are any doors in the land where you have gone through which you can creep out to look at me to-night? I hope that there are none. Death must indeed be a hell if the dead can see and feel and take measure of the forgetful faithlessness of their beloved. Well, I will go to bed and try to get a little rest. I am not so young or so strong as I was, and this wedding wears me out. I wish that the whole thing were done or had never been begun.

What was that? It was not the wind, for it never makes that sound here, and it was not the rain, since the rain has ceased its surging for a moment; nor was it the howling of a dog, for I keep none. It was more like the crying of a woman's voice; but what woman can be abroad on such a night or at such an hour—half-past one in the morning?

There it is again—a dreadful sound; it makes the blood turn chill, and yet has something familiar about it. It is a woman's voice calling round the house. There, she is at the window now, and rattling it, and, great heavens! she is calling me.

"Frank! Frank! Frank!" she calls.

I strive to stir and unshutter that window, but before I can get there she is knocking and calling at another.

Gone again, with her dreadful wail of "Frank! Frank!" Now I hear her at the front door, and, half mad with a horrible fear, I run down the long, dark hall and unbar it. There is nothing there—nothing but the wild rush of the wind and the drip of the rain from the portico. But I can hear the wailing voice going round the house, past the patch of shrubbery. I close the door and listen. There, she has got through the little yard, and is at the back door now. Whoever it is, she must know the way about the house. Along the hall I go again, through a swing door, through the servants' hall, stumbling down some steps into the kitchen, where the embers of the fire are still alive in the grate, diffusing a little warmth and light into the dense gloom.

Whoever it is at the door is knocking now with her clenched hand against the hard wood, and it is wonderful, though she knocks so low, how the sound echoes through the empty kitchens.

*****

There I stood and hesitated, trembling in every limb; I dared not open the door. No words of mine can convey the sense of utter desolation that overpowered me. I felt as though I were the only living man in the whole world.

"*Frank! Frank!*" cries the voice with the dreadful familiar ring in it. "Open the door; I am so cold. I have so little time."

My heart stood still, and yet my hands were constrained to obey. Slowly, slowly I lifted the latch and unbarred the door, and, as I did so, a great rush of air snatched it from my hands and swept it wide.

The black clouds had broken a little overhead, and there was a patch of blue, rain-washed sky with just a star or two glimmering in it fitfully. For a moment I could only see this bit of sky, but by degrees I made out the accustomed outline of the great trees swinging furiously against it, and the rigid line of the coping of the garden wall beneath them. Then a whirling leaf hit me smartly on the face, and instinctively I dropped my eyes on to something that as yet I could not distinguish—something small and black and wet.

"What are you?" I gasped. Somehow I seemed to feel that it was not a person—I could not say, *Who* are you?

"Don't you know me?" wailed the voice, with the far-off familiar ring about it. "And I mayn't come in and show myself. I haven't the time. You were so long opening the door, Frank, and I am so cold—oh, so bitterly cold! Look there, the moon is coming out, and you will be able to see me. I suppose that you long to see me, as I have longed to see you."

As the figure spoke, or rather wailed, a moonbeam struggled through the watery air and fell on it. It was short and shrunken, the figure of a tiny woman. Also it was dressed in black and wore a black covering over the whole head, shrouding it, after the fashion of a bridal veil. From every part of this veil and dress the water fell in heavy drops.

The figure bore a small basket on her left arm, and her hand—such a poor thin little hand—gleamed white in the moonlight. I noticed that on the third finger was a red line, showing that a wedding-ring had once been there. The other hand was stretched towards me as though in entreaty.

All this I saw in an instant, as it were, and as I saw it, horror seemed to grip me by the throat as though it were a living thing, for as the voice had been familiar, so was the form familiar, though the churchyard had received it long years ago. I could not speak—I could not even move.

"Oh, don't you know me yet?" wailed the voice; "and I have come from so far to see you, and I cannot stop. Look, look," and she began to pluck feverishly with her poor thin hand at the black veil that enshrouded her. At last it came off, and, as in a dream, I saw what in a dim frozen way I had expected to see—the white face and pale yellow hair of my dead wife. Unable to speak or to stir, I gazed and gazed. There was no mistake about it, it was she, ay, even as I had last seen her, white with the whiteness of death, with purple circles round her eyes and the grave-cloth yet beneath her chin. Only her eyes were wide open and fixed upon my face; and a lock of the soft yellow hair had broken loose, and the wind tossed it.

"You know me now, Frank—don't you, Frank? It has been so hard to come to see you, and so cold! But you are going to be married to-morrow, Frank; and I promised—oh, a long time ago—to think of you when you were going to be married wherever I was, and I have kept my promise, and I have come from where I am and brought a present with me. It was bitter to die so young! I was so young to die and leave you, but I had to go. Take it—take it; be quick, I cannot stay any longer. *I could not give you my life, Frank, so I have brought you my death—take it!*"

The figure thrust the basket into my hand, and as it did so the rain came up again, and began to obscure the moonlight.

"I must go, I must go," went on the dreadful, familiar voice, in a cry of despair. "Oh, why were you so long opening the door? I wanted to talk to you before you married Annie; and now I shall never see you again—never! never! *never!* I have lost you for ever! ever! *ever!*"

As the last wailing notes died away the wind came down with a rush and a whirl and the sweep as of a thousand wings, and threw me back into the house, bringing the door to with a crash after me.

I staggered into the kitchen, the basket in my hand, and set it on the table. Just then some embers of the fire fell in, and a faint little flame rose and glimmered on the bright dishes on the dresser, even revealing a tin candlestick, with a box of matches by it. I was well-nigh mad with the darkness and fear, and, seizing the matches, I struck one, and held it to the candle. Presently it caught, and I glanced round the room. It was just as usual, just as the servants had left it, and above the mantelpiece the eight-day clock ticked away solemnly. While I looked at it it struck two, and in a dim fashion I was thankful for its friendly sound.

Then I looked at the basket. It was of very fine white plaited work with black bands running up it, and a chequered black-and-white handle. I knew it well. I have never seen another like it. I bought it years ago at Madeira, and gave it to my poor wife. Ultimately it was washed overboard in a gale in the Irish Channel. I remember that it was full of newspapers and library books, and I had to pay for them. Many and many is the time that I have seen that identical basket standing there on that very kitchen table, for my dear wife always used it to put flowers in, and the shortest cut from that part of the garden where her roses grew was through the kitchen. She used to gather the flowers, and then come in and place her basket on the table, just where it stood now, and order the dinner.

All this passed through my mind in a few seconds as I stood there with the candle in my hand, feeling indeed half dead, and yet with my mind painfully alive. I began to wonder if I had gone asleep, and was the victim of a nightmare. No such thing. I wish it had only been a nightmare. A mouse ran out along the dresser and jumped on to the floor, making quite a crash in the silence.

What was in the basket? I feared to look, and yet some power within me forced me to it. I drew near to the table and stood for a moment listening to the sound of my own heart. Then I stretched out my hand and slowly raised the lid of the basket.

"I could not give you my life, so I have brought you my death!" Those were her words. What could she mean—what could it all mean? I must know or I would go mad. There it lay, whatever it was, wrapped up in linen.

Ah, heaven help me! It was a small bleached human skull!

A dream! After all, only a dream by the fire, but what a dream! And I am to be married to-morrow.

Can I be married to-morrow?

Barbara Who Came Back

CHAPTER I. THE RECTORY BLIND

This is the tale of Barbara, Barbara who came back to save a soul alive.

The Reverend Septimus Walrond was returning from a professional visit to a distant cottage of his remote and straggling parish upon the coast of East Anglia. His errand had been sad, to baptise the dying infant of a fisherman, which just as the rite was finished wailed once feebly and expired in his arms. The Reverend Septimus was weeping over the sorrows of the world. Tears ran down his white but rounded face, for he was stout of habit, and fell upon his clerical coat that was green with age and threadbare with use. Although the evening was so cold he held his broad-brimmed hat in his hand, and the wind from the moaning sea tossed his snow-white hair. He was talking to himself, as was his fashion on these lonely walks.

"I think that fresh milk would have saved that child," he said, "but how was poor Thomas to buy fresh milk at fourpence a quart? Laid up for three months as he has been and with six children, how was he to buy fresh milk? I ought to have given it to him. I could have done without these new boots till spring, damp feet don't matter to an old man. But I thought of my own comfort—the son that doth so easily beset me—and so many to clothe and feed at home and poor Barbara, my darling Barbara, hanging between life and death."

He sobbed and wiped away his tears with the back of his hand, then began to pray, still aloud.

"O God of pity, in the name of the loving and merciful Christ, help me and poor Thomas in our troubles."

"I ought to have put Thomas's name first—my selfishness again," he ejaculated, then went on:

"Give consolation to Thomas who loved his baby, and if it pleases Thee in Thy infinite wisdom and foresight, spare my dearest Barbara's life, that she may live out her days upon the earth and perhaps in her turn give life to others. I know I should not ask it; I know it is better that she should go and be with Thee in the immortal home Thou hast prepared for us unhappy, suffering creatures. Yet—pity my poor human weakness—I do ask it. Or if Thou decreest otherwise, then take me also, O God, for I can bear no more. Four children gone! I can bear no more, O God."

He sobbed again and wiped away another tear, then muttered:

"My selfishness, always my selfishness! With six remaining to be looked after, that is counting Barbara if she still lives, I dare to ask to be relieved of the burdens of the flesh! Pitiful Christ, visit not my wickedness on me or on others, and O Thou that didst raise the daughter of Jairus, save my sweet Barbara and comfort the heart of poor Thomas. I will have faith. I *will* have faith."

He thrust his hat upon his head, pulling it down over his ears because of the rough wind, and walked forward quite jauntily for a few yards.

"What a comfort these new boots are," he said. "If I had stepped into that pool with the old ones my left foot would be wet through now. Let me thank God for these new boots. Oh! how can I, when I remember that the price of them should have been spent in milk for the poor baby? If I were really a Christian I ought to take them off and walk barefoot, as the old pilgrims used to do. They say it is healthy, and I tried to think so because it is cheap, though I am sure that this was the beginning of poor little Cicely's last illness. With her broken chilblains she could not stand the snow; at any rate, the chill struck upwards. Well, she has been in bliss three years, three whole years, and how thankful I ought to be for that. How glad she will be to see Barbara too, if it pleases God in His mercy to take Barbara; she always was her favourite sister. I ought to remember that; I ought to remember that what I lose here I gain there, that my store is always growing in Heaven. But I can't, for I am a man still. Oh!

curse it all! I can't, and like Job I wish I'd never been born. Job got a new family and was content, but that's their Eastern way. It's different with us Englishmen."

He stumbled on for a hundred yards or more, vacuously, almost drunkenly, for the hideous agony that he was enduring half paralysed his brain, and by its very excess was bringing him some temporary relief. He looked at the raging sea to his right, and in a vague fashion wished that it had swallowed him. He looked at the kind earth of the ploughed field to his left, and wished vividly, for the idea was more familiar, that six feet of it lay above him. Then he remembered that just beyond that sand-heap he had found a plover's nest with two eggs in it fifty years ago when he was a boy, and had taken one egg and left the other, or rather had restored it because the old bird screamed so pitifully about him. In some strange manner that little, long-forgotten act of righteousness brought a glow of comfort to his tormented spirit. Perhaps God would deal so by him.

In its way the evening was very beautiful. The cold November day was dying into night. Clear, clear was the sky save for some black and heavy snow clouds that floated on it driven before the easterly wind that piped through the sere grasses and blew the plovers over him as though they were dead leaves. Where the sun had vanished long bars of purple lay above the horizon; to his excited fancy they looked like the gateway of another and a better world, set, as the old Egyptians dreamed, above the uttermost pylons of the West. What lay there beyond the sun? Oh! what lay beyond the sun? Perhaps, even now, Barbara knew!

A figure appeared standing upon a sand dune between the pathway and the sea. Septimus was short-sighted and could not tell who it was, but in this place at this hour doubtless it must be a parishioner, perhaps one waiting to see him upon some important matter. He must forget his private griefs. He must strive to steady his shaken mind and attend to his duties. He drew himself together and walked on briskly.

"I wish I had not been obliged to give away Jack," he said. "He was a great companion, and somehow I always met people with more confidence when he was with me; he seemed to take away my shyness. But the license was seven-and-sixpence, and I haven't got seven-and-sixpence; also he has an excellent home with that stuffy old woman, if a dull one, for he must miss his walk. Oh! it's you, Anthony. What are you doing here at this time of night? Your father told me you had a bad cold and there's so much sickness about. You should be careful, Anthony, you know you're not too strong, none of you Arnotts are. Well, I suppose you are shooting, and most young men will risk a great deal in order to kill God's other creatures."

The person addressed, a tall, broad-shouldered, rather pale young man of about twenty-one, remarkable for his large brown eyes and a certain sweet expression which contrasted somewhat oddly with the general manliness of his appearance, lifted his cap and answered:

"No, Mr. Walrond, I am not shooting to-night. In fact, I was waiting here to meet you."

"What for, Anthony? Nothing wrong up at the Hall, I hope."

"No, Mr. Walrond; why should there be anything wrong there?"

"I don't know, I am sure, only as a rule people don't wait for the parson unless there is something amiss, and there seems to be so much misfortune in this parish just now. Well, what is it, my boy?"

"I want to know about Barbara, Mr. Walrond. They tell me she is very bad, but I can't get anything definite from the others, I mean from her sisters. They don't seem to be sure, and the doctor wouldn't say when I asked him."

The Reverend Septimus looked at Anthony and Anthony looked at the Reverend Septimus, and in that look they learned to understand each other. The agony that was eating out this poor father's heart was not peculiar to him; another shared it. In what he would have called his "wicked selfishness" the Reverend Septimus felt almost grateful for this sudden revelation. If it is a comfort to share our joys, it is a still greater comfort to share our torments.

"Walk on with me, Anthony," he said. "I must hurry, I have every reason to hurry. Had it not been a matter of duty I would not have left the house, but, so to speak, a clergyman has many children; he cannot prefer one before the other."

"Yes, yes," said Anthony, "but what about Barbara? Oh! please tell me at once."

"I can't tell you, Anthony, because I don't know. From here to the crest of Gunter's Hill," and he pointed to an eminence in front of them, "is a mile and a quarter. When we get to the crest of Gunter's Hill perhaps we shall know. I left home two hours ago, and then Barbara lay almost at the point of death; insensible."

"Insensible," muttered Anthony. "Oh! my God, insensible."

"Yes," went on the clergyman in a voice of patient resignation. "I don't understand much about such things, but the inflammation appears to have culminated that way. Now either she will never wake again, or if she wakes she may live. At least that is what they tell me, but they may be wrong. I have so often known doctors to be wrong."

They walked on together in silence twenty yards or more. Then he added as though speaking to himself:

"When we reach the top of Gunter's Hill perhaps we shall learn. We can see her window from there, and if she had passed away I bade them pull the blind down; if she was about the same, to pull it half down, and if she were really better, to leave it quite up. I have done that for two nights now, so that I might have a little time to prepare myself. It is a good plan, though very trying to a father's heart. Yesterday I stood for quite a while with my eyes fixed upon the ground, not daring to look and learn the truth."

Anthony groaned, and once more the old man went on:

"She is a very unselfish girl, Barbara, or perhaps I should say was, perhaps I should say was. That is how she caught this horrible inflammation. Three weeks ago she and her sister Janey went for a long walk to the Ness, to—to—oh! I forget why they went. Well, it came on to pour with rain; and just as they had started for home, fortunately, or rather unfortunately, old Stevens the farmer overtook them on his way back from market and offered them a lift. They got into the cart and Barbara took off the mackintosh that her aunt gave her last Christmas—it is the only one in the house, since such things are too costly for me to buy—and put it over Janey, who had a cold. It was quite unnecessary, for Janey was warmly wrapped up, while Barbara had nothing under the mackintosh except a summer dress. That is how she caught the chill."

Anthony made no comment, and again they walked forward without speaking, perhaps for a quarter of a mile. Then the horror of the suspense became intolerable to him. Without a word he dashed forward, sped down the slope and up that of the opposing Gunter's Hill, more swiftly perhaps than he had ever run before, although he was a very quick runner.

"He's gone," murmured Septimus. "I wonder why! I suppose that I walk too slowly for him. I cannot walk so fast as I used to do, and he felt the wind cold."

Then he dismissed the matter from his half-dazed mind and stumbled on wearily, muttering his disjointed prayers.

Thus in due course he began to climb the little slope of Gunter's Hill. The sun had set, but there was still a red glow in the sky, and against this glow he perceived the tall figure of Anthony standing quite still. When he was about a hundred yards away the figure suddenly collapsed, as a man does if he is shot. The Reverend Septimus put his hand to his heart and caught his breath.

"I know what that means," he said. "He was watching the window, and they have just pulled down the blind. I suppose he must be fond of her and it—affects him. Oh! if I were younger I think this would kill me, but, thank God! as one draws near the end of the road the feet harden; one does not feel the thorns so much. 'The Lord gave and the Lord hath taken away, bl—bl—yes, I *will* say it—blessed be the Name of the Lord.' I should remember that she is so much better where she is; that this is a very hard world; indeed, sometimes I think it is not a world, but a hell. Oh! Barbara, my sweet Barbara!" and he struggled forward blindly beating at the rough wind with his hands as though it were a visible foe, and so at last came to the crest of the hill where Anthony Arnott lay prone upon his face.

So sure was Septimus of the cause of his collapse that he did not even trouble to look at the Rectory windows in the hollow near the church two hundred yards or so away. He only looked at Anthony, saying:

"Poor lad, poor lad! I wonder how I shall get him home; I must fetch some help."

As he spoke, Anthony sat up and said, "You see, you see!"

"See what?"

"The blind; *it is quite up*. When I got here it was half down, then someone pulled it up. That's what finished me. I felt as though I had been hit on the head with a stick."

The Reverend Septimus stared, then suddenly sank to his knees and returned thanks in his simple fashion.

"Don't let us be too certain, Anthony," he exclaimed at length. "There may be a mistake, or perhaps this is only a respite which will prolong the suspense. Often such things happen to torment us; I mean that they are God's way of trying and purifying our poor sinful hearts."

CHAPTER II. THE NEW YEAR FEAST

Barbara did not die. On the contrary, Barbara got quite well again, but her recovery was so slow that Anthony only saw her once before he was obliged to return to college. This was on New Year's

Day, when Mr. Walrond asked him to dinner to meet Barbara, who was coming down for the first time. Needless to say he went, taking with him a large bunch of violets which he had grown in a frame at the Hall especially for Barbara. Indeed, she had already received many of those violets through the agency of her numerous younger sisters.

The Rectory dinner was at one o'clock, and the feast could not be called sumptuous. It consisted of a piece of beef, that known as the "aitch-bone," which is perhaps the cheapest that the butcher supplies when the amount of eating is taken into consideration; one roast duck, a large Pekin, the New Year offering of the farmer Stevens; and a plum pudding somewhat pallid in appearance. These dainties with late apples and plenty of cold water made up the best dinner that the Walrond family had eaten for many a day.

The Rectory dining-room was a long, narrow chamber of dilapidated appearance, since between meals it served as a schoolroom also. A deal bookcase in the corner held some tattered educational works and the walls that once had been painted blue, but now were faded in patches to a sickly green, were adorned only with four texts illuminated by Barbara. These texts had evidently served as targets for moistened paper pellets, some of which still stuck upon their surface.

Anthony arrived a little late, since the picking of the violets had taken longer than he anticipated, and as there was no one to open the front door, walked straight into the dining-room. In the doorway he collided with the little maid-of-all-work, a red-elbowed girl of singularly plain appearance, who having deposited the beef upon the table, was rushing back for the duck, accompanied by two of the young Walronds who were assisting with the vegetables. The maid, recoiling, sat down with a bump on one of the wooden chairs, and the Walrond girls, a merry, good-looking, unkempt crew (no boy had put in an appearance in all that family), burst into screams of laughter. Anthony apologised profusely; the maid, ejaculating that she didn't mind, not she, jumped up and ran for the duck; and the Reverend Septimus, a very different Septimus to him whom we met a month or so before, seizing his hand, shook it warmly, calling out:

"Julia, my dear, never mind that beef. I haven't said grace yet. Here's Anthony."

"Glad to see him, I am sure," said Mrs. Walrond, her eyes still fixed upon the beef, which was obviously burnt at one corner. Then with a shrug, for she was accustomed to such accidents, she rose to greet him.

Mrs. Walrond was a tall and extremely good-looking lady of about fifty-five, dark-eyed and bright complexioned, whose chestnut hair was scarcely touched with grey. Notwithstanding all the troubles and hardships that she had endured, her countenance was serene and even happy, for she was blessed with a good heart, a lively faith in Providence, and a well-regulated mind. Looking at her, it was easy to see whence Barbara and her other daughters inherited their beauty and air of breeding.

"How are you, Anthony?" she went on, one eye still fixed upon the burnt beef. "It is good of you to come, though you are late, which I suppose is why the girl has burnt the meat."

"Not a bit," called out one of the children, it was Janey, "it is very good of us to have him when there's only one duck. Anthony, you mustn't eat duck, as we don't often get one and you have hundreds."

"Not I, dear, I hate ducks," he relied automatically, for his eyes were seeking the face of Barbara.

Barbara was seated in the wooden armchair with a cushion on it, near the fire of driftwood, advantages that were accorded to her in honour of her still being an invalid. Even to a stranger she would have looked extraordinarily sweet with her large and rather plaintive violet eyes over which the long black lashes curved, her waving chestnut hair parted in the middle and growing somewhat low upon her forehead, her tall figure, very thin just now, and her lovely shell-like complexion heightened by a blush.

To Anthony she seemed a very angel, an angel returned from the shores of death for his adoration and delight. Oh! if things had gone the other way—if there had been no sweet Barbara seated in that wooden chair! The thought gripped his heart with a hand of ice; he felt as he had felt when he looked at the window-place from the crest of Gunter's Hill. But she *had* come back, and he was sure that they were each other's for life. And yet, and yet, life must end one day and then, what? Once more that hand of ice dragged at his heart strings.

In a moment it was all over and Mr. Walrond was speaking.

"Why don't you bid Barbara good-day, Anthony?" he asked. "Don't you think she looks well, considering? We do, better than you, in fact," he added, glancing at his face, which had suddenly grown pale, almost grey.

"He's going to give Barbara the violets and doesn't know how to do it," piped the irrepressible Janey. "Anthony, why don't you ever bring *us* violets, even when we have the whooping cough?"

"Because the smell of them is bad for delicate throats," he answered, and without a word handed the sweet-scented flowers to Barbara.

She took them, also without a word, but not without a look, pinned a few to her dress, and reaching a cracked vase from the mantelpiece, disposed of the rest of them there till she could remove them to her own room. Then Mr. Walrond began to say grace and the difficulties of that meeting were over.

Anthony sat by Barbara. His chair was rickety, one of the legs being much in need of repair; the driftwood fire that burned brightly about two feet away grilled his spine, for no screen was available, and he nearly choked himself with a piece of very hot and hard potato. Yet to tell the truth never before did he share in such a delightful meal. For soon, when the clamour of "the girls" swelled loud and long, and the attention of Mr. and Mrs. Walrond was entirely occupied with the burnt beef and the large duck that absolutely refused to part with its limbs, he found himself almost as much alone with Barbara as though they had been together on the wide seashore.

"You are really getting quite well?" he asked.

"Yes, I think so." Then, after a pause and with a glance from the violet eyes, "Are you glad?"

"You know I am glad. You know that if you had—died, I should have died too."

"Nonsense," said the curved lips, but they trembled and the violet eyes were a-swim with tears. Then a little catch of the throat, and, almost in a whisper, "Anthony, father told me about you and the window-blind and—oh! I don't know how to thank you. But I want to say something, if you won't laugh. Just at that time I seemed to come up out of some blackness and began to dream of you. I dreamed that I was sinking back into the blackness, but you caught me by the hand and lifted me quite out of it. Then we floated away together for ever and for ever and for ever, for though sometimes I lost you we always met again. Then I woke up and knew that I wasn't going to die, that's all."

"What a beautiful dream," began Anthony, but at that moment, pausing from her labours at the beef, Mrs. Walrond said:

"Barbara, eat your duck before it grows cold. You know the doctor said you must take plenty of nourishment."

"I am going to, mother," answered Barbara, "I feel dreadfully hungry," and really she did; her gentle heart having fed full, of a sudden her body seemed to need nourishment.

"Dear me!" said Mr. Walrond, pausing from his labours and viewing the remains of the duck disconsolately, for he did not see what portion of its gaunt skeleton was going to furnish him with dinner, and duck was one of his weaknesses, "dear me, there's a dreadful smell of burning in this room. Do you think it can be the beef, my love?"

"Of course it is not the beef," replied Mrs. Walrond rather sharply. "The beef is beautifully done."

"Oh!" ejaculated one of the girls who had got the calcined bit, "why, mother, you said it was burnt yourself."

"Never mind what I said," replied Mrs. Walrond severely, "especially as I was mistaken. It is very rude of your father to make remarks about the meat."

"Well, something *is* burning, my love."

Janey, who was sitting next to Anthony, paused from her meal to sniff, then exclaimed in a voice of delight:

"Oh! it is Anthony's coat tails. Just look, they are turning quite brown. Why, Anthony, you must be as beautifully done as the beef. If you can sit there and say nothing, you are a Christian martyr wasted, that's all."

Anthony sprang up, murmuring that he thought there was something wrong behind, which on examination there proved to be. The end of it was that the chairs were all pushed downwards, with the result that for the rest of that meal there was a fiery gulf fixed between him and Barbara which made further confidences impossible. So he had to talk of other matters. Of these, as it chanced, he had something to say.

A letter had arrived that morning from his elder brother George, who was an officer in a line regiment. It had been written in the trenches before Sebastopol, for these events took place in the mid-Victorian period towards the end of the Crimean War. Or rather the letter had been begun in the trenches and finished in the military hospital, whither George had been conveyed, suffering from "fever and severe chill," which seemed to be somewhat contradictory terms, though doubtless they were in fact compatible enough. Still he wrote a very interesting letter, which, after the pudding had been consumed to the last spoonful, Anthony read aloud while the girls ate apples and cracked nuts with their teeth.

"Dear me! George seems to be very unwell," said Mrs. Walrond.

"Yes," answered Anthony, "I am afraid he is. One of the medical officers whom my father knows, who is working in that hospital, says they mean to send him home as soon as he can bear the journey, though he doesn't think it will be just at present."

This sounded depressing, but Mr. Walrond found that it had a bright side.

"At any rate, he won't be shot like so many poor fellows; also he has been in several of the big battles and will be promoted. I look upon him as a made man. He'll soon shake off his cold in his native air——"

"And we shall have a real wounded hero in the village," said one of the girls.

"He isn't a wounded hero," answered Janey, "he's only got a chill."

"Well, that's as bad as wounded, dear, and I am sure he would have been wounded if he could." And so on.

"When are you going back to Cambridge, Anthony?" asked Mrs. Walrond presently.

"To-morrow morning, I am sorry to say," he answered, and Barbara's face fell at his words. "You see, I go up for my degree this summer term, and my father is very anxious that I should take high honours in mathematics. He says that it will give me a better standing in the Bar. So I must begin work at once with a tutor before term, for there's no one near here who can help me."

"No," said Mr. Walrond. "If it had been classics now, with a little refurbishing perhaps I might. But mathematics are beyond me."

"Barbara should teach him," suggested one of the little girls slyly. "She's splendid at Rule of Three."

"Which is more than you are," said Mrs. Walrond in severe tones, "who always make thirteen out of five and seven. Barbara, love, you are looking very tired. All this noise is too much for you, you must go and lie down at once in your own room. No, not on the sofa, in your own room. Now say good-bye to Anthony and go."

So Barbara, who was really tired, though with a happy weariness, did as she was bid. Her hand met Anthony's and lingered there for a little, her violet eyes met his brown eyes and lingered there a little; her lips spoke some few words of commonplace farewell. Then staying a moment to take the violets from the cracked vase, and another moment to kiss her father as she passed him, she walked, or rather glided from the room with the graceful movement that was peculiar to her, and lo! at once for Anthony it became a very emptiness. Moreover, he grew aware of the hardness of his wooden seat and that the noise of the girls was making his head ache. So presently he too rose and departed.

CHAPTER III. AUNT MARIA

Six months or so had gone by and summer reigned royally at Eastwich, for thus was the parish named of which the Reverend Septimus Walrond had spiritual charge. The heath was a blaze of gold, the cut hay smelt sweetly in the fields, the sea sparkled like one vast sapphire, the larks beneath the sun and the nightingales beneath the moon sang their hearts out on Gunter's Hill, and all the land was full of life and sound and perfume.

On one particularly beautiful evening, after partaking of a meal called "high tea," Barbara, quite strong again now and blooming like the wild rose upon her breast, set out alone upon a walk. Her errand was to the cottage of that very fisherman whose child her father had baptised on the night when her life trembled in the balance. Having accomplished this she turned homewards, lost in reverie, events having happened at the Rectory which gave her cause for thought. When she had gone a little way some instinct led her to look up. About fifty yards away a man was walking towards her to all appearance also lost in reverie. Even at that distance and in the uncertain evening light she knew well enough that this was Anthony. Her heart leapt at the sight of him and her cheeks seemed to catch the hue of the wild rose on her bosom. Then she straightened her dress a little and walked on.

In less than a minute they had met.

"I heard where you had gone and came to meet you," he said awkwardly. "How well you are looking, Barbara, how well and——" he had meant to add "beautiful," but his tongue stumbled at the word and what he said was "brown."

"If I were an Indian I suppose I should thank you for the compliment, Anthony, but as it is I don't know. But how well *you* are looking, how well and by comparison—fat."

Then they both laughed, and he explained at length how he had been able to get home two days earlier than he expected; also that he had taken his degree with even higher honours than he hoped.

"I am so glad," she said earnestly.

"And so am I; I mean glad that you are glad. You see, if it hadn't been for you I should never have done so well. But because I thought you would be glad, I worked like anything."

"You should have thought of what your father would feel, not of—of—well, it has all ended as it should, so we needn't argue. How is your brother George?" she went on, cutting short the answer that was rising to his lips. "I suppose I should call him Captain Arnott now, for I hear he has been promoted. We haven't seen him since he came home last week, from some hospital in the South of England, they say."

Anthony's face grew serious.

"I don't know; I don't quite like the look of him, and he coughs such a lot. It seems as though he could not shake off that chill he got in the trenches. That's why he hasn't been to call at the Rectory."

"I hope this beautiful weather will cure him," Barbara replied rather doubtfully, for she had heard a bad report of George Arnott's health. Then to change the subject she added, "Do you know, we had a visitor yesterday, Aunt Maria in the flesh, in a great deal of flesh, as Janey says."

"Do you mean Lady Thompson?"

She nodded.

"Aunt Thompson and her footman and her pug dog. Thank goodness, she only stayed to tea, as she had a ten mile drive back to her hotel. As it was, lots of things happened."

"What happened?"

"Well, first when she got out of the carriage, covered with jet anchor chains—for you know Uncle Samuel died only three months ago and left her all his money—she caught sight of our heads staring at her out of the drawing-room window, and asked father if he kept a girls' school. Then she made mother cry by remarking that she ought to be thankful to Providence for having taken to its bosom the four of us who died young —you know she has no children herself and so can't feel about them. Also father was furious because she told him that at least half of us should have been boys. He turned quite pink and said:

"'I have been taught, Lady Thompson, that these are matters which God Almighty keeps in His own hands, and to Him I must refer you.'

"'Good gracious! don't get angry,' she answered. 'If you clergymen can cross-examine your Maker, I am not in that position. Besides, they are all very good-looking girls who may find husbands, if they ever see a man. So things might have been worse.'

"Then she made remarks about the tea, for Uncle Samuel was a tea-merchant; and lastly that wicked Janey sent the footman to take the pug dog to walk past the butcher's shop where the fighting terrier lives. You can guess the rest."

"Was the pug killed?" asked Anthony.

"No, though the poor thing came back in a bad way. I never knew before that a pug's tail was so long when it is quite uncurled. But the footman looked almost worse, for he got notice on the spot. You see he went into the 'Red Dragon' and left the pug outside."

"And here endeth Aunt Maria and all her works," said Anthony, who wanted to talk of other things.

"No, not quite."

He looked at her, for there was meaning in her voice.

"In fact," she went on, "so far as I'm concerned it ought to run, 'Here beginneth Aunt Maria.' You see, I have got to go and live with her to-morrow."

Anthony stopped and looked at her.

"What the devil do you mean?" he asked.

"What I say. She took a fancy to me and she wants a companion—someone to do her errands and read to her at night and look after the pug dog and so forth. And she will pay me thirty pounds a year with my board and dresses. And" (with gathering emphasis) "we cannot afford to offend her who have half lived upon her alms and old clothes for so many years. And, in short, Dad and my mother thought it best that I should go, since Joyce can take my place, and at any rate it will be a mouth less to feed at home. So I am going to-morrow morning by the carrier's cart."

"Going?" gasped Anthony. "Where to?"

"To London first, then to Paris, then to Italy to winter at Rome, and then goodness knows where. You see, my Aunt Maria has wanted to travel all her life, but Uncle Samuel, who was born in Putney, feared the sea and lived and died in Putney in the very house in which he was born. Now Aunt Maria wants a change and means to have it."

Then Anthony broke out.

"Damn the old woman! Why can't she take her change in Italy or wherever she wishes, and leave you alone?"

"Anthony!" said Barbara in a scandalised voice. "What do you mean, Anthony, by using such dreadful language about my aunt?"

"What do I mean? Well" (this with the recklessness of despair), "if you want to know, I mean that I can't bear your going away."

"If my parents," began Barbara steadily——

"What have your parents to do with it? I'm not your parents, I'm your——"

Barbara looked at him in remonstrance.

"—old friend, played together in childhood, you know the kind of thing. In short, I don't want you to go to Italy with Lady Thompson. I want you to stop here."

"Why, Anthony? I thought you told me you were going to live in chambers in London and read for the Bar."

"Well, London isn't Italy, and one doesn't eat dinners at Lincoln's Inn all the year round, one comes home sometimes. And heaven knows whom you'll meet in those places or what tricks that horrible old aunt of yours will be playing with you. Oh! it's wicked! How can you desert your poor father and mother in this way, to say nothing of your sisters? I never thought you were so hard-hearted."

"Anthony," said Barbara in a gentle voice, "do you know what we have got to live on? In good years it comes to about 150 pounds, but once, when my father got into that lawsuit over the dog that was supposed to kill the sheep, it went down to 70 pounds. That was the winter when two of the little ones died for want of proper food—nothing else—and I remember that the rest of us had to walk barefoot in the mud and snow because there was no money to buy us boots, and only some of us could go out at once because we had no cloaks to put on. Well, all this may happen again. And so, Anthony, do you think that I should be right to throw away thirty pounds a year and to make a quarrel with my aunt, who is rich and kind-hearted although very over-bearing, and the only friend we have? If my father died, Anthony, or even was taken ill, and he is not very strong, what would become of us? Unless Aunt Thompson chose to help we should all have to go to the workhouse, for girls who have not been specially trained can earn nothing, except perhaps as domestic servants, if they are strong enough. I don't want to go away and read to Aunt Maria and take the pug dog out walking, although it is true I should like to see Italy, but I must—can't you understand—I must. So please reproach me no more, for it is hard to bear—especially from you."

"Stop! For God's sake, stop!" said Anthony. "I am a brute to have spoken like that, and I'm helpless; that's the worst of it. Oh! my darling, don't you understand? Don't you understand——?"

"No," answered Barbara, shaking her head and beginning to cry.

"That I love you, that I have always loved you, and that I always shall love you until—until—the moon ceases to shine?" and he pointed to that orb which had appeared above the sea.

"They say that it is dead already, and no doubt will come to an end like everything else," remarked Barbara, seeking to gain time.

Then for a while she sought nothing more, who found herself lost in her lover's arms.

So there they plighted their troth, that was, they swore, more enduring than the moon, for indeed they so believed.

"Nothing shall part us except death," he said.

"Why should death part us?" she answered, looking him bravely in the eyes. "I mean to live beyond death, and while I live and wherever I live death shall *not* part us, if you'll be true to me."

"I'll not fail in that," he answered.

And so their souls melted into rapture and were lifted up beyond the world. The song of the nightingales was heavenly music in their ears, and the moon's silver rays upon the sea were the road by which their linked souls travelled to the throne of Him who had lit their lamp of love, and there made petition that through all life's accidents and death's darkness it might burn eternally.

For the love of these two was deep and faithful, and already seemed to them as though it were a thing they had lost awhile and found once more; a very precious jewel that from the beginning had shone upon their breasts; a guiding-star to light them to that end which is the dawn of Endlessness.

Who will not smile at such thoughts as these?

The way of the man with the maid and the way of the maid with the man and the moon to light them and the birds to sing the epithalamium of their hearts and the great sea to murmur of eternity in their opened ears. Nature at her sweet work beneath the gentle night—who is there that will not say that it was nothing more?

Well, let their story answer.

CHAPTER IV. A YEAR LATER

Something over a year had gone by, and Barbara, returned from her foreign travels, sat in the drawing-room of Lady Thompson's house in Russell Square.

That year had made much difference in her, for the sweet country girl, now of full age, had blossomed into the beautiful young woman of the world. She had wintered in Rome and studied its antiquities and art. She had learned some French and Italian, for nothing was grudged to her in the way of masters, and worked at music, for which she had a natural taste. She had seen a good deal of society also, for Lady Thompson was at heart proud of her beautiful niece, and spared no expense to bring her into contact with such people as she considered she should know.

Thus it came about that the fine apartment they occupied in Rome had many visitors. Among these was a certain Secretary of Legation, the Hon. Charles Erskine Russell, who, it was expected, would in the course of nature succeed to a peerage. He was a very agreeable as well as an accomplished and wealthy man, and—he fell in love with Barbara. With the cleverness of her sex she managed to put him off and to avoid any actual proposal before they left for

Switzerland in the early summer. Thither, happily, he could not follow them, since his official duties prevented him from leaving the Embassy. Lady Thompson was much annoyed at what she considered his bad conduct, and said as much to Barbara.

Her niece listened, but did not discuss the matter, with the result that Lady Thompson's opinion of the Hon. Charles Russell was confirmed. Was it not clear that there had been no proposal, although it was equally clear that he ought to have proposed? Poor Barbara! Perhaps this was the only act of deception of which she was ever guilty.

So things went on until the previous day, the Monday after their arrival in London, when, most unhappily, Lady Thompson went out to lunch and met the Hon. Charles Russell, who was on leave in England.

Next morning, while Barbara was engaged in arranging some flowers in the drawing-room, who should be shown in but Mr. Russell. In her alarm she dropped a bowl and broke it, a sign that he evidently considered hopeful, setting it down to the emotion which his sudden presence caused. To emotion it was due, indeed, but not of a kind he would have wished. Recovering herself, Barbara shook his hand and then told the servant who was picking up the pieces of the bowl to inform her ladyship of the arrival of this morning caller.

The man bowed and departed, and as he went Barbara noticed an ominous twinkle in the pleasant blue eyes of the Hon. Charles Russell.

The rest of the interview may be summed up in a few words. Mr. Russell was eloquent, passionate and convincing. He assured Barbara that she was the only woman he had ever loved with such force and conviction that in the end she almost believed him. But this belief, if it existed, did not in the least shake her absolutely definite determination to have nothing whatsoever to do with her would-be lover.

Not until she had told him so six times, however, did he consent to believe her, for indeed he had been led to expect a very different answer.

"I suppose you care for someone else," he said at last.

"Yes," said Barbara, whose back, metaphorically, was against the wall.

"Somebody much more—suitable."

"No," said Barbara, "he is poor and not distinguished and has all his way to make in the world."

"He might change his mind, or—die."

"If so, I should not change mine," said Barbara. "Very likely I shall not marry him, but I shall not marry anyone else."

"In heaven's name, why not?"

"Because it would be a sacrilege against heaven."

Then at last Mr. Russell understood.

"Allow me to offer you my good wishes and to assure you of my earnest and unalterable respect," he said in a somewhat broken voice, and taking her hand he touched it lightly with his lips, turned, and departed out of Barbara's sight and life.

Ten minutes later Lady Thompson arrived, and her coming was like to that of a thunderstorm. She shut the door, locked it, and sat down in an armchair in solemn, lurid silence. Then with one swift flash the storm broke.

"What is this I hear from Mr. Russell?"

"I am sure I don't know what you have heard from Mr. Russell," answered Barbara faintly.

"Perhaps, but you know very well what there was to hear, you wicked, ungrateful girl."

"Wicked!" murmured Barbara, "ungrateful!"

"Yes, it is wicked to lead a man on and then reject him as though he were—rubbish. And it is ungrateful to throw away the chances that a kind aunt and Providence put in your way. What have you against him?"

"Nothing at all, I think him very nice."

Lady Thompson's brow lightened; if she thought him "very nice" all might yet be well. Perhaps this refusal was nothing but nonsensical modesty. Mr. Russell, being a gentleman, had not told her everything.

"Then I say you shall marry him."

"And I say, Aunt, that I will not and cannot."

"Why? Have you been secretly converted to the Church of Rome, and are you going into a nunnery? Or is there—another man?"

"Yes, Aunt."

"Where is he?" said Lady Thompson, looking about her as though she expected to find him hidden under the furniture. "And how did you manage to become entangled with him, you sly girl, under my very nose? And who is he? One of those bowing and scraping Italians, I suppose, who think you'll get my money. Tell me the truth at once."

"He is somebody you have never seen, Aunt. One of the Arnotts down at home."

"Oh, that Captain! Well, I believe they have a decent property, about 2,000 pounds a year, but all in land, which Sir Samuel never held by. Of course, it is nothing like the Russell match, which would have made a peeress of you some day and given you a great position meanwhile. But I suppose we must be thankful for small mercies."

"It is not Captain Arnott, it is his younger brother Anthony."

"Anthony! Anthony, that youth who is reading for the Bar. Why, the property is all entailed, and he will scarcely have a half-penny, for his mother brought no money to the Arnotts. Oh, this is too much! To throw up Mr. Russell for an Anthony. Are you engaged to him with your parents' consent, may I ask, and if so, why was the matter concealed from me, who would certainly have declined to drag an entangled young woman about the world?"

"I am not engaged, but my father and mother know that we are attached to each other. It happened the day after you came to Eastwich, or they would have told you. My father made me promise that we would not correspond while I was away, as he thought that we were too young to bind ourselves to each other, especially as Anthony has no present prospects or means to support a wife."

"I am glad they had so much sense. It is more than might have been expected of my sister after her own performance, for which doubtless she is sorry enough now. Like you, she might have married a title instead of a curate and beggary."

"I am quite sure that my mother is not sorry, Aunt," replied Barbara, whose spirit was rising. "I know that she is a very happy woman."

"Look here, Barbara, let's come to the point. Will you give up this moon-calf business of yours or not?"

"It is not a moon-calf business, whatever that may be, and I will not give it up."

"Very well, then, I can't make you as you are of age. But I have done with you. You will go to your room and stop there, and to-morrow morning you will return to your parents, to whom I will write at once. You have betrayed my hospitality and presumed upon my kindness; after all the things I have given you, too," and her eyes fixed themselves upon a pearl necklace that Barbara was wearing. For Lady Thompson could be generous when she was in the mood.

Barbara unfastened the necklace and offered it to her aunt without a word.

"Nonsense!" said Lady Thompson. "Do you think I want to rob you of your trinkets because I happen to have given them to you? Keep them, they may be useful one day when you have a husband and a family and no money. Pearls may pay the butcher and the rent."

"Thank you for all your kindness, Aunt, and good-bye. I am sorry that I am not able to do as you wish about marriage, but after all a woman's life is her own."

"That's just what it isn't and never has been. A woman's life is her husband's and her children's, and that's why—but it is no use arguing. You have taken your own line. Perhaps you are right, God knows. At any rate, it isn't mine, so we had better part. Still, I rather admire your courage. I wonder what this young fellow is like for whose sake you are prepared to lose so much; more than you think, maybe, for I had grown fond of you. Well, good-bye, I'll see about your getting off. There, don't think that I bear malice although I am so angry with you. Write to me when you get into a tight place," and rising, she kissed her, rather roughly but not without affection, and flung out of the room like one who feared to trust herself there any longer.

On the evening of the following day Barbara, emerging from the carrier's cart at the blacksmith's corner at Eastwich, was met by a riotous throng of five energetic young sisters who nearly devoured her with kisses. So happy was that greeting, indeed, that in it she almost forgot her sorrows. In truth, as she reflected, why should she be sorry at all? She was clear of a suitor whom she did not wish to marry, and of an aunt whose very kindness was oppressive and whose temper was terrible. She had fifty pounds in her pocket and a good stock of clothes, to say nothing of the pearls and other jewellery, wealth indeed if measured by the Walrond standard. Her beloved sisters were evidently in the best of health and spirits; also, as she thought, better-looking than any girls she had seen since she bade them farewell. Her father and mother were, as they told her, well and delighted at her return; and lastly, as she had already gathered, Anthony either was or was about to be at the Hall. Why then should she be sorry? Why indeed should she not rejoice and thank God for these good things?

On that evening, however, when supper was done, she had a somewhat serious interview with her father and mother who sat on either side of her, each of them holding one of her hands, for they could scarcely bear her out of their sight. She had told all the tale of the Hon. Charles Russell and of her violent dismissal by her aunt, of which story they were not entirely ignorant, for Lady Thompson had already advised them of these events by letter.

The Reverend Septimus shook his head sadly. He was not a worldly-minded man; still, to have a presumptive peer for a son-in-law, who would doubtless also become an ambassador, was a prospect that at heart he relinquished with regret. Also this young Arnott business seemed very vague and unsatisfactory, and there were the other girls and their future to be considered. No wonder, then, that he shook his kindly grey head and looked somewhat depressed.

But his wife took another line.

"Septimus," she said, "in these matters a woman must judge by her own heart, and you see Barbara is a woman now. Once, you remember, I had to face something of the same sort, and I do not think, dear, notwithstanding all our troubles, that either of us have regretted our decision."

Then they both rose and solemnly kissed each other over Barbara's head.

CHAPTER V. WEDDED

Next day, oh! joy of joys, Barbara and Anthony met once more after some fifteen months of separation. Anthony was now in his twenty-fourth year, a fine young man with well-cut features, brown eyes and a pleasant smile. Muscularly, too, he was very strong, as was shown by his athletic record at Cambridge. Whether his strength extended to his constitution was another matter. Mrs. Walrond, noticing his unvarying colour, which she thought unduly high, and the transparent character of his skin, spoke to her husband upon the matter.

In his turn Septimus spoke to the old local doctor, who shrugged his shoulders and remarked that the Arnotts had been delicate for generations, "lungy," he called it. Noticing that Mr. Walrond looked serious, and knowing something of how matters stood between Anthony and Barbara, he hastened to add that so far as he knew there was no cause for alarm, and that if he were moderately careful he thought that Anthony would live to eighty.

"But it is otherwise with his brother," he added significantly, "and for the matter of that with the old man also."

Then he went away, and there was something in the manner of his going which seemed to suggest that he did not wish to continue the conversation.

From Anthony, however, Barbara soon learned the truth as to his brother. His lungs were gone, for the chill he took in the Crimea had settled on them, and now there was left to him but a little time to live. This was sad news and marred the happiness of their meeting, since both of them were far too unworldly to consider its effect upon their own prospects, or that it would make easy that which had hitherto seemed impossible.

"Are you nursing him?" she asked.

"Yes, more or less. I took him to the South of England for two months, but it did no good."

"I am glad the thing is not catching," she remarked, glancing at him.

"Oh, no," he replied carelessly, "I never heard that it was catching, though some people say it runs in families. I hope not, I am sure, as the poor old chap insists upon my sleeping in his room whenever I am at home, as we used to do when we were boys."

Then their talk wandered elsewhere, for they had so much to say to each other that it seemed doubtful if they would ever get to the end of it all. Anthony was particularly anxious to learn what blessed circumstance had caused Barbara's sudden re-appearance at Eastwich. She fenced for a while, then told him all the truth.

"So you gave up this brilliant marriage for me, a fellow with scarcely a half-penny and a very few prospects," he exclaimed, staring at her.

"Of course. What would you have expected me to do—marry one man while I love another? As for the rest it must take its chance," and while the words were on her lips, for the first time it came into Barbara's mind that perhaps Anthony had no need to trouble about his worldly fortunes. For if it were indeed true that Captain Arnott was doomed, who else would succeed to the estate?

"I think you are an angel," he said, still overcome by this wondrous instance of fidelity and of courage in the face of Lady Thompson's anger.

"If I had done anything else, I think, Anthony, that you might very well have called me—whatever is the reverse of an angel."

And thus the links of their perfect love were drawn even closer than before.

Only three days later Mr. Walrond was summoned hastily to the Hall. When he returned from his ministrations it was to announce in a sad voice that Captain Arnott was sinking fast. Before the following morning he was dead.

A month or so after the grave had closed over Captain Arnott the engagement of Anthony and Barbara was announced formally, and by the express wish of Mr. Arnott. The old gentleman had for years been partially paralysed and in a delicate state of health, which the sad loss of his elder son had done much to render worse. He sent for Barbara, whom he had known from her childhood, and told her that the sooner she and Anthony were married the better he would be pleased.

"You see, my dear," he added, "I do not wish the old name to die out after we have been in this place for three hundred years, and you

Walronds are a healthy stock, which is more than we can say now. Worn out, I suppose, worn out! In fact," he went on, looking at her sharply, "it is for you to consider whether you care to take the risks of coming into this family, for whatever the doctors may or may not say, I think it my duty to tell you straight out that in my opinion there is some risk."

"If so, I do not fear it, Mr. Arnott, and I hope you will not put any such idea into Anthony's head. If you do he might refuse to marry me, and that would break my heart."

"No, I dare say you do not fear it, but there are other—well, things must take their course. If we were always thinking of the future no one would dare to stir."

Then he told her that when first he heard of their mutual attachment he had been much disturbed, as he did not see how they were to marry.

"But poor George's death has changed all that," he said, "since now Anthony will get the estate, which is practically the only property we have, and it ought always to produce enough to keep you going and to maintain the place in a modest way."

Lastly he presented her with a valuable set of diamonds that had belonged to his mother, saying he might not be alive to do so when the time of her marriage came, and dismissed her with his blessing.

In due course all these tidings, including that of the diamonds, came to the ears of Aunt Thompson, and wondrously softened that lady's anger. Indeed, she wrote to Barbara in very affectionate terms, to wish her every happiness and say how glad she was to hear that she was settling herself so well in life. She added that she should make a point of being present at the wedding. A postscript informed her that Mr. Russell was about to be married to an Italian countess, a widow.

Barbara's wedding was fixed for October. At the beginning of that month, however, Anthony was seized with some unaccountable kind of illness, in which coughing played a considerable part. So severe were its effects that it was thought desirable to postpone the ceremony. The doctor ordered him away for a change of air. On the morning of his departure he spoke seriously to Barbara.

"I don't know what is the matter with me," he said, "and I don't think it is very much at present. But, dear, I have a kind of presentiment that I am going to become an invalid. My strength is nothing like what it was, and at times it fails me in a most unaccountable manner. Barbara, it breaks my heart to say it, but I doubt whether you ought to marry me."

"If you were going to be a permanent invalid, which I do not believe for one moment," answered Barbara steadily, "you would want a nurse, and who could nurse you so well as your wife? Therefore unless you had ceased to care for me, I should certainly marry you."

Then, as still he seemed to hesitate, she flung her arms about him and kissed him, which was an argument that he lacked strength to resist.

A day or two afterwards her father also spoke to Barbara.

"I don't like this illness of Anthony's, my dear. The doctor does not seem to understand it, or at any rate so he pretends, and says he has no doubt it will pass off. But I cannot help remembering the case of his brother George; also that of his mother before him.. In short, Barbara, do you think—well, that it would be wise to marry him? I know that to break it off would be dreadful, but, you see, health is so very important."

Barbara turned on her father almost fiercely.

"Whose health?" she asked. "If you mean mine, it is in no danger; and if it were I should care nothing. What good would health be to me if I lost Anthony, who is more to me than life? But if you mean his health, then the greatest happiness I can have is to nurse him."

"Yes, yes, I understand, dear. But, you see, there might be—others."

"If so, father, they must run their risks as we do; that is if there are any risks for them to run, which I doubt."

"I dare say you are quite right, dear; indeed, I feel almost sure that you are right, only I thought it my duty to mention the matter, which I hope you will forgive me for having done. And now I may tell you I have a letter from Anthony, saying that he is ever so much better, and asking if the fifteenth of November will suit us for the wedding."

On the fifteenth of November, accordingly, Anthony and Barbara were made man and wife by the bride's father with the assistance of the clergyman of the next parish. Owing to the recent death of the bridegroom's brother and the condition of Mr. Arnott's health the wedding was extremely quiet. Still, in its own way it was as charming as it was happy. All her five sisters acted as Barbara's bridesmaids, and many gathered in that church said they were the most beautiful bevy of maidens that ever had been seen. But if so, Barbara outshone them all, perhaps because of her jewels and fine clothes and the radiance on her lovely face.

Anthony, who seemed to be quite well again, also looked extremely handsome, while Aunt Thompson, who by now had put off her mourning, shone in that dim church as the sun shines through a morning mist.

In short, all went as merrily as it should, save that the bride's mother seemed depressed and wept a little.

This, said her sister to someone in a loud voice, was in her opinion nothing short of wicked. What business, she asked, has a woman with six portionless daughters to cry because one of them is making a good marriage; "though it is true," she added, dropping her voice to a confidential whisper, "that had Barbara chosen she might have made a better one. Yes, I don't mind telling you that she might have been a peeress, instead of the wife of a mere country squire."

In truth, Mrs. Walrond was ill at ease about this marriage, why she did not know. Something in her heart seemed to tell her that her dear daughter's happiness would not be of long continuance. Bearing in mind his family history, she feared for Anthony's health; indeed, she feared a hundred things that she was quite unable to define. However, at the little breakfast which followed she seemed quite to recover her spirits and laughed as merrily as anyone at the speech which Lady Thompson insisted upon making, in which she described Barbara as "her darling, beautiful and most accomplished niece, who indeed was almost her daughter."

CHAPTER VI. PARTED

Hard indeed would it be to find a happier marriage than that of Anthony and Barbara. They adored each other. Never a shadow came between them. Almost might it be said that their thoughts were one thought and their hearts one heart. It is common to hear of twin souls, but how often are they to be met with in the actual experience of life? Here, however, they really might be found, or so it would seem. Had they been one ancient entity divided long ago by the working of Fate and now brought together once more through the power of an overmastering attraction, their union could not have been more complete. To the eye of the observer, and indeed to their own eyes, it showed neither seam nor flaw. They were one and indivisible.

About such happiness as this there is something alarming, something ominous. Mrs. Walrond felt it from the first, and they, the two persons concerned, felt it also.

"Our joy frightens me," said Anthony to Barbara one day. "I feel like that Persian monarch who threw his most treasured ring into the sea because he was too fortunate; you remember the sea refused the offering, for the royal cook found it in the mouth of a fish."

"Then, dear, he was doubly fortunate, for he made his sacrifice and kept his ring."

Anthony, seeing that Barbara had never heard the story and its ending, did not tell it to her, but she read something of what was passing in his mind, as very often she had the power to do.

"Dearest," she said earnestly, "I know what you think. You think that such happiness as ours will not be allowed to last for long, that something evil will overtake us. Well, it may be so, but if it is, at least we shall have had the happiness, which having been, will remain for ever, a part of you, a part of me; a temple of our love not built with hands in which we shall offer thanks eternally, here and—beyond," and she nodded towards the glory of the sunset sky, then turned and kissed him.

As it chanced, that cruel devouring sea which rages at the feet of all mankind was destined ere long to take the offering that was most precious to these two. Only this was flung to its waters, not by their hands, but by that of Fate, nor did it return to them again.

After their marriage Anthony and Barbara hired a charming little Georgian house at Chelsea near to the river. The drawback to the dwelling was that it stood quite close to a place of public entertainment called "The Gardens," very well known in those days as the nightly haunt of persons who were not always as respectable as they might have been. During their sojourn in London they never entered these Gardens, but often in the summer evenings they passed them when out for the walks which they took together, since Anthony spent most of his days at the Temple, studying law in the chambers of a leading barrister. Thus their somewhat fantastic gateway became impressed upon Barbara's mind, as did the character of the people who frequented them. As, however, their proximity reduced the rent of their own and neighbouring houses by about one-half, personally they were grateful to these Gardens, since the noise of the bands and the dancing did not trouble them much, and those who danced could always be avoided.

When they had been married nearly a year a little daughter was born to them, a sweet baby with violet eyes like to those of Barbara. Now indeed their bliss was complete, but it was not fated that it should remain, since the hungry sea took its sacrifice. The summer was very hot in London, and many infants sickened there of some infantile complaint, among them their own child. Like hundreds of others, it died when only a few months old and left them desolate.

Perhaps Anthony was the more crushed of the two, since here Barbara's vivid faith came to her aid.

"We have only lost her for a little while," she said, choking back her tears as she laid some flowers on the little grave. "We shall find her again; I know that we shall find her again, and meanwhile she will be happier than she could have been with us in this sad world."

Then they walked back home, pushing their way through the painted crowds that were gathering at the gates of "The Gardens," and listening to the strains of the gay music that jarred upon their ears.

In due course, having been called to the Bar, Anthony entered the chambers of an eminent Common Law leader. Although his prospects were now good, and he was ere long likely to be independent of the profession, he was anxious to follow it and make a name and fortune for himself. This indeed he would have found little difficulty in doing, since soon he showed that he had studied to good purpose; moreover, his gifts were decidedly forensic. He spoke well and without nervousness; his memory was accurate and his mind logical. Moreover, he had something of that imaginative and sympathetic power which brings an advocate success with juries.

Already he had been entrusted with a few cases which he held as "devil" for somebody else, when two events happened which between them brought his career as a lawyer to an end. In the November after the death of their baby his father suddenly died. On receiving the news of his fatal illness Anthony hurried to Eastwich without even returning home to fetch a warm coat, and as a result took a severe cold. During the winter following the funeral this cold settled on his lungs. At last towards the spring the crisis came. He was taken seriously ill, and on his partial recovery several doctors held a consultation over him. Their verdict was that he must give up his profession, which fortunately now he was in a position to do, live in the country and as much in the open air as possible, spending the worst months of the winter either in the South of England or in some warmer land. These grave and learned men told him outright that his lungs were seriously attacked, and that he must choose between following their advice and a speedy departure from the world.

Anthony would have defied them, for that was his nature. He wished to go on with his work and take the risk. But Barbara persuaded him to obedience. She said she agreed with him that the matter of his health was greatly exaggerated. At the same time, she pointed out that as they were now very well off she saw no reason why he should continue to slave at a profession which might or might not bring him an adequate return fifteen or twenty years later. She added that personally she detested London, and would like nothing better than to live at Eastwich near her own people. Also she showed him that his rather extensive estate needed personal attention, and could be much improved in value if he were there to care for it.

The end may be guessed; Anthony gave up the Bar and the house in Chelsea. After staying at Torquay for a few of the winter months, where his health improved enormously, they moved to Eastwich during the following May. Here their welcome was warm indeed, not only from the Rectory party, who rejoiced to have Barbara back among them, but from the entire neighbourhood, including the tenants and labourers on the property.

The ensuing summer was one of the happiest of their married life. Anthony became so much better that Barbara began to believe he had thrown off his lung weakness. Certain repairs and rearrangements of their old Elizabethan house agreeably occupied their time, and, to crown all, on Christmas Eve Barbara gave birth to a son, an extraordinarily fine and vigorous child, red-haired, blue-eyed, and so far as could be seen at that early age entirely unlike either of his parents.

The old doctor who ushered him into the world remarked that he had never seen a more splendid and perfect boy, nor one who appeared to possess a robuster constitution.

In due course Mr. Walrond christened him by the name of Anthony, after his father, and a dinner was given to the tenants and labourers in honour of the event.

That same month, there being a dearth of suitable men with an adequate knowledge of the law, Anthony, who already was a magistrate, though so young, was elected a Deputy-Chairman of Quarter Sessions for his county. This local honour pleased him very much, since now he knew that his legal education would not be wasted, and that he would have an opportunity of turning it to use as a judge of minor cases.

Yet this grateful and conciliatory appointment in the end brought him evil and not good. The first Quarter Sessions at which he was called upon to preside in one of the courts fell in February, when he ought to have been out of the East of England. The calendar was heavy, and Anthony acquitted himself very well in the trial of some difficult cases, earning the compliments of all concerned. But on leaving the hot court after a long day he caught a heavy cold, which awoke his latent complaint, and from that time forward he began to go down hill.

Still, watched, fought against by Barbara, its progress was slow. The winter months they spent in warmer climates, only residing in Eastwich from May to November. During the summer Anthony occupied himself on matters connected with the estate and principally with the cultivation of the home farm. Indeed, as time went on and increasing weakness forced him to withdraw himself more and more from the world and its affairs, the interests of this farm loomed ever larger in his eyes, as largely indeed as though he depended upon it alone for his daily bread. Moreover, it brought him into touch with Nature, and now that they were so near to parting, his friendship with her grew very close.

This was one of his troubles, that when he died, and he knew that before very long he must die, even if he continued to live in some other form, he must bid farewell to the Nature that he knew.

Of course, there was much of her, her cruel side, that he would rejoice to lose. He could scarcely conceive a future existence framed upon those lines of struggle, which in its working involves pain and cruelty and death. Putting aside sport and its pleasures, which he had abandoned because of the suffering and extinction entailed upon the shot or hunted creatures, to him it seemed inexpressibly sad that even his honest farming operations, at least where the beasts were concerned, should always culminate in death. Why should the faithful horse be knocked on the head when it grew old, or the poor cow go to the butcher as a reward for its long career of usefulness and profit?

What relentless power had thus decreed? In any higher life surely this decree would be rescinded, and of that side of Nature he had seen more than enough upon the earth. It was her gentler and harmless aspects from which he did not wish to part—from the flower and the fruit, from the springing blade and the ripened corn; from the beauty that brooded over sea and land; from the glory of the spreading firmament alive with light, and the winds that blew beneath it, and the rains that washed the face of earth; from the majestic passage of the glittering stars shedding their sweet influences through the night. To bid farewell to such things as these must, to his mind, indeed be terrible.

Once he said as much to Barbara, who thought a while and answered him:

"Why should we be taken beyond all things? If seems scarcely reasonable. I know we have not much to go on, but did not the Christ speak of drinking the fruit of the vine 'new with you in my Father's kingdom'? Therefore surely there must be a growing plant that produces the fruit and a process directed by intelligence that turns it into wine. There must be husbandmen or farmers. There must be mansions or abiding places, also, for they are spoken of, and flowers and all things that are beautiful and useful; a new earth indeed, but not one so different to the old as to be utterly unfamiliar."

Anthony said no more of the matter at this time, but it must have remained in his mind. At any rate, a month or two later when he woke up one morning he said to Barbara:

"Will you laugh very much if I tell you of a dream that came to me last night—if it was a dream, for I seemed to be still awake?"

"Why should I laugh at your dream?" she asked, kissing him. "I often think that there is as much truth in dreams as in anything else. Tell it to me."

"I dreamed that I saw a mighty landscape which I knew was not of the earth. It came to me like a picture, and a great stillness brooded over it. At the back of this landscape stood a towering cliff of stern rock thousands of feet high. Set at intervals along the edge of the cliff were golden figures, mighty and immovable. Whether they were living guards or only statues I do not know, for I never came near to them. Here and there, miles apart, streams from the lands beyond poured over the edge of the cliff in huge cascades of foam that became raging torrents when they reached its lowest slopes. One of these rivers fed a lake which lay in a chasm on the slopes, and from either end of this lake poured two rivers which seemed to me about twenty miles apart, as we should judge. They ran through groves of cedars and large groups of forest trees not unlike to enormous oaks and pines, and yet not the same.

"One river, that to the right if I looked towards the lake, was very broad, so broad that after it reached the plain and flowed slowly, great ships could have sailed upon it. The other, that to the left, was smaller and more rapid, but it also wandered away across the plain till my sight could follow it no farther. I observed that the broad, right-hand river evidently inundated its banks in seasons of flood, much as the Nile does, and that all along those banks were fields filled with rich crops, of what sort I do not know. The plain itself, which I take it was a kind of delta, the gift of the great river, was limitless. It stretched on and on, broken only by forests, along the edges of which moved many animals.

"When first I saw this landscape it was suffused with a sweet and pearly light, that came not from sun or moon or stars, but from a luminous body in shape like a folded fan, of which the handle rested on the earth. By degrees this fan began to open; I suppose that it was the hour of dawn. Its ribs of gorgeous light spread themselves from one side of heaven to the other and were joined together by webs of a thousand colours, of such stuff as the rainbow, only a hundred times more beautiful. The reflection from these rainbow webs lay upon the earth, divided by and sometimes mingled with those from the bars of light, and made it glorious.

"All these things I saw from an eminence on which I stood that rose between the rivers at the head of the plain. At length, overcome by the splendour, drunk as it were with beauty, I turned to look behind me, and there, quite close, in the midst of stately gardens with terraces and trees and fountains and banks of flowers, I saw a house, and—now indeed you will laugh—for so far as I can recollect it, in general style it was not unlike our own; that is to say, its architecture seemed to be more or less Elizabethan. If one who was acquainted with Elizabethan buildings had gone to that land and built a house from memory, but with more beautiful materials, he might have produced such a one as I imagined in my dream.

"Presently from the door of the house emerged two figures. One of these was my brother George and the other, Barbara, was our baby grown to a little fair-haired child. The child perceived me first and ran to me through the flowers. It leapt into my arms and kissed me. Then my brother came and said—I do not mean he spoke, but his meaning was conveyed to me:

"'You see, we are making your home ready. We hope that you will like it when you come, but if not you can change it as you wish.'

"Then I woke up, or went to sleep—I do not know which."

Barbara made light of Anthony's dream, which seemed to her to be after all but a reflection or an echo of earthly things tricked out with some bizarre imagination. Was not this obvious? The house? A vague replica of his own house. The river? Something copied from the Nile, delta and all. The waterfalls? Niagara on a larger scale. The great trees? Doubtless their counterparts grew in America. The brother and the babe—would he not naturally be thinking of his brother and his babe? The thing stood self-convicted. Echo, echo, echo, flung back in mockery of our agonised pleadings from the cliffs of the Beyond.

And yet this dream haunted her, especially as it returned to him more than once, always with a few added details. They often talked of this supernatural landscape and of the great radiant fan which closed at night and opened itself by day, wherewith it was illuminated. Barbara thought it strange that Anthony should have imagined so splendid a thing. And yet why should he not have done so? If she could picture it in her own mind, why should he not be able to originate it in his.

She told him all this, only avoiding allusions to the child, the baby Barbara whom they had lost. For of this child, although she longed to ask him details as to her supposed appearance, she could not bring herself to speak. Supposing that he were right, supposing that their daughter was really growing up yonder towards some celestial womanhood, and waiting for him and waiting for her, the mother upon whose breast she had lain, the poor, bereaved mother. Oh! then would not all be worth while?

Anthony listened and said that he agreed with her; as a lawyer he had analysed the dream and found in it nothing at all. Nothing more, for instance, than on analysis is to be found in any and every religion.

"And yet," he added, with that pleasant smile of his which was beginning to grow so painfully sweet and plaintive in its character, "and yet, it is very odd how real that landscape and that house are becoming to me. Do you know, Barbara, that the other night I seemed to be sitting in it in a great cool room, looking out at the river and the vast fertile plain. Then you came in, my dear, clad in a beautiful robe embroidered with violets. Yes, you came in glancing round you timidly like one who had lost her way, and saw me and cried aloud."

Towards the end Anthony grew worse with a dreadful swiftness. He was to have gone abroad as usual that winter, but when the time came his state was such that the doctors shrugged their shoulders and said that he might as well stop at home in comfort.

Up to the middle of October he managed to get out upon the farm on fine days to see to the drilling of the wheat and so forth. One rather rough afternoon he went out thus, not because he wished to, but for the sake of his spaniel dog, Nell, which bothered him to come into the fresh air. Not finding something that he sought, he was drawn far afield and caught in a tempest of rain and wind, through which he must struggle home. Barbara who, growing anxious, had gone to seek him, found him leaning against an oak unable to speak, with a little stream of blood trickling from the corner of his mouth. Indeed, it was the dog, which seemed distressed, that discovered her and led her to him.

This was Anthony's last outing, but he lived till Christmas Eve, his son's eighth birthday. That morning the boy was brought into his room to receive some present that his father had procured for him, and warned that he must be very quiet. Quiet, however, he would not be; his tumultuous health and strength seemed to forbid it. He racketed about the room, teasing the spaniel which lay by the side of the bed, until the patient beast growled at him and even bit, or pretended to bite him. Thereon he set up such a yell of pain, or anger, or both, that his father struggled from the bed to see what was the matter, and so brought on the haemorrhage which caused his death.

"I am afraid you will have trouble with that child, Barbara," he gasped shortly before the end. "He seems to be different from either of us; but he is our son, and I know that you will do your best for him. I leave him in your keeping. Good night, dearest, I want to go to sleep."

Then he went to sleep, and Barbara's heart broke.

CHAPTER VII. BARBARA'S SIN

The months following Anthony's death were to Barbara as a bad dream. Like one in a dream she saw that open, wintry grave beneath the tall church tower about whose battlements the wind-blown rooks wheeled on their homeward way. She noted a little yellow aconite that had opened its bloom prematurely in the shadow of the wall, and the sight of it brought her some kind of comfort. He had loved aconites and planted many of them, though because of his winter absences years had gone by since he had seen one with his eyes, at any rate in England. That this flower among them all should bloom on that day and in that place seemed to her a message and a consolation, the only one that she could find.

His sad office over, her father accompanied her home, pouring into her ear the words of faith and hope that he was accustomed to use to those broken by bereavement, and with him came her mother. But soon she thanked them gently and bade them leave her to herself. Then they brought her son to her, thinking that the sight of him would thaw her heart. For a while the child was quiet and subdued, for there was that about his mother's face which awed him. At last, weary of being still, he swung round on his heel after a fashion that he had, and said:

"Cook says that now father is dead I'm master here, and everyone will have to do what I tell them."

Barbara lifted her head and looked at him, and something in her fawn-like eyes, a mute reproach, pierced to the boy's heart. At any rate, he began to whimper and left the room.

There was little in the remark, which was such as a vulgar servant might well make thoughtlessly. Yet it brought home to Barbara the grim fact of her loss more completely perhaps than anything had done. Her beloved husband was dead, of no more account in the world than those who had passed from it at Eastwich a thousand years ago. He was dead, and soon would be forgotten by all save her, and she was alone; in her heart utterly alone.

The summer came and everyone grew cheerful. Aunt Thompson arrived at the Hall to stay, and urged Barbara to put away past things and resign herself to the will of Providence—as she had done in the case of the departed Samuel.

"After all," she said, "it might have been worse. You might have been called upon to nurse an invalid for twenty years, and when at last he went, have found the best part of your life gone, as I did," and she sighed heavily. "As it is, you still look quite a girl, having kept your figure so well; you are comfortably off and have a good position, and in short there is no knowing what may happen in the future. You must come up and stay with me this winter, dear, instead of poking yourself away in this damp old house, where everybody seems to die of consumption. Really it is a sort of family vault, and if you stop here long enough you will catch something too."

Barbara thanked her with a sad little smile, and answered that she would think over her kind invitation and write to her later. But in the end she never went to London, at least not to stay, perhaps it reminded her too vividly of her life there with Anthony. At Eastwich she could bear such memories, but for some unexplained reason it was otherwise in London.

Indeed, in the course of time her aunt gave up the attempt to persuade her, and devoted herself to forwarding the fortunes of her other pretty nieces, Barbara's sisters, two of whom, it should be said, already she had settled comfortably in life. Also she took a fancy to the boy, in whose rough, energetic nature she found something akin to her own.

"I am sick of women," she said; "it is a comfort to have to do with a male thing."

So it came about that after he went to school young Anthony spent a large share of his holidays at his great-aunt's London house. It may be added that he got no good from these visits, since Lady Thompson spoilt him and let him have his way in everything. Also she gave him more money than a boy ought to have. As a result, or partly so, Barbara found that her son grew more and more uncontrollable. He mixed with grooms and low characters, and when checked flew into fits of passion which frightened her.

Oddly enough, during these paroxysms, which were generally followed by two or three days of persistent sulking, the only person who seemed to have any control over him was a certain under-housemaid named Bess Cotton, the daughter of a small farmer in the neighbourhood. This girl, who was only about three years older than Anthony, was remarkable for her handsome appearance and vigour of body and mind. Her hair and large eyes were so dark that probably the local belief that she had gipsy or other foreign blood in her veins was true. Her complexion, however, was purely English, and her character had all the coarseness of those who have lived for generations in the Fens, whence her father came, uncontrolled by higher influences, such as the fellowship of gentle-bred and educated folk.

Bess was an excellent and capable servant, one, moreover, who soon obtained a sort of mastery in the household. On a certain occasion the young Squire, as they called him, was in one of the worst of his rages, having been forbidden by his mother to go to a coursing meeting which he wished to attend. In this state he shut himself up in the library, swearing that he would do a mischief to anyone who came near him, a promise which, being very strong for his years, he was quite capable of keeping. The man-servant was told to go in and bring him out, but hung back.

"Bless you," said Bess, "I ain't afraid," and without hesitation walked into the room and shut the door behind her.

Barbara, listening afar off, heard a shout of "Get out!" followed by a fearful crash, and trembled, for all violence was abominable to her nature.

"He will injure that poor girl," she said to herself, and rose, proposing to enter the library and face her son.

As she hurried down the long Elizabethan corridor, however, she heard another sound that came to her through an open window, that of Anthony laughing in his jolliest and most uproarious manner and of the housemaid Bess, laughing with him. She stayed where she was and listened. Bess had left the library and was coming across the courtyard, where one of the other servants met her and asked some question that Barbara did not catch. The answer in Bess's ringing voice was clear enough.

"Lord!" she said, "they always gave me the wild colts to break upon the farm. It is a matter of eye and handling, that's all. He nearly got me with that plaster thing, so I went for him and boxed his ears till he was dazed. Then I kissed him afterwards till he laughed, and he'll never be any more trouble, at least with me. That mother of his don't know how to handle him. She's another breed."

"Yes," said the questioner, "the mistress is a lady, she is, and gentle like the squire who's gone. But how did they get such a one as Master Anthony?"

"Don't know," replied Bess, "but father says that when he was a boy in the Fens they'd have told that the fairy folk changed him at birth. Anyway, I like him well enough, for he suits me."

Barbara went back to her sitting-room, where not long afterwards the boy came to her. As he entered the doorway she noted how handsome he looked with his massive head and square-jawed face, and how utterly unlike any Arnott or Walrond known to her personally or by tradition. Had he been a changeling, such as the girl Bess spoke of, he could not have seemed more different.

He came and stood before her, his hands in his pockets and a smile upon his face, for he could smile very pleasantly when he chose.

"Well, Anthony," she said, "what is it?"

"Nothing, mother dear, except that I have come to beg your pardon. You were quite right about the coursing meeting; they are a low lot, and I oughtn't to mix with them. But I had bets on some of the dogs and wanted to go awfully. Then when you said I mustn't I lost my temper."

"That was very evident, Anthony."

"Yes, mother; I felt as though I could have killed someone. I did try to kill Bess with that bust of Plato, but she dodged like a cat and the thing smashed against the wall. Then she came for me straight and gave me what I deserved, for she was too many for me. And presently all my rage went, and I found that I was laughing while she tidied my clothes. I wish you could do the same, mother."

"Do you, Anthony? Well, I cannot."

"I know. Where did I get my temper from, mother? Not from you, or my father from all I have heard and remember of him."

"Your grandfather would say it was from the devil, Anthony."

"Yes, and perhaps he is right; only then it is rather hard luck on me, isn't it? I can't help it—it comes."

"Then make it go, Anthony. You are to be confirmed soon. Change your heart."

"I'll try. But, mother dear, though I am so bad to you, you are the only one who will ever change me. When that wild-cat of a girl got the better of me just now, it was you I thought of, not her. If I lost you I don't know what would become of me."

"We have to stand or fall alone, Anthony."

"Perhaps, mother. I don't know; I am not old enough. Still, don't leave me alone, for if you do, then I am sure which I shall do," and bending down he kissed her and left the room.

After this scene Anthony's behaviour improved very much; his reports from school were good, for he was quick and clever, and his great skill in athletics made him a favourite. Also his grandfather, who prepared him for confirmation, announced that the lad's nature seemed to have softened.

So things remained for some time, to be accurate, for just so long as the girl Bess was a servant at the Hall.

Anthony might talk about his mother's influence over him, and without doubt when he was in his normal state this was considerable. Also it served to prevent him from breaking out. But when he did break out, Bess Catton alone could deal with him. Naturally it would be thought that there was some mutual attraction between these young people. Yet this was not so, at any rate on the part of the girl, who had been overheard to tell Anthony to his face that she hated the sight of him and "would cut him to ribbons" if she were his mother.

At any rate, there were others, or one other, of whom Bess did not hate the sight, and in the end her behaviour caused such scandal that Barbara was obliged to send her out of the house.

"All right, ma'am," she said, "I'll go, and be glad of a change. You may ring your own bull-calf now and I wish you joy of the job, since there's none but me that can lead him."

A few days later Anthony returned from school. With him came a letter from the head master, who wrote that he did not wish to make any scandal, and therefore had not expelled the boy. Still, he would be obliged if his mother would refrain from sending him back, as he did not consider him a suitable member of a public school. He suggested, in the lad's own interest, that it might be wise to place him in some establishment where a speciality was made of the training of unruly youths. He added that he wrote this with the more regret since Anthony's father and grandfather had been scholars at —— in their day, and her son possessed no mean intellectual abilities. This would be shown by the fact that he was at the head of his class, and might doubtless under other circumstances have risen to a high place in the sixth form.

Then followed the details of his misdoings, of which one need only be mentioned. He had fought another boy, who, it may be added, was older than himself, and beaten him. But the matter did not end there, since after his adversary had given up the fight Anthony flew at him and maltreated him so ferociously before they could be separated, that for a while the poor lad was actually in danger of collapse.

When reproached he expressed no penitence, but said only that he wished that he had killed him. This he repeated to his mother's face; moreover, he was furious when he found that Bess Catton had been sent away and demanded her return. When told that this was impossible he announced quietly that he would make the place a hell, and kept his word.

For a year or more before this date Barbara had not been well. She suffered from persistent colds which she was unable to shake off, and with these came great depression of spirit. Now in her misery the poor woman went to her room, and falling on her knees prayed with all her heart that she might die. The burden laid upon her was more than she could bear. Only one consolation could she find, that her beloved husband had not lived to share it, for she knew it would have crushed him as it crushed her.

Her father was now very old, and so feeble that everyone screened him from trouble so far as might be. But this particular trouble could not be hid, and Barbara told him all.

"Do not give way, my dearest daughter," he said, "and above all do not seek to fly from your trial, which doubtless is sent to you for some good purpose. Troubles that we strive to escape nearly always recoil upon our heads, whereas if they are faced, often they melt away. If you remain in the world to watch and help him, your son's nature, bad as it seems to be, may yet alter, for after all I know that he loves you. But if you give up and leave the world, who can tell what will happen to him when he is quite uncontrolled and in possession of his fortune?"

Barbara recognised the truth of her father's words, and while he lived tried to act up to them. But as it happened Mr. Walrond did not live long, for one evening he was found dead in the church, whither he often went to pray.

About this time the doctors told Barbara that her condition of health was somewhat serious. It seemed that her lungs also showed signs of being affected. Perhaps she had contracted the disease from her husband, and now that she was so broken in spirit, it asserted itself. They added, however, that if she took certain precautions, and above all went away from Eastwich, there was every reason to hope that she would quite recover her health.

In the end Barbara did not go away. At the time Anthony was being instructed by a tutor who resided at the Hall to prepare him for the University and ultimately for the Army. Needless to say, she was employed continually in trying to compose the differences between him and this tutor. How then could she go away and leave that poor gentleman and her old mother, who when she was not staying with one of her other married daughters now made her home at the Hall?

Thus she argued to herself, but the truth was that she did not wish to go. Her dearest associations were in the churchyard yonder, the churchyard where she hoped ere long she would be laid. She hated life, she sought and craved for death. This was her sin.

Night by night she lay awake and thought of Anthony, her darling, her beloved. She remembered that dream of his about a home that awaited him in another world, and she loved to fancy him as dwelling in that place of peace and making ready for her coming.

Nobody thought of him now except herself and his old dog Nell. The dog thought of him, she was sure, for it would sleep beneath his empty bed, and at times sit up, look at it and whine. Then it would come and rest its head upon her as she slept, and she would wake to find it looking at her with a question in its eyes. One night in the darkness it did this, then left her and broke into a joyous whimpering, such as it used to make when its master was going to take it out. She even heard it jumping up as though to paw at him, and wondered dreamily what it could mean.

When she woke in the morning she saw the poor beast lying stiff and cold upon the bed that had been Anthony's, and though she wept over it, her tears were perhaps those of envy rather than of sorrow, for she was sure that it had found Anthony.

More and more Barbara threw out her soul towards Anthony. Across the void of Nothingness she sent it travelling, nor did it return with empty hands. Something of Anthony had greeted it, though she could not remember the greeting, had spoken with it, though she could not interpret the words. Of this at least she was sure, she had been near to Anthony.

Once she seemed to see him. In the infinite, infinite distance, millions of miles away, the sky opened as it were. There in the opening was Anthony talking with one whom she knew for their daughter, the baby that had died, talking of her. In a minute they were gone, but she had seen them, she was sure that she had seen them, and the knowledge warmed her heart.

So there was no error, the Bible was true, more or less; Faith was not built on running water or on sand. Life was not a mere hellish mockery, where tiaras turned to crowns of thorn and joy was but an inch rule by which to measure the alps of human pain. Life was a door, a gateway. The door dreadful, the gate perilous, if you will, but beyond it lay no dream, no empty blackness. Beyond it stretched the Promised Land peopled with the lost who soon would be the found.

Barbara's last illness was rapid. When she began to go she went swiftly.

"Can't you save her?" asked her son of one of the doctors.

"The disease has gone too far," he answered. "Moreover, it is impossible to save one who seeks to die."

"Why does she seek to die?" blurted Anthony, glaring at him.

"Perhaps, young gentleman, you are in a better position to answer that question than I am," replied the doctor, who knew of Anthony's cruel conduct to his mother and had reproached him with it, not once but on several occasions.

"You mean that I have killed her," said Anthony savagely.

"No," replied the doctor, "she is dying of tuberculosis of the lungs. What were the primary causes which induced that disease I cannot be sure. All I said was that she appears to welcome it, or rather its issue. And I will add this on my own account, that when she does die the world will lose one of the sweetest women that ever walked upon it. Good morning."

"I know what he means," said Anthony to himself, as he watched the retreating form. "He means that I have murdered her, and perhaps I have. She is sick of me and wants to get back to my father, who was so different. That's why she won't go on living when she might.

She is committing suicide—of a holy sort. Well, what made me a brute and her an angel? And when she's gone how will the brute get on without the angel? Why should I be filled with fury and wickedness and she of whom I was born with sweetness and light? Let God or the devil answer that if they can. My mother, oh! my mother!" and this violent, sinister youth hid his face in his hands and wept.

Barbara sank down and down into a very whirlpool of nothingness. Bending over it, as it were, she saw the face of her aged mother, the faces of some of her dear sisters, the face of the kindly doctor, and lastly the agonised face of her handsome son.

"Mother! Don't leave me, mother. Mother! for God's sake come back to me, mother, or we shall never meet again. Come back to save me!"

These were the last words that Barbara heard.

CHAPTER VIII. THE ATONEMENT

Now these are the things that seemed to happen to Barbara after her earthly death. Or rather some of the things, for most of them have faded away and been lost to her mortal memory.

Consciousness returned to her, but at first it was consciousness in an utter dark. Everywhere was blackness, and in it she was quite alone. The whole universe seemed to centre in her solitary soul. Still she felt no fear, only a kind of wonder at this infinite blank through which she was being borne for millions and millions of miles.

Lights began to shine in the blackness like to those of passing ships upon a midnight sea. Now she was at rest, and the rest was long and sweet. Every fear and sad thought, every sensation of pain or discomfort left her. Peace flowed into her.

Presently she became aware of a weight upon her knee, and wondered by what it could be caused, for it reminded her of something; became aware also that there was light about her. At length her eyes opened and she perceived the light, though dimly, and that it was different to any she had known, purer, more radiant. She perceived also that she lay upon a low couch, and that the weight upon her knee was caused by something shaped like the head of a dog. Nay, it *was* the head of a dog, and one she knew well, Anthony's dog, that had died upon his bed. Now she was sure that she dreamed, and in her dream she tried to speak to the dog. The words that her mind formed were:

"Nell! Is that you, Nell?" but she could not utter them.

Still they were answered, for it appeared to her that the dog thought, and that she could read its thought, which was:

"Yes, it is I, who though but a dog, having been the last to leave you, am allowed to be the first to greet you," and it lifted its head and looked at her with eyes full of a wonderful love.

Her heart went out towards the faithful beast in a kind of rapture, and her intelligence formed another question, it was:

"Where am I, and if you, a creature, are here, where are the others?"

"Be patient. I only watch you till they come," was the answer.

"Till they come. Till who come?" she murmured.

Something within told her to inquire no more. But oh! was it possible —was the earth dream coming true?

A long while went by. She looked about her, and understood that she was lying in a great and beautiful room beneath a dome which seemed to be fashioned of translucent ivory or alabaster. At the end of the room were curtains woven of some glittering stuff that gave out light. At length these curtains were drawn, and through them, bearing a cup in her hand, passed a shape like to that of a mortal woman, only so radiant that Barbara knew that had she been alive with the old life she would have felt afraid.

This shape also was clad in garments that gave out light, and in its hair were jewelled flowers. It glided to her side and looked at her with loving, mysterious eyes. Then it held the cup to her lips, and said, or rather thought, for the speech of that land declared itself in thought and vision:

"Drink of this new wine."

She drank of the wine, and a wonderful life fell upon her like a glory.

"Who are you, O Vision?" she asked, and by way of answer there rose up within her a picture of herself, Barbara, leaning over a cot and looking at the white face of a dead child in a certain room in London. Then she knew that this was her daughter, and stretched out her arms towards her and received her in her arms.

Presently she looked again, and there around the bed appeared four other shapes of beauty.

"You have forgotten us, Barbara," said one of them, "but we are your sisters who died in infancy."

For the third time she looked, and behold! kneeling at her side, just as he had been found kneeling in the church, was her adored father, grown more young. Once more she looked, and last of all, breathing ineffable love, came her lost darling, Anthony himself.

From heart to heart flashed their swift thoughts, like lightnings from cloud to cloud, till all her being was a very sea of joy. Now the great room was full of presences, and now the curtains were gone and all space beyond was full of presences, and from that glorious company of a sudden there arose a song of welcome and beneath the burden of its sweetness she swooned to sleep.

Barbara dwelt in joy with those she loved and learned many things. She learned that this sweet new life of hers was what she had fashioned on the earth with her prayers and strivings; that the seeds of love and suffering sown down in the world's rank soil had here blossomed to this perfect flower. Now she knew what was meant by the saying that the kingdom of Heaven is within you, and by the other saying that as man sows so shall he reap. She learned that in this world beyond the world, and that yet itself was but a rung in the ladder of many universes, up which ladder all souls must climb to the ultimate judgment, there was sorrow as well as bliss, there were both suffering and delight.

Here the sinful were brought face to face with the naked horror of their sins, and from it fled wailing and aghast. Here the cruel, the covetous, the lustful and the liar were as creatures dragged from black caverns of darkness into the burning light of day. These yearned back to their darkness and attained sometimes to other coverings of a mortal flesh, or to some land of which she had no knowledge. For such was their fate if in them there was no spark of repentant spirit that in this new world could be fanned to flame.

Upwards or downwards, such is the law of the universe in which nothing can stand still. Up from the earth which Barbara had left came the spirit shape of all that lived and could die, even to that of the flower. But down to the earth it seemed that much of it was whirled again, to ascend once more in an age to come, since though the stream of life pulses continually forward, it has its backwash and its eddies.

Barbara learned that though it is blessed to die young and sinless, like to that glorious child of hers with whom she walked in this heavenly creation, and whose task it was to instruct her in its simpler mysteries, to live and to repent is yet more blessed. In this life or in that all have sinned, but not all have repented, and therefore, it appeared to Barbara, again and again such must know the burden of the flesh.

Also she saw many wonders and learned many secrets of that vast, spiritual universe into which this world of ours pours itself day by day. But if she remembers anything of these she cannot tell them.

Oh! happy was her life with Anthony, for there, though now sex as we know it had ceased to be, spirit grew ever closer to spirit, and as below they dreamed and hoped, their union had indeed become an altar on which Love's perfect fire flamed an offering to Heaven. Happy, too, was her communion with those other souls that had been mingled in her lot, and with many more whom she had known aforetime and elsewhere and long forgotten. For Barbara learned that life is an ancient story of which we spell out the chapters one by one.

Yet amidst all this joy and all the blessed labours of a hallowed world in which idleness was not known, nor any weariness in well-doing, a certain shadow met Barbara whichever way she turned.

"What is it?" asked Anthony, who felt her trouble.

"Our son," she answered, and showed him all the tale, or so much of it as he did not know, ending, "And I chose to leave him that I might take my chance of finding you. I died when I might have lived on if I had so willed. That is my sin and it haunts me."

"We are not the parents of his soul, which is as ancient as our own, Barbara."

"No, but for a while it was given into my hand and I deserted it, and now I am afraid. How can I tell what has chanced to the soul of this son of ours? Here there is no time. I know not if I bade it farewell yesterday or ten thousand years ago. Long, long since it may have passed through this world, where it would seem we dwell only with those whom we seek or who seek us. Or it may abide upon the earth and there grow foul and hateful. Let us search out the truth, Anthony. There are those who can open its gates to us if the aim be pure and good."

"After I died, Barbara, I strove to learn how things went with you, and strove in vain."

"Not altogether, Anthony, for sometimes you were very near to me, or so I dreamed. Moreover, the case was different."

"Those who search sometimes find more than they seek, Barbara."

"Doubtless. Still, it is laid on me. Something drives me on."

So by the means appointed they sought to know the truth as to this son of theirs, and it was decreed that the truth should be known to them.

In a dream, a vision, or perchance in truth—which they never knew—they were drawn to the world that they had left, and the reek of its sins and miseries pierced them like a spear.

They stood in the streets of London near to a certain fantastic gateway that was familiar to them, the gateway of "The Gardens." From within came sounds of music and revelling, for the season was that of summer. A woman descended from a carriage. She was finely dressed, dark and handsome. Barbara knew her at once for the girl Bess Catton, who alone could control her son in his rages and whom she had dismissed for her bad conduct. She entered the place and they entered with her, although she saw them not. Bess sat down, and presently a man whom she seemed to know drew out of the throng and spoke to her. He was a tall man of middle age, with heavy eyes. Looking into his heart, they saw that it was stained with evil. The soul within him lay asleep, wrapped round with the webs of sin. This man said:

"We are going to have a merry supper, Bess. Come and join us."

"I'd like to well enough," she answered, "for I'm tired of my grand life; it's too respectable. But suppose that Anthony came along. He's my lawful spouse, you know. We had words and I told him where I was going."

"Oh, we'll risk your Anthony! Forget your marriage ring and have a taste of the good old times."

"All right. I'm not afraid of Anthony, never was, but others are. Well, it's your look-out."

She went with the man to a pavilion where food was served, and accompanied him to a room separated by curtains from the main hall. It had open windows which looked out on to the illuminated garden and the dancing. In this room, seated round a table, was a company of women gaudily dressed and painted, and with them were men. One of these was a mere boy now being drawn into evil for the first time, and Barbara grieved for him.

These welcomed the woman Bess and her companion noisily, and made room for them in seats near to the window. Then the meal began, a costly meal at which not much was eaten but a great deal was drunk. The revellers grew excited with wine; they made jests and told doubtful stories.

Barbara's son Anthony entered unobserved and stood with his back against the curtains. He was a man now, tall, powerful, and in his way handsome, with hair of a chestnut red. Just then he who had brought Bess to the supper threw his arm about her and kissed her, whereat she laughed and the others laughed also.

Anthony sprang forward. The table was overthrown. He seized the man and shook him. Then he struck him in the face and hurled him through the open window to the path below. For a few seconds the man lay there, then rose and ran till presently he vanished beneath the shadow of some trees. There was tumult and confusion in the room; servants rushed in, and one of the men, he who seemed to be the host, talked with them and offered them money. The woman Bess began to revile her husband.

He took her by the arm and said:

"Will you follow that fellow through the window, or will you come with me?"

Glancing at him, she saw something in his face that made her silent. Then they went away together.

The scene changed. Barbara knew that now she saw her Aunt Thompson's London house. In that drawing-room where she had parted from Mr. Russell, her son and his wife stood face to face.

"How dare you?" she gasped through her set lips, glaring at him with fierce eyes.

"How dare *you*?" he answered. "Did I marry you for this? I have given you everything, my name, the wealth my old aunt left to me; you, you the peasant's child, the evil woman whom I tried to lift up because I loved you from the first."

"Then you were a fool for your pains, for such as I can't be lifted up."

"And you," he went on, unheeding, "go back to your mire and the herd of your fellow-swine. You ask me how I dare. Go on with these ways, and I tell you I'll dare a good deal more before I've done. I'll be rid of you if I must break your neck and hang for it."

"You can't be rid of me. I'm your lawful wife, and you can prove nothing against me since I married. Do you think I want to be such a one as that mother of yours, to have children and mope myself to the grave——"

"You'd best leave my mother out of it, or by the devil that made you I'll send you after her. Keep her name off your vile lips."

"Why should I? What good did she ever do you? She pretended to be such a saint, but she hated you, and small wonder, seeing what you were. Why she even died to be rid of you. Oh, I know all about it, and you told me as much yourself. If my child is ever born I hope for your sake it will be such another as you are, or as I am. You can take your choice," and with a glare of hate she rushed from the room.

On a table near the fireplace stood spirits. The maddened husband went to them, filled a tumbler half full with brandy, added a little water and drank it off.

He poured more brandy into the glass and began to think. To Barbara his mind was as an open book and she read what was passing there. What she saw were such thoughts as these: "My only comfort, and yet till within two years ago, whatever else I did, I never touched drink. I swore to my mother that I never would, and had she been alive to-day——. But Bess always liked her glass, and drinking alone is no company. Ah! if my mother had lived everything would have been different, for I outgrew the bad fit and might have become quite a decent fellow. But then I met Bess again by chance, and she had the old hold on me, and there was none to keep me back, and she knew how to play her fish until I married her. The old aunt never found it out. If she had I shouldn't have 8,000 pounds a year to-day. I lied to her about that, and I wonder what she thinks of me now, if she can think where she is gone. I wonder what my mother thinks also, and my father, who was a good man by all accounts, though nobody seems to remember much about him. Supposing that they could see me now, supposing that they could have been at that supper party and witnessed the conjugal interview between me and the female creature who is my legal wife, what would they think? Well, they are dead and can't, for the dead don't come back. The dead are just a few double handfuls of dirt, no more, and since no doubt I shall join them before very long, I thank God for it, or rather I would if there were a God to thank. Here's to the company of the Dead who will never hear or see or feel anything more from everlasting to everlasting. Amen."

Then he drank off the second half tumbler of brandy, hid his face in his hands and began to sob, muttering:

"Mother, why did you leave me? Oh, mother, come back to me, mother, and save my soul from hell!"

Barbara and Anthony awoke from their dream of the dreadful earth and looked into each other's hearts.

"It is true," said their hearts, which could not lie, and with those words all the glory of their state faded to a grey nothingness.

"You have seen and heard," said Barbara. "It was my sin which has brought this misery on our son, who, had I lived on, might have been saved. Now through me he is lost, who step by step of his own will must travel downwards to the last depth, and thence, perhaps, never be raised again. This is the thing that I have done, yes, I whom blind judges in the world held to be good."

"I have seen and heard," he answered, "and joy has departed from me. Yet what wrong have you worked, who did not know?"

"Come, my father," called Barbara to that spirit who in the flesh had been named Septimus Walrond, "come, you who are holy, and pray that light may be given to us."

So he came and prayed and from the Heavens above fell a vision in answer to his prayer. The vision was that of the fate of the soul of the son of Anthony and Barbara through a thousand, thousand ages that were to come, and it was a dreadful fate.

"Pray again, my father," said Barbara, "and ask if it may be changed."

So the spirit of Septimus Walrond prayed, and the spirits of his daughters and of the daughter of Anthony and Barbara prayed with him. Together they kneeled and prayed to the Glory that shone above.

There came another vision, that of a little child leading a man by the hand, and the child was Barbara and the man was he who had been her son. By a long and difficult path—upwards, ever upwards—she led him, and the end of that path was not seen.

Then these spirits prayed that the meaning of this vision might be made more clear. But to that prayer there came no answer.

Barbara went apart into a wilderness where thorns grew and there endured the agony of temptation. On the one hand lay the pure life of joy which, like the difficult path that had been shown to her, led upwards, ever upwards to yet greater joy, shared with those she loved. On the other hand lay the seething hell of Earth, to be once more endured through many mortal years and—a soul to save alive. None might counsel her, none might direct her. She must choose and choose alone. Not in fear of punishment, for this was not possible to her. Not in hope of glory, for that she must inherit, but only for the hope's sake that she might—save a soul alive.

Out of her deep heart's infinite love and charity thus she chose in atonement of her mortal sin. And as she chose the great arc of Heaven above her, that had been grey and silent, burst to splendour and to song.

So Barbara for a while bade farewell to those who loved her, bade farewell to Anthony her heart's heart. Once more, alone, utterly alone, she laid her on the couch in the great chamber with the translucent dome and thence her spirit was whirled back through nothingness to the hell of Earth, there to be born again in the child of the evil woman, that it might save a soul alive.

Thus did the sweet and holy Barbara—Barbara who came back—in atonement of her sin.

For her reward, as she fights on in hope, she has memory and such visions as are written here.

THE END

www.ingramcontent.com/pod-product-compliance
Lightning Source LLC
LaVergne TN
LVHW041800060526
838201LV00046B/1066